10/10
8

8/19
9

8/00

3 48

D0914350

Martin Luther King Jr.

Other Titles in the
People Who Made History Series

Martin Luther King Jr.

Thomas Siebold, *Book Editor*

David L. Bender, *Publisher*
Bruno Leone, *Executive Editor*
Bonnie Szumski, *Editorial Director*
David M. Haugen, *Managing Editor*
Scott Barbour, *Series Editor*

Greenhaven Press, Inc., San Diego, CA

Every effort has been made to trace the owners of copyrighted material. The articles in this volume may have been edited for content, length, and/or reading level. The titles have been changed to enhance the editorial purpose. Those interested in locating the original source will find the complete citation on the first page of each article.

Library of Congress Cataloging-in-Publication Data

Martin Luther King, Jr. / Thomas Siebold, book editor.
     p.   cm. — (People who made history)
     Includes bibliographical references and index.
     ISBN 0-7377-0227-3 (lib. bdg. : alk. paper). —
ISBN 0-7377-0226-5 (pbk. : alk. paper)
     1. King, Martin Luther, Jr., 1929–1968. 2. Afro-
Americans—Civil rights. 3. Civil rights movements—
United States—History—20th century. 4. Afro-Americans
Biography. 5. Civil rights workers—United States
Biography. 6. Baptists—United States—Clergy Biography.
I. Series
E185.97.K5M288   2000
323'.092—dc21   99-38367
     [B]   CIP

Cover photo: Archive Photos
Library of Congress: 25

Copyright ©2000 by Greenhaven Press, Inc.
PO Box 289009
San Diego, CA 92198-9009
Printed in the U.S.A.

CONTENTS

Martin's dedication to Gandhian spirituality and his devotion to the cause of nonviolent change.

Chapter 2: King's Social and Political Ideology

Chapter 3: King's Role in the Civil Rights Movement

FOREWORD

In the vast and colorful pageant of human history, a handful of individuals stand out. They are the men and women who have come variously to be called "great," "leading," "brilliant," "pivotal," or "infamous" because they and their deeds forever changed their own society or the world as a whole. Some were political or military leaders—kings, queens, presidents, generals, and the like—whose policies, conquests, or innovations reshaped the maps and futures of countries and entire continents. Among those falling into this category were the formidable Roman statesman/general Julius Caesar, who extended Rome's power into Gaul (what is now France); Caesar's lover and ally, the notorious Egyptian queen Cleopatra, who challenged the strongest male rulers of her day; and England's stalwart Queen Elizabeth I, whose defeat of the mighty Spanish Armada saved England from subjugation.

Some of history's other movers and shakers were scientists or other thinkers whose ideas and discoveries altered the way people conduct their everyday lives or view themselves and their place in nature. The electric light and other remarkable inventions of Thomas Edison, for example, revolutionized almost every aspect of home-life and the workplace; and the theories of naturalist Charles Darwin lit the way for biologists and other scientists in their ongoing efforts to understand the origins of living things, including human beings.

Still other people who made history were religious leaders and social reformers. The struggles of the Arabic prophet Muhammad more than a thousand years ago led to the establishment of one of the world's great religions—Islam; and the efforts and personal sacrifices of an American reverend named Martin Luther King Jr. brought about major improvements in race relations and the justice system in the United States.

Each anthology in the People Who Made History series begins with an introductory essay that provides a general overview of the individual's life, times, and contributions. The group of essays that follow are chosen for their accessibility to a young adult audience and carefully edited in consideration of the reading and comprehension levels of that audience. Some of the essays are by noted historians, professors, and other experts. Others are excerpts from contemporary writings by or about the pivotal individual in question. To aid the reader in choosing the material of immediate interest or need, an annotated table of contents summarizes the article's main themes and insights.

Each volume also contains extensive research tools, including a collection of excerpts from primary source documents pertaining to the individual under discussion. The volumes are rounded out with an extensive bibliography and a comprehensive index.

Plutarch, the renowned first-century Greek biographer and moralist, crystallized the idea behind Greenhaven's People Who Made History when he said, "To be ignorant of the lives of the most celebrated men of past ages is to continue in a state of childhood all our days." Indeed, since it is people who make history, every modern nation, organization, institution, invention, artifact, and idea is the result of the diligent efforts of one or more individuals, living or dead; and it is therefore impossible to understand how the world we live in came to be without examining the contributions of these individuals.

MARTIN LUTHER KING JR.: CRUSADER FOR SOCIAL JUSTICE

On December 1, 1955, a forty-two-year-old seamstress named Rosa Parks boarded a city bus in Montgomery, Alabama. As whites got on the bus, the driver told Parks to vacate her seat and move further back into the Negro section. She remained quiet, sat still, and refused to give up her seat. As the rest of the passengers watched passively, the angry bus driver called a policeman, who arrested Rosa Parks and took her to the courthouse. Although Parks's action was hardly revolutionary, it served as a poignant starting point of a revolutionary, nonviolent protest movement.

Rosa Parks's protest stirred the feelings of blacks throughout Montgomery, including the minister at the Dexter Avenue Baptist Church, Martin Luther King Jr., a new father and a recent arrival to the city. The city's black leadership asked King and other ministers to organize a bus boycott. As the boycott successfully unfolded, Martin Luther King Jr. discovered his capacity to inspire and motivate people, a gift that would ultimately change his life and the lives of all Americans. Sensing the symbolic importance of the boycott, King remarked, "It is one of the splendid ironies of our day that Montgomery, the Cradle of the Confederacy, is being transformed into Montgomery, the cradle of freedom and justice."[1] Out of the Montgomery experience King emerged as a courageous and determined leader who knew that protest with dignity and love could inject new meaning into the consciousness of a nation. At Montgomery, King's struggle for righteousness was just beginning, and from that day forward he would face seemingly insurmountable odds, intense hatred, and entrenched political and social forces. He would be jailed, threatened, and finally murdered; he would win voting rights for blacks, the Nobel Prize for Peace, and over four hundred other awards; and, as one of modern

America's most charismatic figures, he would lead a crusade to transform the moral landscape of America.

EARLY YEARS

Martin Luther King Jr. was born on January 15, 1929, in Atlanta, Georgia. Martin's father, Martin Luther King Sr., told the attending physician, Dr. Charles Johnson, to simply put a "junior" on the birth certificate. Since Dr. Johnson knew King Sr. as "Mike," he erroneously wrote the infant's name as Michael Luther King Jr. The error remained in place until 1958 when Martin applied for a passport, discovered the mistake, and finally made the correction. Martin was the second of three children born to Reverend Martin Luther King Sr. and Alberta Williams King. Daughter Willie Christine was one year older than Martin, born in 1928, and Alfred Daniel, called A.D., was one year younger, born in 1930. The King children grew up in a pleasant Victorian house on Atlanta's Auburn Avenue, located in a comfortable neighborhood that contained some of the city's most successful black-owned businesses.

Martin's father was known to his family as "Daddy King." Daddy King came from a family of ten children and, like many black families at the time, they lived a life of extreme poverty and hardship, sometimes living without much hope as their father, James King, lapsed further and further into alcoholism. In order to contribute to the family income, Daddy King curried mules. When he was sixteen he packed up his meager belongings and walked to Atlanta, determined to make a success of himself. In Atlanta he worked odd jobs, went to school at night, and, because he was deeply religious, preached in several small churches just outside of Atlanta. His preaching was powerful and inspired and reflected his inner resolve. Even after he was married and raising a family, Daddy King continued to improve himself, finally graduating from high school and earning a college degree from Morehouse College. Reflecting on his father's character, Martin writes in his book *Stride Toward Freedom*,

> I remember riding with him . . . when he accidentally drove past a stop sign. A policeman pulled up to the car and said: "All right, boy, pull over and let me see your license." My father replied indignantly, "I'm no boy." Then, pointing to me, "This is a boy. I'm a man, and until you call me one, I will not listen to you." The policeman was so shocked that he wrote the ticket up nervously, and left the scene as quickly as possible.[2]

While working part-time as a preacher, Daddy King met Alberta Christine Williams. Alberta was the daughter of Reverend Adam Daniel Williams, a well-respected pastor at the Ebenezer Baptist Church on Auburn Avenue. At the time, Alberta, a graduate of the prestigious Spelman College in Atlanta, was teaching school. They fell in love, Daddy King, a sharecropper's son who had met the brutalities of life early, and Alberta, who had grown up in relative comfort and protected from the worst side of discrimination. After they were married, the couple moved into the Williams's home and Daddy King joined Alberta's father as an assistant preacher. When Reverend Williams died of a heart attack in 1931, Daddy King became head pastor of Ebenezer Church.

The Kings maintained an orderly, loving home. Daddy King, who was proud of all his children, particularly liked to brag that Martin loved to recite Scriptures before he was five, sing hymns from memory, listen to preachers, and study the dictionary to add big words to his vocabulary. Martin's wife, Coretta Scott King, suggests that Daddy King's characterization, although truthful, wrongly portrays Martin as a stuffy, precocious child when, in reality, "He always had a playful sense of humor and liked practical jokes. As a child he was small, but very strong and quick, good at sports. When he got older, he was quarterback of the football team at Morehouse College, because in spite of light weight, his compact body and tremendous spirit made him very hard to stop."[3]

Throughout his life, even as a youngster, Martin disliked violence, preferring his ability to persuade and influence others with language. Although Martin's early years were comfortable, secure, and somewhat sheltered from Jim Crow abuses, he was nonetheless introduced to the ugliness of bigotry at an early age. Certainly Martin, like all black Southern children, knew that there were places blacks could not go: swimming pools, rest rooms, water fountains, certain seats on the bus, and particular restaurants and businesses. But firsthand, personal discrimination hit him directly when the mother of his two white preschool playmates told Martin that he could not play with her sons anymore because he was black. Martin's mother consoled him but the sting of rejection and injustice hit him hard.

Like his father, Martin Luther King Jr. liked school. He attended Young Street Elementary for his first two years, then finished through sixth grade at David T. Howard Elementary. For secondary school he followed his sister to the Laboratory High School of Atlanta University until it closed after Martin's second year of attendance. In 1942, at age thirteen, he transferred to the only black high school in Atlanta, Booker T. Washington; he graduated in 1944. Throughout his schooling, Martin studied hard; participated in activities, particularly sports; enjoyed his classmates; dated; and wore smart clothes. His love of clothing and fine shoes continued throughout his life, and because of it he was good-naturedly nicknamed "Tweed."

MARTIN'S COLLEGE YEARS

At the age of fifteen, Martin matriculated at the same college his father had attended, Morehouse. His years at Morehouse from 1944 to 1948 had a great impact on his development as a speaker, social activist, preacher, and thinker. His teachers at the all-black college expected their students to rise above the hostile and segregated society in which they lived and work to be successful, maintain humanitarian values, and provide leadership for their people. Martin majored in sociology and minored in English. Both subjects served him well later in life: His study of English trained him to be a more cogent and powerful speaker and writer, and his study of sociology led him to understand the political, social, and economic forces that shaped America, especially the connection between economic inequalities and racism.

During the summer months and his college holidays Martin took temporary jobs as a common laborer, despite the fact that his father's influence with successful Atlanta businessmen could have connected him with easier and better paying work. He labored on a tobacco plantation, worked for Atlanta's Railway Express Company unloading trucks, and he helped in the stockroom at the Southern Spring Bed Mattress Company. He discovered how blacks received less pay than whites for the same work, how they were given the worst jobs, and how they were trapped in lives with little hope and limited prospects for their families. Perhaps because of these firsthand experiences and the social activism that they inspired, Martin joined the National Association for the Advancement of Colored People (NAACP). Participation in the NAACP and his exposure to various interracial college groups helped Martin to ease his tension and hostility toward white people. After meeting more compassionate whites,

Martin began to understand how the destiny of blacks is tied to America's destiny. He formulated a philosophical position that "in the final analysis the white man cannot ignore the Negro problem, because he is part of the Negro and the Negro is part of him. The Negro's agony diminishes the white man, and the Negro's salvation enlarges the white man."[4]

It was also in college that Martin reevaluated an earlier rejection of the ministry. At Morehouse he listened to the eloquent and scholarly preaching of the Reverend Dr. Benjamin Mays and the head of the Theological Department, Dr. George D. Kelsey. Martin learned that the spiritual nature of self can meaningfully be blended with one's intellectual self. At age seventeen, just after he finished his junior year, Martin alerted Daddy King that he felt inspired to join the ministry. Elated, Daddy King suggested that his son deliver a sermon to a small group in an auxiliary room at Ebenezer Church. When the word got out that the young King was going to preach, enough people showed up that the service was moved to the main sanctuary. Martin demonstrated his natural gift for oratory, and the sermon was hugely successful. Martin became very serious about his call to the ministry and his desire to serve.

CROZER THEOLOGICAL SEMINARY

At age nineteen Martin graduated from Morehouse and accepted a scholarship to Crozer Theological Seminary near Philadelphia, studying there from 1948 to 1951. At Crozer, an integrated school, Martin made many friends, both black and white. He even fell in love with a white girl for a short time and was the first black to be elected student body president.

Martin worked very hard studying ethics, social philosophy, and church history and graduated with a straight-A average in 1951. He was awarded the Pearl Plafker Award as an outstanding student and the J. Lewis Crozer Fellowship for graduate study. At Crozer, Martin was profoundly influenced by the work of theologian Walter Rauschenbusch, whose social ideas helped form Martin's conviction that "any religion which professes to be concerned about the souls of men and is not concerned about the social and economic conditions that scar the soul, is a spiritually moribund religion."[5] The young theological student also embraced the ideas of the influential Indian religious reformer Mahatma Gandhi. Gandhi, who believed that the pathway to social change was through love and peacefulness, had freed India from harsh British rule using the power of nonviolent resistance. In his work *Stride Toward Freedom: The Montgomery Story* Martin wrote, "As the days unfolded . . . the inspiration of Mahatma Gandhi began to exert its influence. I had come to see early that the Christian doctrine of love operating through the Gandhian method of nonviolence was one of the most potent weapons available to the Negro in his struggle for freedom."[6] The tactics of Gandhi and the ethics of Jesus Christ would serve as the guiding forces of Martin's leadership.

In 1951 Martin went to Boston University to earn a Ph.D. There he came in contact with a strong, secure black community. He dated frequently, engaged in philosophical discussions, enjoyed sports, and went with friends to local nightclubs in Boston's black neighborhoods. As his Ph.D. studies progressed, Martin came to the realization that he had a moral obligation to return to the South to help his people rise above poverty and segregation. The South, after all, was his home; the South offered him a sense of place and the blacks there were his people. He wrote once that "despite the existence of Jim Crow which kept reminding us at all times of the color of our skin, we had the feeling that something remarkable was unfolding in the South, and we wanted to be on hand to witness it."[7]

Through a mutual friend, Martin met Coretta Scott, a young woman from Alabama who was training in Boston at the New England Conservatory of Music. The daughter of a successful landowner in Marion, Alabama, Coretta went first to Antioch College in Ohio and then to Boston to pursue a career as a concert soprano. The gifted singer enchanted Martin immediately with her beauty, wit, and intelligence. At the end of their first date together Martin uncharacteristically blurted out, "You have all the qualities that I expect to find in the girl I'd like to have for a wife."[8] They were together constantly, walking, discussing philosophy and life, attending concerts, dancing, and, of course, revealing their feelings and beliefs about the future. Coretta initially resisted Martin's hints at marriage because she was determined to establish her own singing career and because she was leery of the demands of being a minister's wife. Moreover, Daddy King was pressuring Martin to marry a prominent young woman whom Martin had dated in Atlanta. But Martin would not be denied, and Reverend King Sr. performed the marriage ceremony on June 18, 1953. The newlyweds returned to Boston so Martin could complete his Ph.D. residency and Coretta could finish her course work in music.

MONTGOMERY

In January of 1954 the sophisticated congregation of the Dexter Avenue Baptist Church in Montgomery, Alabama, invited Martin to present a trial sermon. They were enthralled with the sincerity and profundity of Martin's thought and offered him the job as pastor. After much consideration the Kings moved to Montgomery. Reflecting back on this point in their lives, Coretta Scott King wrote, "Though I had been opposed to going to Montgomery, I realize now that it was an inevitable part of a greater plan for our lives. Even in 1954 I felt that my husband was being prepared—and I too—for a special role about which we would learn more later."[9] During the next fifteen months, the Kings settled peacefully into their new life in Montgomery. Martin completed his dissertation, he received his Ph.D. from Boston University, and he and his wife Coretta had their first child, Yolanda Denise (Yoki), on November 17, 1955. Within a month of the birth, however, the quiet life of a successful minister came to an end when Rosa Parks was arrested for refusing to give up her seat to a white person on a Montgomery bus.

The timing of Rosa Parks's action was fortuitous. Montgomery blacks were feeling bitter about an unfair trial of a black man who was unjustly accused of attacking a white woman; they were tired of repeated indignities like Rosa's, particularly since they made up over 70 percent of the passengers on Montgomery bus lines; they were encouraged by the 1954 U.S. Supreme Court's decision in *Brown v. Board of Education*, which outlawed racial segregation in public schools; and they were strengthened by the government's ruling against segregation on buses traveling across state lines. The time to act was at hand, and Rosa Parks provided the impetus.

Rosa Parks's minister, Reverend Ralph Abernathy, asked Martin to join a committee to organize a boycott of the city buses. Several factors made Martin reluctant to take action: He was a new father, he was just settling into his role as a minister, and he had concerns about the resolve of his fellow black ministers to stick with a long and arduous boycott. But Martin acquiesced and initiated the boycott by distributing forty thousand leaflets encouraging blacks to avoid the buses starting on Monday, December 5. On the first day of the boycott, Coretta ran into the kitchen and told Martin to come quickly: "I put down my cup and ran toward the living room. As I approached the front window Coretta pointed joyfully to a slowly moving bus: 'Darling, it's empty!' I could hardly believe what I saw."[10] Soon, bus after bus rolled by; all were virtually empty. That same day Martin was elected as president of the Montgomery Improvement Association (MIA), a newly formed committee to improve all areas of life in which blacks were treated differently than whites. That night he spoke to a huge crowd, telling them that they were protesting in order to give birth to justice and that black people, a great people, have the opportunity to "inject new meaning and dignity into the veins of our civilization."[11] The boycott lasted 381 tumultuous days until November 13, 1956, when the U.S. Supreme Court unanimously upheld a District Court ruling that segregation on Alabama's buses was unconstitutional.

Throughout the boycott Martin and other black leaders held mass meetings to teach and encourage nonviolence. The success of the nonviolent boycott unleashed the rage of the white segregationists, particularly members of the White Citizens Council and the Ku Klux Klan (KKK). The night after the Supreme Court ruling, forty carloads of hooded KKK members menacingly drove through the black neighborhood. Instead of retreating and cowering from the obvious threat, blacks, in a gesture of defiance, turned on all their lights and stood out on the curb mocking the KKK caravan as if they were watching clowns in a parade. Martin's success made him and his family targets of racist behavior. He and Coretta received phone calls at all hours of the night filled with racist slurs and death threats, he was harassed by the police and Montgomery city fathers, he was arrested, and, on January 30, 1956, the King house was bombed. At the time of the bombing Martin was gone but Coretta, a friend, and Yolanda were home. In *My Life with Martin Luther King Jr.* Coretta recalls that at 9:30 in the evening she heard a thump on the front porch. Instinctively she and her friend ran to the back of the house. "We moved fast—not through the hall, which would have taken us nearer the sound, but straight back through the guest bedroom. We were in the middle of it when there was a thunderous blast.

Then smoke and the sound of breaking glass."[12] Luckily no one was hurt. Despite the danger, Martin held fast to his stance of nonviolence. After returning to find his home bombed, he calmly told the crowd that had gathered, "I want you to go home and put down your weapons. We cannot solve this problem through retaliatory violence. We must meet violence with nonviolence."[13]

MARTIN'S CALL TO THE NATION

The experiences in Montgomery deepened Martin's commitment to interconnecting spirituality and nonviolence to bring about social reform. To this end he traveled widely preaching, he wrote his first book entitled *Stride Toward Freedom: The Montgomery Story*, and he broadened the base of the civil rights movement by establishing the Southern Christian Leadership Conference (SCLC). Encouraged by the cooperation of the black ministers in Montgomery, as well as sporadic protests in other Southern cities, Martin hoped to focus and mobilize social change efforts using the SCLC as a central organizing body. Approximately one hundred church leaders gathered at Ebenezer Baptist Church in Atlanta to create this social action arm of the black church. When the SCLC held its first formal meeting in New Orleans on February 14, 1957, Martin was elected its first president. Martin articulated five goals of the SCLC:

> First, to stimulate nonviolent, direct mass action to expose and remove the barriers of segregation and discrimination; second to disseminate the creative philosophy and techniques of nonviolence through local and area workshops; third to secure the right and unhampered use of the ballot for every citizen; fourth to achieve full citizenship rights, and the total integration of the Negro into American life; and fifth, to reduce the cultural lag through our citizenship training program.[14]

One of Martin's first actions was to send a letter to President Eisenhower asking him to initiate a White House conference on civil rights. When their request was denied, Martin and the SCLC organized a Prayer Pilgrimage to be held at the Abraham Lincoln Memorial in Washington, D.C. On May 17, 1957, three years to the day after the *Brown v. Board of Education* decision, Martin, along with Roy Wilkens, the executive secretary of the NAACP, and other black leaders from around the nation, spoke to the largest civil rights crowd in history to date, approximately thirty-seven thousand. In his keynote address, Martin called on both the Democrats and Republicans to support their struggle for freedom and he appealed to President Eisenhower for legislation to protect blacks' right to vote. The crowd chanted "Give us the ballot." Later President Eisenhower agreed to meet with Martin and a small contingency of black leaders. Despite their discussion about voting rights and the need for police protection from the rising violence against blacks, Eisenhower took no action.

Martin's work load had increased tremendously. He was the president of the Montgomery Improvement Association and the SCLC, he fulfilled numerous public appearances, he wrote prolifically, and he was a busy pastor of Dexter Avenue Baptist Church. Moreover, the Kings had their second child, Martin Luther III, a son born in Montgomery on October 23, 1957. Martin was extremely overworked and the tension was intense. To make matters worse, in 1958 Martin was attacked by a mentally ill woman while autographing his book in a New York department store. A forty-two-year-old black woman named Izola Curry approached Martin's table and asked if he was Dr. King. When Martin answered, she murmured, "Luther King, I've been after you for five years," and without hesitation she plunged a sharp letter opener into his chest. Martin remained calm, which was fortunate since the point of the knife was dangerously close to his heart and any sudden movement might have been fatal. During the operation, the doctors removed two ribs to free the knife safely. At first there was some talk of a conspiracy to kill Martin, but Curry turned out to be criminally insane, motivated by some vague notion that ministers were to blame for her hard life.

After Martin recuperated the Kings took a month-long trip to India as guests of Prime Minister Nehru to study Gandhi's techniques of nonviolence. Upon his return to America, Martin knew that he would have to reorganize his life so he could devote more time to the civil rights movement. Consequently he made the difficult decision to resign his position as head minister at Dexter Avenue Baptist Church and join his father as assistant pastor at Ebenezer Baptist Church in Atlanta, the headquarters of SCLC. Violence was mounting throughout the South as many hostile whites expressed outrage toward the changes that blacks were demanding. In response, the SCLC increased its nonviolent protests. One tactic that proved to be effective was the sit-in. The first sit-in took place in Greensboro, North Carolina, at the Woolworth drug store lunch counter. Four black freshmen from a local college quietly sat down at the all-white counter and ordered lunch. When they were refused service, they sat there all day, impeding Woolworth's lunch business. Martin introduced another protest strategy called selective buying. Dr. King and the SCLC encouraged blacks to avoid purchasing products from businesses that practiced segregation, stating bluntly that it is immoral for blacks to patronize organizations that oppress them.

In 1960 approximately seventy-five students invited Martin to join their sit-in at the segregated lunch counter at Atlanta's largest department store, Rich's. When all were arrested, including Martin, the protest made national headlines. All of the students were eventually released, but Martin was jailed for violating a one-year probation that he had been given for an earlier minor traffic violation. Martin was sentenced to four months of hard labor at Reidsville State Prison. At four thirty in the morning guards at the local jail put Martin in handcuffs and leg irons and took him four hundred miles to Reidsville. Senator John F. Kennedy, who was in a tight presidential race against the Republican Richard Nixon, made a highly publicized telephone call to Coretta, who was five months pregnant with her third child, Dexter Scott, expressing his regrets and his support. Meanwhile, Kennedy's brother, Robert, convinced the county judge to release Dr. King on bail after only one day in prison. This gesture was a shrewd political move on the part of Kennedy who, with the election just one month away, earned, with Martin's support, over 75 percent of the black vote.

Shortly after Kennedy's inauguration in 1961 students from another civil rights group, the Congress of Racial Equality (CORE), supported by the SCLC, initiated the Freedom Rides. Motivated by the U.S. Supreme Court's ruling banning segregation on interstate buses, the Freedom Riders intended to not only test the law but also to check Kennedy's commitment to act on civil rights issues. They informed the Kennedy administration of their intent, and interracial groups of students boarded Greyhound and Trailways buses in Washington, D.C., and headed south to challenge policies of segregated restaurants, rest rooms, and bus stations. Along the way the highly publicized riders met hostility: A bus was burned in Alabama, riders were arrested in Mississippi, and violence exploded in Birmingham and Montgomery. The white mob in Montgomery, numbering approximately one thousand, beat up the riders so viciously that Attorney General Robert F. Kennedy ordered over four hundred federal marshals to restore order. The Freedom Rides pushed the civil rights movement into the remotest areas of the South and helped raise the level of awareness throughout the entire country.

THE ALBANY AND BIRMINGHAM CAMPAIGNS

The next major civil rights confrontation happened in Albany in November 1961 when three young black students were denied service at the city bus terminal dining room. When they refused to leave, they were arrested. Shortly thereafter a group of Freedom Riders arrived in Albany to help local black leaders integrate public facilities, and they too were arrested. Exasperated, black organizers called Martin for help. White city officials acted quickly and had Martin, who was leading a procession of protesters, arrested for obstructing the sidewalk and marching in a parade without a permit. He was jailed for two days. Through the course of the prolonged Albany campaign Martin would be arrested three times. Despite the fact that Martin and others preached nonviolence, the Albany movement turned violent. A large crowd of frustrated and angry blacks blocked the streets and threw rocks and bottles at one hundred Albany police. This time the police did not retaliate; instead they retreated, making very few arrests. The incident was televised nationally and to the TV viewers the incident looked like Martin's pledge of nonviolence had collapsed and things were spiraling out of control. With momentum seemingly on their side, Albany officials secured a federal injunction that outlawed any further demonstrations for ten days.

Albany turned out to be Martin's greatest failure: local leadership was not sharply organized, Martin was successfully portrayed in the media as an outside troublemaker, parts of the campaign had a feel of aggression rather than nonviolence, and the public facilities were not immediately desegregated. Martin also acknowledged that the Albany campaign lacked focus because he and his supporters attempted to overturn segregation in all public facilities rather than concentrating on one or two targets. Reflecting on the movement, Martin stated that "our protest was so vague that we got nothing."[15] He knew that the message broadcast to the nation made the campaign appear muddled and random. Despite its lack of clarity, Martin felt that the Albany protest had unified black churches, that it had taught Martin and the SCLC the need to define their movement with clear, reachable objectives, and that it had empowered the black people of Albany.

The mistakes made in Albany were not repeated in the successful 1963 Birmingham, Alabama, campaign. Martin intuitively understood that Birmingham was a crisis point for his people, realizing from the outset that a failure in Birmingham might mean the breakdown of nonviolence and a shift to violent revolt. Martin often referred to Birmingham as the most thoroughly segregated city in America. Blacks were shamefully subjugated in Birmingham: They were discriminated against in employment, able to secure only low-paying menial jobs with no benefits or hope of improved wages; they made up a very small percentage of registered voters, despite constituting over 40 percent of the population; the NAACP was outlawed; and blacks had been repeatedly victimized by racial violence and property damage—several had been murdered by whites who walked away without penalty. Perhaps Birmingham's racial position, particularly on the police force, was best symbolized by the popular commissioner of public safety, Eugene "Bull" Connor, when he demeaned blacks by stating, "If you ask half of them what freedom means, they couldn't tell you."[16] Martin once stated that in "Connor's Birmingham, the silent password was fear. It was a fear not only on the part of the black oppressed, but also in the hearts of the white oppressors. Guilt was a part of their fear."[17] Martin knew that Birmingham would be the centerpiece of the civil rights movement. "If Birmingham could be cracked," he recalled later, "the direction of the entire nonviolent movement in the South could take a significant turn. It was our faith that 'as Birmingham goes, so goes the South.'"[18]

In the summer of 1962 Martin, the SCLC, Birmingham church leaders, and Reverend Fred Shuttlesworth, Birmingham's foremost freedom fighter, whose house had recently been dynamited by racists, planned Operation "C," signifying confrontation. Operation "C" had a clear goal: the desegregation of restaurants and easier access to better jobs for blacks. Volunteer leaders were trained in nonviolent tactics that stressed that fighting the Birmingham police would be playing into the authorities' hands. At first the sit-ins, demonstrations, and boycotts of Birmingham businesses went without incident. However, on April 7, 1963, the police broke loose and charged into a crowd of demonstrators, beating them with sticks and unleashing police dogs. In response, on April 12, Martin and Ralph Abernathy led a large crowd toward central Birmingham singing the movement's rallying song *We Shall Overcome*. This march stood out in Martin's mind: "All along the way Negroes lined the streets. We were singing, and they were joining in. Occasionally the singing from the sidewalks was interspersed with applause. As we neared the downtown area, Bull Connor ordered his men to arrest us. Ralph and I were hauled off by two muscular policemen, clutching the backs of our shirts in handfuls."[19] Over fifty protesters were taken to jail and Martin was placed in solitary confinement and denied the right to make a telephone call for over twenty-four hours. During his eight days in jail, Martin composed "Letter from Birmingham Jail," one of the most insightful statements of the civil rights movement. Immediately upon his release, Martin and Ralph Abernathy drew up plans for the next phase of the Birmingham strategy, a children's crusade for freedom. On May 2, 1963, over a thousand black schoolchildren, ranging in age from six to eighteen, marched toward downtown singing freedom songs. Again Bull Connor unleashed the police, who used dogs and fire hoses to break up the crowd and arrest hundreds of young people. The images of nonviolent children attacked by police dogs and violently swept off their feet with surging water streams shocked the viewing public and resulted in a national outcry of protest.

The reaction in Washington, D.C., was so overwhelming that President Kennedy was compelled to send a delegated representative and three thousand federal troops to Birmingham to force a settlement. On May 10, Birmingham officials agreed to desegregate city facilities and drop the charges against demonstrators who had been arrested. Enraged and frustrated, hard-core white segregationists turned once more to violence by bombing the Birmingham headquarters of the SCLC and the house of Martin's brother, A.D. King. Tensions cooled somewhat when President Kennedy publicly supported the Birmingham crusade, and just three weeks later he asked Congress to enact a comprehensive

Civil Rights Bill. The segregated South would never be the same again.

THE MARCH ON WASHINGTON

After Birmingham, Martin's popularity grew throughout the nation. His voice was being heard and his nonviolent civil rights strategy was working. Martin himself maintained a rigorous speaking tour, preaching to thousands in Chicago, Detroit, and Los Angeles. In total he traveled over 250,000 miles and delivered over 350 speeches. But horrendous acts of racism continued: Medgar Evers, Mississippi's state chairman of the NAACP, was shot to death in the driveway of his home; the governor of Alabama, George Wallace, stood defiantly in a school doorway to block blacks from entering and desegregating public schools; and the Sunday school at the Birmingham Sixteenth Avenue Baptist Church was bombed, killing four little girls.

Late in the summer of 1963 Martin organized his Lincoln Memorial Prayer Pilgrimage in Washington, D.C., a site chosen for its symbolic meaning. This demonstration, called the March on Washington for Jobs and Freedom, generated an outpouring of support, far outstripping the 1957 rally at the same site. After lengthy preparations and discussions with

Martin Luther King Jr. delivering his "I Have a Dream" speech during the March on Washington, August 28, 1963.

President Kennedy, the march was sanctioned, and on August 28 an estimated 250,000 people, both black and white, came to Washington from across the nation. Following numerous speakers, Martin stepped to the podium as the keynote speaker and delivered his address outlining his dream for America. Martin's "I Have a Dream" speech touched the national conscience by portraying an America where "all of God's children, black men and white men, Jews and Gentiles, Protestants and Catholics, will be able to join hands and sing in the words of the old Negro spiritual, 'Free at last! Free at last! Great God Almighty, we are free at last!'"[20] Coretta wrote that these last words drifted out onto an awed silence and then the crowd broke, "They kept on shouting in one thunderous voice, and for that brief moment the Kingdom of God seemed to have come to earth."[21] Three months later, however, darkness descended when President John F. Kennedy, the nation's most potent voice for human rights, was assassinated in Dallas.

1964

The January 4, 1964, issue of *Time* magazine named Martin Luther King Jr. "Man of the Year" for 1963, making Martin the first black American to receive the honor. The *Time* article praised the civil rights struggle and Martin's role as its foremost leader. Indeed, just two months after the *Time* accolade, the House of Representatives, urged on by the new president, Lyndon B. Johnson, passed the Civil Rights Bill and sent it on to the Senate. After eighty-three days of heated debate, the bill ultimately won approval and was signed by President Johnson on July 2. As an invited guest, Martin witnessed the signing of the most comprehensive civil rights legislation in history. The 1964 Civil Rights Act guaranteed blacks the right to vote, banned discrimination in all organizations that received money from the government, and provided blacks full access to public facilities.

Martin's stature as an inspirational leader was celebrated in October 1964 when Martin, at age thirty-five, was chosen to receive the coveted Nobel Peace Prize. He was awarded the prize in Oslo, Norway, for his struggle for freedom and his adherence to nonviolence. While most Americans rejoiced at Martin's honor, J. Edgar Hoover, the longtime head of the FBI, was critical. Hoover hated Martin and saw the black struggle for freedom as nothing more than a breeding ground for communist infiltrators. Martin was continually under surveillance, his phones were tapped, and once, Coretta received FBI evidence alleging proof of Martin's sexual indiscretions. Hoover, who once called Martin the most notorious liar in the country, was obsessed with smearing the reputation of the civil rights leader and thwarting the SCLC's freedom efforts.

Despite Martin's honors and some encouraging signs of positive change in government, the summer of 1964 revealed an entrenched racist meanness in the nation. Martin's demonstrations in St. Augustine, Florida, were met with hostile and violent reactions from white segregationists; riots erupted in New York City's Harlem when a teenage black student was beaten by a white police officer; and three civil rights workers were savagely attacked and shot to death in Mississippi. Martin was also deeply concerned about the growing popularity of another black leader, Malcolm X. Although Martin agreed with Malcolm X's plea for black pride and his passionate call for a racial renaissance, he was afraid of Malcolm's Black Power philosophy, an approach to reform that did not rule out violence. Martin responded to the Black Power movement by thoughtfully stating "that it talks unceasingly about not imitating the values of white society, but in advocating violence it is imitating the worst, the most brutal and most uncivilized value of American life."[22] Undaunted, Martin continued to work tirelessly to secure black rights, particularly voting rights. The SCLC launched a Southern offensive to get blacks to register to vote. Martin selected Selma, Alabama, as a target for voter registration because it was at the heart of the state's black-belt counties where very few blacks voted; in fact, in some counties not a single black voter was even registered. In Selma only one in fifty blacks actually voted. One of Martin's goals was to pressure President Johnson to enact legislation to protect the rights of blacks to vote and to provide federal inspectors to guarantee that they were not threatened during the voter registration process.

SELMA

With the advance of federal desegregation, white citizens of Selma organized a White Citizen's Council to coordinate efforts to keep blacks from obtaining power and rights. Many of the efforts of this council were overseen by a tough county sheriff, James Clark. In January 1965 Martin orchestrated imposing demonstrations protesting voter registration practices in Selma. Five hundred blacks marched to the county courthouse to register, but police maneuvered them into an out-of-the-way, roped-off area in an alley. Despite waiting there all day, none were registered. These humiliating stall tactics lasted for approximately two weeks; each day James Clark and his officers arrested anyone who protested the procedure. When a federal order was issued to prevent voter harassment, city officials admitted only one registrant at a time, requiring each one to spend a lengthy amount of time completing useless and unfair forms and questionnaires.

Again, Martin was arrested, this time for leading an illegal parade. Frustrated, more than 250 protesters locked arms outside the courthouse and sang songs, joined later by 500 children who left school to participate. An angry James Clark had the adults arrested and the children charged with juvenile delinquency. This predictable overreaction by racist authorities attracted a great deal of publicity, which eventually reaped benefits when the U.S. Department of Justice decreed that the Selma registration process must be discarded and a minimum of 100 registrants must be processed a day. This victory spread throughout Alabama as more and more blacks demanded their right to register. In hopes of emphasizing the importance of voter registration, Martin planned a march from Selma to Montgomery. Alabama's governor, George Wallace, promptly banned the march, but undeterred, 500 protesters led by Martin's close associate, Hosea Williams, marched in defiance of the order. Just outside of Selma the road was blocked by state troopers who told them to disperse and go back to their churches. Quietly, following their nonviolent tactics, the marchers knelt down. While white spectators cheered them on, the troopers charged, brutally beating and seriously injuring many of the kneeling marchers with clubs, bullwhips, cattle prods, and tear gas. The news of the horrific event spread, labeled by the media as "Bloody Sunday." Shocked, but not intimidated, Martin made plans for another Selma to Montgomery march.

Two weeks after Bloody Sunday, Martin led a group of three thousand blacks and whites down the same road as the earlier march. At the outset, Martin told the protesters, "I can't promise that you won't get beaten; I can't promise you won't get your house bombed; I can't promise that you won't get scarred up a bit, but we must stand up for what is right."[23] The march was orderly, peaceful, and uneventful. The police did not attack, and Martin, after a prayer session on the highway, quietly asked the marchers to return to Selma. The march had been somewhat of a compromise, each side seeming to score a victory: The protesters established their right to march, and the authorities turned them back. Perhaps things would have ended there, but a foolish, hateful act stirred the animosities once again. That night a white Unitarian minister, James Reeb, ate dinner with two other clergymen at a black-owned restaurant and, as they were leaving, four Klansmen attacked them, shouting, "White niggers!" and crushed Reeb's skull with a wooden club. He died a short time later.

Reports of the Reeb killing, added with the appalling news footage of Bloody Sunday, horrified much of the nation. President Johnson finally broke his silence and addressed a joint congressional session. Broadcast on national television, Johnson concluded that "what happened in Selma is part of a far larger movement which reaches into every section and state of America. It is the effort of American Negroes to secure for themselves the full blessings of American life. . . . Their cause must be our cause, too. Because it is not just Negroes but really all of us, who must overcome the crippling legacy of bigotry and injustice. And we shall overcome!"[24] Martin and the freedom fighters were encouraged and gratified by the president's message. Later that year, President Johnson signed the 1965 Voting Rights Act, which barred literacy tests as a registration requirement and allowed federal authorities to intervene when the right to vote was obstructed.

THE FREEDOM MOVEMENT PUSHES INTO THE NORTH

Martin knew that the freedom struggle was not confined to the South. This was emphatically punctuated during the summer of 1965, when violent riots exploded in Watts, a black ghetto of Los Angeles, resulting in over thirty-five hundred arrests and thirty-five deaths. At a Baltimore meeting of the SCLC Martin decided to push his campaign to selected northern cities in order to fight poverty, inadequate housing, and unemployment. Martin understood that to simply calm the rioting was not enough; real social and political change for equality had to take place or violence would erupt over and over again.

Early in 1966 Martin established an SCLC office in Chicago and the King family, in order to understand the daily life of the downtrodden, moved into a dingy little tenement apartment in a Chicago ghetto. Martin's arrival in Chicago was not appreciated by the city's powerful and influential mayor, Richard Daley, who saw King as a troublemaking outsider. Immediately Martin and workers for the SCLC began to organize the neighbors, explaining that they could unify as renters to demand housing improvements. Martin wanted the poor to understand that even they could exercise legal and legitimate power. In the summer of 1966 Martin led a rally, named "Freedom Sunday," of over fifty thousand people at Soldier Field demanding better housing, jobs, city services, and schools. Tensions rose quickly: Some whites felt that Martin's activities, though nonviolent, would ultimately generate violence; and militant black leaders wanted more aggressive leadership. Many citizens, both black and white, were fearful and purchased guns to protect themselves from what they believed to be the inevitable "war." Indeed, two black youths were killed in rioting on Chicago's West Side, and the governor of Illinois mobilized the national guard to maintain order. Martin met with Richard Daley to write a Summit Agreement in which the city agreed to end discrimination and help blacks find better housing and jobs. However, the agreement was very general and not sincerely supported by Daley or city officials.

Since substantive changes had not been made, Martin feared that the summer of 1967 would be even more violent than 1966. As early as June 2 riots broke out in Boston where more than sixty people were injured. Before the summer ended, over thirty riots exploded across America, including Detroit, where forty-three died and over three hundred were seriously injured. Martin preached that the boiling unrest could only be eased if the oppressive yoke of poverty was lifted. He stated unflinchingly that "the curse of poverty has no justification in our age. It is socially as cruel and blind as the practice of cannibalism at the dawn of civilization, when men ate each other because they had not yet learned to take food from the soil or to consume the abundant animal life around them. The time has come for us to civilize ourselves by the total, direct, and immediate abolition of poverty."[25] By the end of 1967 Martin had announced a new initiative, the Poor People's Campaign, dedicated to eradicating poverty through the development of meaningful employment for people of all colors.

MARTIN'S DEATH

Martin's work on the Poor People's Campaign was interrupted when the sanitation workers in Memphis, Tennessee, went on strike for better wages and working conditions. Martin's first demonstration in Memphis to support the striking workers turned violent and one black person was killed. Chagrined at the violent result of the first demonstration, Martin returned on April 3, 1968, to try another march, one rooted in nonviolence.

The very next day, April 4, 1968, after a successful meeting with his staff, Martin retired to his room at the Lorraine Motel in Memphis. Shortly before six, while standing pensively on his balcony, a gunshot fired by an escaped convict named James Earl Ray mortally wounded Martin in the neck. He died an hour later at Memphis's St. Joseph's Hospital. The day before the assassination, while speaking to a group of supporters, Martin voiced the risks that he was taking. After King's assassination, the media frequently referenced this speech as Martin's premonition of his own death:

> We've got some difficult days ahead, but it doesn't matter with me now. Because I've been to the mountain top. And I don't mind. Like anybody, I would like to live a long life. Longevity has its place. But I'm not concerned about that now. I just want to do God's will. And He's allowed me to go to the mountain. And I've looked over. And I've seen the promised land. I may not get there with you. But I want you to know tonight, that we, as a people will get to the promised land.[26]

People across the nation were shocked at Martin's brutal and senseless slaying. Upon his death riots broke out in over a hundred American cities; thousands were injured, almost fifty were killed, and over twenty thousand were arrested. Grief, shock, and introspective questions were articulated by millions around the world. The fact that the archetype of nonviolence should meet such a violent end dramatized the very anger in American society that Martin had tirelessly struggled against. He once wrote, "The oceans of history are made turbulent by the ever-rising tides of hate. History is cluttered with the wreckage of nations and individuals that pursued that self-defeating path of hate. Love is the key to the solution of the problems of the world."[27] Martin's campaign to free blacks and help the poor was built on love without egotism and selflessness without pride.

The funeral was held at his father's church in Atlanta. The nation mourned as they watched it on television, and the thousands who attended—black and white, rich and poor, notable and ordinary—provided a living tribute to Martin's vision of a unified society. Martin's coffin was taken to the interment on a simple farm wagon drawn by mules, followed by a long, sinuous procession of mourners. Words from a black spiritual, the same words that concluded his famous speech at the Lincoln Memorial, are inscribed on his marble monument: "Free at last! Free at last! Thank God Almighty, I'm free at last." President Johnson proclaimed Sunday, April 7, as a national day of mourning.

Coretta King wrote that "my husband had always talked of his own readiness to give his life for a cause he believed in. He felt that giving himself completely would serve as a redemptive force in its inspiration to other people. This would mean that he would be resurrected in the lives of other people who dedicated themselves to a great cause." [28] Indeed, Martin's cause has had a lasting effect on the nation. Through his personal efforts, inspiration, and courage blacks not only have the right to vote, but are actually registered to vote; blacks have been voted into school boards, mayors' offices, and Congress. Martin's legacy has made discrimination illegal, offering blacks access to all public facilities and schools; Jim Crow laws died at the hands of nonviolent freedom fighters. He led the battle for better employment, and today more and more blacks are entering professional jobs that were unattainable for them when Martin first started preaching. And in just twelve years of struggle, Martin, like Gandhi, raised a nation's understanding of justice and equality, provided sustenance for its moral well-being, and pushed it one step closer toward its democratic ideal. Because minorities are still fighting to attain their rightful share of America's comfortable life, Martin's struggle continues today, and his dream lies somewhere in the future. But every third Monday in January on Martin Luther King Jr. Day millions of Americans feel Martin's spirit and find optimism in his indefatigable capacity for hope: "If you lose hope, somehow you lose the vitality that keeps life moving, you lose that courage to be, that quality that helps you to go on in spite of all. And so today I still have a dream." [29]

This volume for Greenhaven's People Who Made History series is designed to explore Martin Luther King's struggle, his failures, and his victories. It focuses on circumstances and people who shaped his thinking and activism; it investigates how his social and political thinking emerged and evolved; it records his role in the monumental events of the civil rights movement; and it examines his legacy as a key contributor to America's social and moral development.

This anthology works to capture not only the actions of the man, but it also seeks to reveal the essence of his character. King's participation in the black freedom struggle lasted only twelve years, stopped tragically when he was shot to death at the age of thirty-nine. In that time he taught all of America how to live a moral, compassionate, and committed life. His systematic attack on segregation and the denial of minority freedom was built on an unwavering dedication to nonviolence and a philosophy of love; his blueprint of social improvement was predicated on justice and democratic ideals; and his opportunity to change a nation grew from his charismatic ability to motivate people. For many, Martin Luther King Jr. is a fitting metaphor for the best of American idealism.

Dexter Scott King, Martin and Coretta's second son, cogently expressed the value of studying Martin's life and struggles for freedom when, in his introduction to *The Martin Luther King, Jr., Companion,* he wrote,

> To most young people history is just that, with no relevance to the present or future. With our new technologies and new-found freedoms, what can we learn from a civil rights movement that took place before this generation was born? If we cannot understand and respect the lessons which our ancestors learned through hard struggle, then we are condemned to relive those same struggles over and over again. If history has taught us nothing else, it has taught us that.[30]

NOTES

1. Martin Luther King Jr., *Stride Toward Freedom: The Montgomery Story.* New York: Harper & Row, 1958, p. 53.

2. King, *Stride Toward Freedom,* p. 20.

3. Coretta Scott King, *My Life with Martin Luther King, Jr.* New York: Holt, Rinehart and Winston, 1969, p. 81.

4. Martin Luther King Jr., *Where Do We Go from Here: Chaos or Community?* New York: Harper & Row, 1967, p. 101.

5. King, *Stride Toward Freedom,* p. 91.

6. King, *Stride Toward Freedom*, p. 85.

7. King, *Stride Toward Freedom*, p. 22.

8. Quoted in L.D. Reddick, *Crusader Without Violence: A Biography of Martin Luther King, Jr.* New York: Harper & Brothers, 1959, p. 105.

9. King, *My Life with Martin Luther King, Jr.*, p. 97.

10. King, *Stride Toward Freedom*, p. 53.

11. Quoted in King, *My Life with Martin Luther King, Jr.*, p. 118.

12. King, *My Life with Martin Luther King, Jr.*, p. 127.

13. Quoted in King, *My Life with Martin Luther King, Jr.*, p. 129.

14. Quoted in *Playboy* Interview (January 1965) in *A Testament of Hope: The Essential Writings of Martin Luther King, Jr.*, ed. James Melvin Washington. San Francisco: Harper & Row, 1986, p. 350.

15. Quoted in Clayborne Carson, ed., *The Autobiography of Martin Luther King, Jr.* New York: Warner Books, 1998, p. 168.

16. Quoted in Jim Bishop, *The Days of Martin Luther King, Jr.* New York: G.P. Putnam's Sons, 1971, p. 304.

17. Martin Luther King Jr., "Why We Can't Wait," in *A Testament of Hope: The Essential Writings of Martin Luther King, Jr.*, ed. James Melvin Washington. San Francisco: Harper & Row, 1986, p. 220.

18. Quoted in Adam Fairclough, *Martin Luther King, Jr.* Athens: University of Georgia Press, 1995, p. 74.

19. King, "Why We Can't Wait," in *A Testament of Hope*, p. 554.

20. Martin Luther King Jr., "I Have a Dream," in *A Testament of Hope: The Essential Writings of Martin Luther King, Jr.*, ed. James Melvin Washington. San Francisco: Harper & Row, 1986, p. 220.

21. King, *My Life with Martin Luther King, Jr.*, p. 240.

22. King, *Where Do We Go from Here*, p. 64.

23. Quoted in King, *My Life with Martin Luther King, Jr.*, p. 259.

24. Quoted in Stephen B. Oates, *Let the Trumpet Sound: The Life of Martin Luther King, Jr.* New York: Harper & Row, 1982, p. 355.

25. King, *Where Do We Go From Here*, p. 165.

26. Quoted in Oates, *Let the Trumpet Sound*, p. 486.

27. Martin Luther King Jr., Nobel Prize Lecture, December 11, 1964.

28. King, *My Life with Martin Luther King, Jr.*, p. 320.

29. Martin Luther King Jr., *The Trumpet of Conscience.* New York: Harper & Row, 1967, p. 41.

30. Dexter Scott King, "Introduction," in Coretta Scott King, ed., *The Martin Luther King, Jr., Companion.* New York: St. Martin's Press, 1993, p. vi.

CHAPTER 1

The Shaping of King's Activism

Social Conditions and the Emergence of Martin Luther King Jr.

Aldon D. Morris

Aldon D. Morris argues that social conditions of the 1950s converged to produce black leaders like Martin Luther King Jr. According to Morris, black leaders had to learn creative strategies and methodologies to combat a comprehensive environment of white domination that was bolstered by a legal system that sanctioned racial segregation. By mid-century, black migration to the cities worked to strengthen the black community, increase political power, and create communication networks. As a result, three solid social institutions formed the emotional and intellectual breeding ground for leaders like King: the black church, black colleges, and black families.

Morris maintains that the black church formed the organizational framework for most black political, economic, educational, and religious activities. Indeed, King would harness the power of the church to provide the necessary work force and the money to challenge white domination. Morris also concludes that black urbanization allowed for the rapid growth of black colleges. Within their walls black teachers taught students like King to battle intellectually against the racial status quo. Finally, Morris suggests that conditions in the cities helped solidify the black family and consequently provide young people the emotional strength and energy to lead the civil rights struggle.

Aldon D. Morris teaches sociology at the Center for Urban Affairs and Policy Research at Northwestern University, Evanston, Illinois.

Excerpted from "A Man Prepared for the Times: A Sociological Analysis of the Leadership of Martin Luther King Jr.," by Aldon D. Morris, in *We Shall Overcome*, edited by Peter J. Albert and Ronald Hoffman. Copyright ©1990 by United States Capitol Historical Society. Reprinted by permission of Pantheon Books, a division of Random House, Inc.

Oppression has always been—and continues to be—one of the defining characteristics of black life in the United States. Indeed, throughout American history, blacks have struggled against a comprehensive system of domination imposed on them by whites. Powerful whites—landowners, politicians, business elites, and others—have been the architects of this system. Throughout more than two hundred years of slavery and subsequent slave-like conditions, racial domination has enabled whites to build one of the most powerful empires ever known to human civilization. Racial domination in America was constructed in such a manner as to benefit all whites, at least in the short run. Poor and middle class whites benefited because the segregated labor force prevented blacks from competing with them for better-paying jobs. The white ruling class benefited because blacks supplied them with cheap labor and a weapon against the labor movement, the threat to use unemployed blacks as strikebreakers in labor disputes. Finally, most whites benefited from the system's implicit assurance that no matter how poor or uneducated, they were always better than the niggers.

In the 1950s southern blacks experienced this system of domination most acutely. Like their northern counterparts, they found themselves at the bottom of the economic ladder and without any substantial political power, but for them the economic and political oppression was compounded by a legal system of racial segregation that denied them personal freedoms routinely enjoyed by whites. Segregation was an arrangement that set blacks off from the rest of humanity and stigmatized them as an inferior race. Forced to use different toilets, drinking fountains, waiting rooms, parks, schools, and the like, facilities contrasting sharply with the well-kept ones reserved for whites only, blacks were forever reminded of their low status. The "colored" and "white only" signs that dotted the buildings and public places of a typical southern city expressed the reality of a social system committed to the subjugation of blacks and the denial of their human dignity and self-respect.

This perplexing problem of economic, political, and social domination has absorbed the creative energies of black leadership since the days of slavery. Great black leaders, including Frederick Douglass, Booker T. Washington, W.E.B. Du Bois, Marcus Garvey, and A. Philip Randolph, have had to tackle this problem, each in his own way, depending on the resources and changing conditions of the black masses and the larger society at the time. Black leadership, therefore, can be assessed in terms of its response to this tripartite system of domination; any aspiring black leader has had to confront racism with creative strategies and methodologies. It was this system of domination, well entrenched in the South of the 1950s and crippling to the black masses, that confronted Martin Luther King, Jr., and his generation. To understand King's leadership one has to situate it within this social context of domination.

THE SOCIAL IMPACT OF BLACK URBANIZATION

The rapid urbanization of the black population during the first half of the twentieth century was an advantage to King that was not available to the black leaders who preceded him. The quality of the leadership of any oppressed group is directly proportionate to the group's collective strength. The phenomenal migration of rural blacks to southern and northern cities during the first and second world wars enhanced the collective strength of the black community tremendously. Life in the cities contrasted sharply with that found in southern rural settings. The sociologist E. Franklin Frazier described rural black communities as follows: "The cabins are scattered in the open country so that the development of village communities has been impossible. Consequently, communication between rural families as well as the development of rural institutions has been limited by the wide dispersion of the population." Black urbanization created densely populated black communities where blacks could interact freely among themselves. In an urban setting rich social networks flourished, embedded in kinship, religious, and community ties. New political and social organizations, as well as economic enterprises, sprang up, and existing ones were strengthened. In the urban milieu sophisticated communication networks that crisscrossed within and between black communities proliferated and hardened. Although money was scarce and unemployment high, blacks fared slightly better economically in the cities than they had on the farms.

Research has demonstrated that social movements are likely to emerge from groups characterized by solid communication networks, organizational strength, and a variety of resources, of which financial capital is extremely important. By the 1950s, southern black urban communities were fast becoming such sources of emerging movements; it was from these communities that Martin Luther King, Jr., would derive his leadership. Indeed, King's organizational documents reveal that he was acutely aware of these structural developments. "Social and economic forces are bringing about great changes in the South. Urbanization, industrialization, scientific agriculture and mass education are making it possible to remove the barriers to a prosperous, free and creative life for all southerners."

Black urbanization also increased the political strength of the black community, especially in the urban North. As blacks concentrated there, they began to form voting blocs that could not be ignored by the two main political parties. This created a weapon for the black community because the Democratic party in particular had to give lip service to black equality in order to attract the black vote; in effect it had to go on record as supporting the aspirations of the black masses. This stance, coupled with the 1954 Supreme Court ruling declaring segregated schools to be unconstitutional, went far toward legitimizing the black struggle.

THE POWER OF THE BLACK CHURCH

Institution-building within the black community following black urbanization was also important to the rise of the modern civil rights movement and King's leadership. In cities, this institutional development was evident on a number of fronts. The black press, political organizations, barber and beauty shops, and a host of other groups all experienced growth, thanks to black migration. In particular, the institution-building that occurred in the black church, colleges, and the family was crucial to the development of the civil rights movement.

The strength of the black community parallels that of the black church to a considerable degree, and this was especially true in the 1950s. A unique institution, the black church was organized and developed by an oppressed group shut off from the institutional life of the larger society. As a result, it provided the organizational framework for most activities of the community: economic, political, and educational, as well as religious. The church furnished outlets for social and artistic expression, a forum for the discussion of important issues, a social environment that developed, trained, and disciplined potential leaders from all walks of life, and an arena that lent itself to the development of charisma and meaningful symbols to engender hope, enthusiasm, and a resilient group spirit. The church was also a platform where group interests could be collectively articulated and defended.

Two other factors made the church important to the black movement and to King's leadership. First, its principal human resource was its organizational base—the congregation. The black community has always contributed the voluntary labor and financial capital necessary to meet the church's considerable needs in its role as the main community center. Accordingly, it was the church that provided the movement and King with the work force and the money capable of challenging white domination. Second, the black church was the only popularly based institution within the black community that was, for the most part, economically and politically independent of the white community. This independence allowed it to serve as a staging ground for the black protest movement. This, of course, is one of the reasons why a disproportionate number of prominent protest leaders were ministers: their activities could not be derailed by white economic reprisals. Thus, the black church functioned as the institutional bedrock of black resistance.

The urbanization of the black population during the first half of the twentieth century rapidly increased the strength of the black church. For one thing, the membership of the urban church was much larger than that of the rural church. For example, [social scientist] Doug McAdam found that the average membership of southern urban churches was three times greater than that of rural churches. This meant that the urban black church could raise substantial amounts of money and that the capacity of its work force was increased significantly. The urban church, in comparison to its rural counterpart, also enjoyed more sophisticated ministerial leadership. In this regard McAdam found that a far greater proportion of ministers in southern urban churches held advanced degrees than in rural ones. Given the fact that urban ministers earned higher salaries, they were far more likely to function as full-time pastors. Therefore, in terms of organizational strength, the urban church became an institution capable of wielding considerable power. This led [Swedish economist] Gunnar Myrdal to write in 1944 that "potentially, the Negro church is undoubtedly a power institution. It has the Negro masses organized and, if the church bodies decided to do so, they could line the Negroes behind a program." By the 1950s the black church was capable of mass struggle, and Martin Luther King, Jr., would utilize this power for just this purpose.

INFLUENCE OF BLACK COLLEGES

Like the black church, black colleges also underwent significant institution-building during the first half of the twentieth century owing to the urbanization of the black population and the consequent improvement of black economic conditions. McAdam found that from 1941 to mid-century the enrollment in black colleges doubled from 37,203 to 74,526. Moreover, the income for black colleges rose from roughly $8 million to over $38 million between 1930 and 1947. The number of degrees awarded by black colleges also increased dramatically, and during the first half of the twentieth century a significant number of these schools achieved full accreditation.

The extensive growth of black colleges was important to the rise of the modern civil rights movement and its leadership because some of these schools became the institutions where the intellectual battle against racial inequality was waged. Within their walls, students and professors debated and wrote about the injustice of racial segregation and domination and generally agreed that they should embrace and promote the drive toward equality. Around the turn of the twentieth century, W.E.B. Du Bois wrote in *The Souls of Black Folk*, "The function of the Negro college, then, is clear: it must maintain the standards of popular education, it must seek the social regeneration of the Negro, and it must help in the solution of problems of race contact and cooperation." The president of Morehouse College, Benjamin Mays, wrote in his autobiography, *Born to Rebel*, that "in my twenty-seven years as President, I never ceased to raise my voice and pen against the injustices of a society that segregated and discriminated against people because God made them black." Mays pointed out that "the leadership of Morehouse College never accepted the status quo in Negro-white relations" and that "throughout its history, Morehouse's leadership has rebelled against racial injustices."

In a comprehensive study of [early civil rights lawyer]

Charles H. Houston, [American historian and biographer] Genna Rae McNeil has demonstrated that during Houston's years at Howard University he developed a first-rate law school there for the explicit purpose of challenging the legal underpinnings of racial segregation. It was this law school that trained the National Association for the Advancement of Colored People (NAACP) lawyers who won numerous cases against racial segregation, including the Supreme Court's famous 1954 school desegregation decision. [Historian] Daniel Thompson in his thorough study of black colleges captured the essence of the argument: "The central mission . . . of Black colleges . . . is still essentially the same as it was in the beginning . . . to prepare students to make necessary and unique contributions to the survival and advancement of black Americans and to improve the overall social condition of the less-advantaged masses." This is not to claim that black colleges have been totally free of conservatism, corrupt administrators, and political censorship by powerful whites who often controlled the purse strings of the schools. However, the argument here is that in spite of such problems, a substantial number of professors and students in these colleges produced trenchant critiques of the racial status quo and waged the intellectual battle against racial domination.

MOREHOUSE COLLEGE AND MARTIN LUTHER KING JR.

Another responsibility of black colleges was to produce black leaders. Thompson provides an explanation of this: "The sense of leadership responsibility on black campuses has been always stimulated by two interrelated facts: at least 80 percent of the students come from homes and communities where well-prepared, articulate leadership is desperately needed, and because these campuses are relatively small, all students have opportunities, even challenges, to discover and develop their leadership talents." This seems to have been the case at Morehouse where Dr. King received his undergraduate training in the late 1940s. Benjamin Mays wrote, "I found a special, intangible something at Morehouse in 1921 which sent men out into life with a sense of mission, believing that they could accomplish whatever they set out to do. This priceless quality was still alive when I returned in 1940, and for twenty-seven years I built on what I found, instilling in Morehouse students the idea that despite crippling circumstances the sky was their limit." He went on to point out that "it was a few able, dedicated teachers who made the Morehouse man believe that he was 'somebody.'" The size of Morehouse facilitated this social conditioning because "the student body has never been large. In 1967 the college enrolled 910 students." Given the nature and mission of black colleges it is not surprising that they played a major role in producing men and women who would become major leaders in the civil rights movement. Martin Luther King, Jr., was a product of this college environment, and his personality epitomized the leadership characteristics championed by black colleges.

THE INFLUENCE OF THE FAMILY ON BLACK LEADERSHIP

Institution-building within the family was also significant for the rise of the movement and King's leadership. It is not impossible for great leaders to emerge from conditions of extreme poverty and degradation, but it is unlikely; great leaders throughout human history have usually emerged from the middle and upper classes. They have generally had the privilege of receiving formal education and enjoying the necessary leisure time to develop leadership skills. Therefore, family context is a critical variable that plays an enormous role in providing the resources and environment conducive to the development of leadership skills. [American sociologist] Andrew Billingsley has correctly argued that "prominent in the background of Negro men and women of achievement is a strong family life."

The black rural-to-urban migration strengthened the black family. This was true for urban black families in both the North *and* South. It has already been pointed out that in contrast to rural blacks, urban blacks earned more money, lived in stronger communities, and had access to more supportive churches and educational institutions. This general upgrading of the urban black community had positive consequences for the black family. Indeed, Billingsley found that religion, education, money or property, jobs, family ties, and community-centered activities were the chief ingredients of strong family life. He went on to argue that strong black families have a "certain degree of independence and control of the forces affecting the lives of their members" and that they "are often highly influenced by the religious convictions and behavior, the education or educational aspirations of one or more members. They often have an economic footing more secure than the average Negro family in their community. They often have strong emotional ties."

By the 1950s significant numbers of black people had migrated to the cities of the South, hoping to escape the back-breaking poverty and oppression that crippled them and their families in the rural setting. A brief examination of the rural family context of Martin Luther King, Sr.—"Daddy King"—is instructive. Daddy King's childhood was spent in rural Stockbridge, Georgia. His father, James Albert King, was a sharecropper while his mother, Delia King, was a domestic. They had the difficult task of rearing ten children. As a sharecropper Albert King was cheated out of most of his hard-earned annual income by exploitative white landowners. The meager earnings of Delia King contributed to the household but were not enough to raise the family out of poverty. Daddy King recalled that "there was no way to make any money sharecropping." Speaking of the family's overall condition [King biographer] Lawrence Reddick wrote, "life was hard, work and children plentiful, and material rewards slight." As a result, Albert King became an alcoholic and often released his rage by abusing Delia King and the children. This syndrome of black poverty and tense family relations was widespread in the rural South. It engendered an "outward looking" attitude among thousands of rural youths who hungered for city life where they believed opportunities would be greater and social oppression less. During World War I, Martin Luther King, Sr., moved to Atlanta, like thousands of other young blacks who migrated to the city in search of a better life. Within a relatively short period of time he had developed an educational and economic infrastructure for a strong family. And it was in this strong family context that Martin Luther King, Jr., would be nurtured and prepared for his leadership role.

Family Influences on King

Lewis V. Baldwin

Lewis V. Baldwin contends that Martin Luther King Jr. gained much of his strength to withstand adversity from the love and support of his family. His wife Coretta kept the family intact, offering primary care and emotional strength for the children when Martin was away for long periods of time. She also provided Martin with the encouragement to continue during those times when he received unrelenting criticism. To do this, Coretta had to cope with the pressures of death threats, her husband's absence, and, occasionally, financial hardships. Like Martin, Coretta was deeply committed to the civil rights struggle; she understood the necessity to push, at all costs, toward the higher cause for her people. Baldwin writes that both Martin and Coretta acknowledged the likelihood of Martin's death; they talked about it and gained courage from each other. Others, like Martin's teachers, theologians Benjamin Mays and Howard Thurman, helped Martin see death philosophically.

Martin's parents, Daddy King and Alberta, provided Martin additional family strength. Martin viewed his father as an example of courage and a reformer like himself. Baldwin suggests that Martin learned moral power from his father, while Daddy King eventually gained from Martin an understanding of strength through nonviolence. From his mother, Martin acquired the healing power of affection and a trust in optimism. Baldwin concludes that the Kings are a wonderful example of how the black family in America has worked as an instrument of black survival.

Lewis V. Baldwin is a professor of religious studies at the College of Arts and Science, Vanderbilt University, Nashville, Tennessee. He is the author of several works on the civil rights movement.

Martin Luther King, Jr., could not have sustained himself in a protracted battle for freedom without a community that cared for him, embraced him, and accepted him in spite of his mistakes. Faced with many personal sufferings that involved arrests more than twenty times, physical attacks, and victimization through numerous threats against his life and family, King drew strength and courage not from the liberal theology he studied at Crozer Theological Seminary and Boston University, but from a social network built largely around his family. Without the love, comfort, support, and encouragement provided by his family, King could not have maintained the physical strength, mental stability, and moral and spiritual balance necessary to confront the enormous challenges of social reality, external dangers, and rapidly growing fame. King's rise to the forefront of the civil rights movement and the worldwide struggle for justice and peace did not surprise or disturb his wife Coretta, who always said that "my husband was committed to social justice and determined to be successful in life when I met him." Sharing her husband's passion for equal rights and social justice, Coretta determined very early that his burden was hers as well. "As Martin was being made ready to be the leader and the symbol of the Negro movement," she wrote, "so I was being prepared to be his wife and helpmate. It was in Montgomery that I became aware of the contribution I could make in sustaining and helping my husband in what was to come."

Coretta's Supportive Role

For thirteen years prior to her husband's assassination, Coretta King was a working mother and an active father for their children. It was she who constantly explained to the children why their father had to be away from home so much. "I told them that daddy is doing God's work," she explained. "He loves you all, but he also loves other people. I taught this to them in simple terms while they were very young, and I enlarged on that definition as they got older." Coretta was the constant source of comfort and strength for the children as they confronted the devastating consequences of racism in the South in their early years. She also helped them see the relevance of what their father was doing for their own lives and futures, as well as for the destiny of black people and the nation as a whole.

Coretta's support for Martin also found expression in other ways. Many nights when King arrived home after fulfilling a busy schedule, Coretta would meet him at the door with a hug and kiss. "We would often come in off the road at 10 o'clock at night," recounted King's assistant Bernard Lee, "and Coretta would be so glad to see us that she would get up and fix a major meal. Late at night we'd be sitting there eating greens and cornbread." Martin and Coretta would often tease one another and sing together on those occasions, and these times were immensely important in keeping them strong and dedicated to each other and to the cause. When King met a storm of criticism from both blacks and whites because of his expressed opposition to the involvement of the United States in Vietnam, Coretta not only supported him but also made many speeches on Vietnam for him. "I remember saying to him so many times, especially after he received the Nobel Peace Prize," Coretta reminisced, "'I think there is a role you must play in achieving world peace, and I will be so glad when the time comes when you can assume that role.'" It is difficult to measure the significance of this kind of support, especially when one considers that King's own father initially opposed his stance on Vietnam.

CORETTA'S INFLUENCE ON MARTIN

Confronted daily with criticism and threats, it was never easy for Coretta to remain undaunted. At times, her concern for her husband's safety and well-being took priority over other considerations, and understandably so. When officials sentenced King to six months' hard labor in Georgia's State Penitentiary at Reidsville in 1961 for allegedly violating his probation, Coretta burst into tears. This was a very rare occurrence for the woman who had stood by her husband when their home was bombed in Montgomery, when he suffered a near-fatal stabbing in Harlem in 1958, and during the forty or so threatening phone calls he received each day. The pressures of family life, stemming primarily from King's frequent absences and the scarcity of financial resources, did cause tension and differences between the couple at times, but these difficulties were never permitted to fragment the family or to interfere with the movement. Coretta stood by her husband's side because she believed in the essential righteousness of his cause and personal sacrifices, and because she valued his contributions to the uplift of humanity.

She was always amazed, and often disturbed, to discover that her husband cared more about his service to humanity than about money and other material values. King frequently said to her: "People who are doing something don't have time to be worried about all that," an observation to which Coretta seldom responded.

King's own reflections on the supportive role of Coretta are profound and searching. He found great pleasure and consolation in knowing that his wife was aware of the whole struggle and of all his involvements in the struggle. Referring specifically to Coretta's knowledge of and participation in the struggle, King once noted that "I think at many points she educated me":

> When I met her she was very concerned about all the things that we're trying to do now. I never will forget that the first discussion we had when we met was the whole question of racial injustice, economic injustice, and peace. In her college days she had been actively engaged in movements dealing with these problems. So I must admit—I wish I could say, to satisfy my masculine ego, that I led her down this path, but I must say that we went down together.

From the time of the Montgomery Bus Boycott, King knew that Coretta would be one of his greatest sources of support and his most loving critic. The calmness Coretta displayed when their home was bombed in Montgomery in 1956 did much to reinforce this perception. After the bombing, King said to his wife: "Well, Coretta, I don't know what I would have done without you. You have been a real soldier." "I realized then," Coretta recalled, "how much it meant to him for me to continue to be strong and to give him support, not only in terms of words, but in terms of actually feeling this way and being this way." For King, Coretta was always "a most understanding wife, who has given me consolation when I needed it most." It is not an insignificant point that he dedicated his first book, *Stride Toward Freedom: The Montgomery Story* (1958), "To Coretta, my beloved wife and co-worker."

THE PROSPECT OF MARTIN'S DEATH

The manner in which Coretta adjusted to the possibility of her husband's assassination was a source of inspiration and instruction for him. Death was frequently a topic of conversation in the King home, and that helped to prepare Coretta emotionally, spiritually, and philosophically for what would be the inevitable. Shortly before he was killed in Memphis, King alluded to his wife's amazing adjustment to the fact that he was exposing himself to the constant danger of assassination:

> The interesting thing is that she's adjusted to this, and she's adjusted by looking at it philosophically. She's realistic enough to know that emotions are high on this issue and that something can happen. There are many sick people in our society—people who are corroded with hatred, and they will use violence, and they will assassinate leaders of the movement. . . . My wife is very conscious of this, but it does not stop her in her commitment in going about her daily work. If one worried about these things all the time, one certainly couldn't function. So we must go on with the faith that the cause is right, and that if something happens in the process, it will serve that cause in a way that we may not be able to see at this time.

Because of the understanding and support of Coretta and other members of the King family, who believed strongly in an afterlife, King did not have to face the possibility of his own death alone. Others who were very close to the King family, such as the black theologians Benjamin E. Mays and Howard Thurman, helped King to accept the reality of death without crippling fear through their counseling and teachings. Philip Lenud [Martin's roommate in college] claims that Thurman's brilliant and extensive reflections on transcendence were of great inspirational value to King as he confronted the reality and the possible meaning of his own death. The significance of family and other black folk sources should be carefully considered over against the common assumption that [German philosopher] Martin Heidegger and other existentialists were primarily responsible for King's ability to deal courageously, creatively, and philosophically with the imminent possibility of his own death. . . .

THE INFLUENCE OF DADDY AND ALBERTA KING

The relationship between King and his father during the movement was rooted in a mutual love and understanding that almost defies definition. In the early stages of the Montgomery struggle, when the forces of racism moved against his son with power that seemed almost invincible, Daddy King wept and advised young Martin to turn the reins of leadership over to someone else. This experience helped Daddy King discipline himself, and he never displayed such emotions in his son's presence again. From that point, he assured Martin, Jr.: "Well, son, you know that whatever you decide to do, you can count on Daddy." Daddy King was very proud of his son and of the spiritual and moral power he imparted to the family and to the entire nation. Martin, Jr., continued to view Daddy King as a profile in courage, and he once spoke of his father's role and his own role "as historical phases of the same process":

> I think my father and I have worked together a great deal in the last few years, trying to grapple with the same problem. . . . He was working in the area of civil rights before I was born and when I was just a kid, and I grew up in the kind of atmosphere that had a real civil rights concern. I do think its the same problem that we are grappling with—its the same historical process. . . .

On another occasion King evoked the name of the great Protestant Reformer Martin Luther, noting that "Both father and I have fought all our lives for reform, and perhaps we've earned our right to the name." Much of the power of the relationship between young Martin and Daddy King stemmed not only from the tradition of social action that bound them together but also from what they learned and experienced from each other. Martin, Jr., frequently alluded to the impelling spiritual and moral power he received from his father, a power that helped him grow in wisdom and fortitude. In a similar vein, Daddy King credited his son with introducing him to the most powerful method available to humans in their quest for social justice. "I never thought I would be nonviolent," Daddy King commented on one occasion, "but M.L. has convinced me that nonviolence is the way to deal with these white folks." On another occasion he declared that "I love what my son taught me and thousands of other people in this country about the enormous personal power of nonviolence."

The spiritual and moral power that drew Martin, Jr., and Alberta King together in a chain of mutual love and support took on a somewhat unique character. Alberta, with her rich and warm displays of motherly love, afforded her son an example of human energy and resourcefulness that no one else in the King family could have provided in a time of conflict and crisis. Aside from becoming one with young Martin in suffering, in struggle, and in the celebration of the liberation of humanity, Alberta shared with him nourishing food, confidential advice, and vital portions of the accumulated lore of the folk. The tie of affection that marked this mother-son relationship was revealed most profoundly during those times when King chatted with his mother by telephone. There were times when he and his brother A.D. "would both be on the phone with their mother, laughing and riding each other about their huge appetites and what they were doing to their respective waistlines." At other times they would tease and fool their mother for a while, "disguising their voices, each pretending to be the other." The power that this kind of affection generated helped ease the heavy burdens King was forced to bear daily as a result of his involvement in the movement. To be sure, much of the faith and optimism with which he faced life grew out of those moments of conversation and sharing with his mother and others in the family.

The love and support King received from his family during the thirteen years of his active leadership in the civil rights movement was characteristic of the role that the black family has played since slavery. In the midst of the crises, conflict, and change that marked the 1950s and 1960s, the King family emerged as a supreme example of how the black family has functioned as a flexible and adaptable instrument of black survival.

King's Decision to Become a Minister

James P. Hanigan

James P. Hanigan reports that in a school essay entitled "An Autobiography of Religious Development"
King emphasized the powerful childhood influence
of his father and his maternal grandmother. King
wrote that his upbringing, his unwavering good
health, and the psychological strength that he received from his family shaped his view of the world
and of God. In this same essay he also wrote that the
church, although an integral part of his life, relied
too much on emotionalism and not enough on intellectual meaning.

Hanigan suggests that King went through an intense
skeptical period while at Morehouse College. There he
doubted the literal interpretation of the Bible and turned to
modern, liberal biblical criticism. He knew then he wanted
to help humanity and this, not a mystical conversion,
pushed him to accept the ministry. According to Hanigan,
King refined his religious views at Crozer Theological Seminary, where he honed a highly personal interpretation of the
Christian message. King theorized that the Christian ethic
started with the image of God as Father and humankind as a
brotherhood. For King all human beings are equal parts of a
brotherhood and, therefore, all have worth and dignity.

James P. Hanigan is a professor of philosophy and religion at Villa Maria College, Erie, Pennsylvania. He has written extensively for religious and philosophical journals.

The decision that King made in his junior year at Morehouse
College to become a Baptist minister was not surprising for
a boy of his background and upbringing. Yet the reasons for
his decision have remained somewhat obscure. He himself
tells us very little about them in his published account, and

Excerpted from *Martin Luther King Jr. and the Foundations of Nonviolence*, by James
P. Hanigan. Copyright ©1984 University Press of America. Reprinted with permission.

the reasons have puzzled his biographers. His difficulties with the emotionalism of the ordinary Baptist churches that he knew and with the lack of serious intellectual content in the sermons he heard there are well known. Psychologically, the influence of his father, and of ministers he encountered at Morehouse, particularly Dr. Benjamin Mays and Dr. George Kelsey, was a powerful inducement to the ministry. The latter two men certainly provided an alternative to the emotional performances he so disliked. Yet their example alone is not sufficient to explain his decision.

CHILDHOOD INFLUENCES

While at Crozer [Theological Seminary], King wrote, apparently as an assignment, a paper entitled "An Autobiography of Religious Development," which runs to some fifteen hand-written pages. In the paper he mentions as important influences in his life an intimate family relationship, "a saintly grandmother" (maternal) who was especially dear to him, extraordinary health such that he hardly knows what an ill moment feels like, an above average I.Q., and a precocity both physical and mental. "So it seems that from an hereditary view nature was very kind to me." He mentions a great deal about his father, and in fifteen pages has but one line about his mother. Above all he reveals a spirit fundamentally at peace with itself and with the universe. He writes:

> It is quite easy for me to think of a God of love mainly because I grew up in a family where love was central and lovely relationships were ever present. It is quite easy for me to think of the universe as basically friendly mainly because of my up-lifting hereditary and environmental circumstances. It is quite easy for me to lean more toward optimism than pessimism about human nature mainly because of my childhood experiences.

In the same document King goes on to comment on the ordinariness of life. The church he looked upon as a second home and he cannot remember ever missing it on Sunday. He acknowledges a complete ignorance of the meaning of what was taking place at his baptism, and the best he can say for Sunday school is that it helped him develop the ability to get along with people. Nor did he ever go through a conversion experience, or, as he calls it, "the so-called crisis moment," the experience which is more commonly called, in the evangelical tradition, making a decision for Christ. "Conversion for me," he wrote, "has been the gradual intaking of the noble ideas set forth in my family and my environment, and I must admit this intaking has been largely unconscious."

KING'S SKEPTICISM AT MOREHOUSE COLLEGE

King's mind apparently began to function critically as he reached his teen-age years, for he has reported shocking his Sunday school class at the age of twelve by denying the bodily resurrection of Jesus. That started the doubts and they reached a peak in a period of skepticism during his second year at Morehouse when he began to regret his association with the church. The doubts stemmed largely from the fundamentalistic and unquestioning literal interpretation of the Bible to which he had been continuously exposed. There can be little doubt that it was this skepticism, with the resultant inability to relate meaningfully to the root document of Christian faith, that deterred him from accepting what would appear to have been his natural inheritance, the ministry.

It was a course in the Bible at Morehouse that exposed him at last to modern biblical criticism and helped him over his doubts. "I came to see that behind the legends and myths of the Book were many profound truths which one could not escape." One other kind of doubt also blocked his path to the ministry and it, too, required a college experience to resolve. That doubt was how he could love a race of people who hated him and had destroyed one of his closest childhood friendships. The growing anti-white feeling that gnawed at his soul was only dissipated when he came in contact with white students while taking part in inter-racial organizations.

The call to the ministry had been pressing upon King from his latter high school days, but the doubts had caused him to put it off. His father, he reports, never talked to him about the ministry, but he could scarcely have been unaware of his father's hopes for him. In any case, with the doubts resolved, the call to the ministry returned and he answered it. What that call was is best described in his own words. "My call to the ministry was not a miraculous or supernatural something; on the contrary, it was an inner urge calling me to serve humanity." If asked, but why the ministry as the vehicle of service, King would acknowledge his father's example: "He set forth a noble example that I didn't mine [sic] following. Today I differ a good deal with my father theologically, but that admiration for a real father still remains."

KING'S DEVELOPING LIBERAL CHRISTIANITY

The result of these early experiences was that King was ordained a Baptist Minister and then entered Crozer to begin his formal theological training with the shackles of fundamentalism removed "from my body," and with a readiness to accept the liberal interpretation of Christianity. Ready he was indeed! Nowhere has King recorded any serious doubts or objections to that interpretation. Basically what he had upon entering the seminary was a lively faith in a personal God, very much in the image of his own father, and a deep attachment to the ethical ideals he had grown up unconsciously assimilating. He claimed that even in times of theological doubt he could never turn away from these ideals. Despite the lack of any striking conversion experience, religion was very real to him, very much part of life. "In fact," he wrote, "the two cannot be separated; religion for me is life." The process of honing and refining this nebulous and loose conception of faith took place during his years at Crozer and Boston University.

The liberal interpretation of Christianity which King found himself so ready to accept was, for the most part, a product of European biblical and historical criticism with its roots extending back to the Protestant Reformation. While it was never the intention of either Luther or Calvin to set up every individual as his or her own interpreter of the Christian message, their challenge to the established authority of the Roman Church started individuals on the road of questioning and criticism. The impact that scientific method made upon Christian theology was enormous and often threatening—so enormous, in fact, that the major questions in Christian Protestant theology quickly became methodological. Just what was theology, what were the sources for it, the norm of truth it sought, and how did one go about the construction of a theology?

The development of theological liberalism in Germany and then in France and its transfer to the United States has been recounted elsewhere, but its single most representative example may well be Adolf Harnack's *What Is Christianity?* Harnack's answer to that question was a vast reductive generalization of Christian faith and doctrine to a slogan. The meaning of Christianity, Harnack suggested, is exhausted by the idea of the Fatherhood of God and the brotherhood of man. That slogan came close to exhausting the theological content of liberal Christianity, and became the guiding light of King's theological education.

KING'S DEVELOPING CHRISTIAN ETHIC

In a series of short papers, which appear to date from his Crozer days and were probably outlines for sermons, King included one paper on what a Christian should believe about himself. He wrote that the Christian is a member of a larger family of which God is the Father. And he mentioned explicitly that the Fatherhood of God and the brotherhood of man is the starting point of the Christian ethic. In one of the very rare references to slavery in his notes, he applied this starting point to the preaching done to slaves—"you are not niggers, not slaves, you are God's children."

This God who was the Father of humankind was quite real and personal to King. If one does not grasp just how alive and how central this God was in King's mind and heart, it is likely that he will never comprehend King's message of militant nonviolence. The fact of the matter is that King believed—he entrusted himself to and staked his life upon the God in whom he believed. In writing about his years at Boston University and his study of personalist philosophy while there, he claimed that he had been strengthened in two convictions: "it gave me metaphysical and philosophical grounding for the idea of a personal God, and it gave me a metaphysical basis for the dignity and worth of all human personality." Yet King's God was not the result of metaphysical construction, no product of philosophical investigation, although the terms in which he described the nature and activity of his God are derived from personalist philosophy. In the same set of outlines mentioned just above there is one paper on the character of the Christian God. This God is personal, by which King means self-conscious and self-directing, and is defined as "the personal spirit, perfectly good, who in love creates, sustains, and orders all." He is perfectly good in that he contains in himself all the possible excellence that the human mind can conceive and still transcends in goodness the highest conceptions of the human mind. He is also the original cause of the universe, the perpetual cause that preserves everything in being, and the final cause or the one who governs and directs the universe to a deliberate end. God's motive in all this activity is what King called holy love, which is a combination of his perfect goodness and immeasurable self-giving. This holy love is the substance of God's character and the motive of all his activity in relation to finite existence. How do we know this about God? We learn this, not from empirical observation, not from philosophical analysis, not even from some kind of personal experience. We learn this, insisted King, from Jesus of Nazareth. . . .

This conception of God is not confined to King's doctoral dissertation. It is the operative conception in all his sermons and is also at the root of his espousal of militant nonviolence. He had a variety of ways of expressing this conception of God, but the persistent affirmation that God is both good and powerful, that the two attributes meet in his personality, remained without explanation. The unity of goodness and power in God was based solely upon the oft-repeated slogan that [German philosopher Georg Wilhelm Friedrich] Hegel said the truth is to be found "in an emergent synthesis which reconciles opposites." So, for example, God has a tough mind and a tender heart, he is austere and gentle, just and merciful: such combinations indicate the content of King's preaching. God is, he could say, "tough-minded enough to transcend the world; he is tenderhearted enough to live in it." Or again, the faith that we are to have is "the faith that God is good and just." Or, "Christianity clearly affirms that in the long struggle between good and evil, good will eventually emerge as victor." King also expressed the same idea with a peculiarly Kantian ring to it. "Would not this be a strangely irrational universe if God did not ultimately join virtue and fulfillment . . .", and again, in a wildly optimistic view of human conscience, "God's unbroken hold on us is something that will never permit us to feel right when we do wrong or to feel natural when we do the unnatural." Finally, the same idea was the basis for nonviolent resistance, which "is based on the conviction that the universe is on the side of justice," that in man's struggle for justice he has cosmic companionship, or that there is "some creative force that works for universal wholeness."

The Black Church Tradition

James H. Cone

James H. Cone believes that the black church was the major influence on the theological and intellectual life of Martin Luther King Jr. Although numerous intellectual philosophers and theologians provided a framework for King's beliefs, Cone argues that King was primarily shaped by the tradition of the black church. King's frequent references to Western philosophy were geared primarily for the white listening public.

Cone's judgment is that King's theological perspective is built on two key notions: the oppression of black people and the liberating message of hope and freedom offered by the black church. King knew that his message had to be relevant for the social and political needs of his people. He understood that black people supported him not for his intellectual understanding of theology but because he embodied the faith and hope of their church and their struggle. Cone also adds that King's speaking style was unmistakably from the tradition of the black church and black preaching. He used a tone and movement that expressed the black church spirit of empowerment, hope, and freedom.

James H. Cone is a professor of theology at Union Theological Seminary, New York. He is the author of many books including *Black Theology and Black Power*, *God of the Oppressed*, and *My Soul Looks Back.*

Not much has been written about Martin Luther King, Jr., and the relation of his theology to the black church and the rise of black theology during the late 1960s. Many assume that the black church made no decisive impact upon his intellectual life. To explain his theology, most interpreters turn to his teachers at Crozer Theological Seminary and Boston

Excerpted from James H. Cone, "Martin Luther King Jr., Black Theology–Black Church," *Theology Today*, vol. 40, no. 4 (January 1984), pp. 409–20. Reprinted by permission of *Theology Today*.

University. The implication of this procedure is that his theological perspective was defined exclusively by the intellectual impact of white Western theology and philosophy rather than the black church. While I do not deny the influence of his seminary and university teachers, I think the influence of the black church was much more decisive in shaping his theological perspective.

Because many misunderstand the origin of King's theology in the black church, they also misunderstand his relation to black theology. Many assume that black theology and Martin Luther King, Jr. have completely different theological and political perspectives. Persons who hold this viewpoint often explain the difference by saying that King was concerned primarily with love, non-violence, and the reconciliation between blacks and whites. But black theology, in contrast to King, seldom mentions love or reconciliation between blacks and whites and explicitly rejects non-violence with its endorsement of [black activist leader] Malcolm X's contention that blacks should achieve their freedom "by any means necessary." Some claim that black theology is a separatist and an extremist interpretation of the Christian faith. But King was an integrationist and a moderate who believed that whites can and should be redeemed.

During a decade of writing and teaching Black Theology, the most frequent question that has been addressed to me, publically and privately, by blacks and especially whites, has been: "How do you reconcile the separatist and violent orientation of black theology with Martin Luther King's emphasis on integration, love, and non-violence?" I have always found it difficult to respond to this question because those who ask it seem unaware of the interrelations between King, black theology, and the black church.

While it is not my primary intention to compare King and black theology, I do hope that an explication of his theology in the context of the black church will show, for those interested in a comparison, that black theology and King are not nearly as far apart as some persons might be inclined to think.

THE ORIGIN OF KING'S THEOLOGY

Martin Luther King, Jr. was a product of the black church. When the question is asked, "Who is Martin King?" or "What is his theology?" neither question can be answered properly without giving major attention to the context of King's origin, which is the black church.

Martin King was the son of a Baptist preacher, and he entered the ministry during his student years at Morehouse College. While he was deeply influenced by his teachers at Crozer Theological Seminary and Boston University, the black church was much more decisive in determining his theology, even though he seldom referred to it when he attempted to explain the course of his intellectual development. When asked about the sources of his theological perspective, he referred to such persons as Henry David Thoreau, Mahatma Gandhi, Reinhold Niebuhr, Walter Rauschenbusch, L. Harold DeWolf, and Edgar Sheffield Brightman.

I think it is unquestionably true that these philosophers and theologians, as well as other writers and teachers whom King encountered in graduate school, had a profound effect upon the content, shape, and depth of his theological perspective. They provided the intellectual structure for him to express his ideas about love, non-violence, the value of the human person, and the existence of a moral order in the universe. When King was asked to give an explanation for an action or belief, the question usually came from the white community, and he almost always answered the question by appealing to intellectual sources that were regarded as persuasive authorities in the community from which the questions were derived. Martin King seldom had to defend his perspective to black people, and when he was required, as with the advocates of Black Power [movement for racial pride], white intellectual resources were never mentioned, because that would have been a sure way to lose the argument.

References to the intellectual tradition of Western philosophy and theology were primarily for the benefit of the white public so that King could demonstrate to them that he could think as well or better than any other seminary or university graduate. Furthermore, King knew that he could not receive substantial support from the white community until he explained to their satisfaction what he believed and why. If he had appealed directly to the black church tradition as the primary source of his theological and political perspective, no one in the white community would have taken him seriously, since the black church is usually not thought of as being the origin of intellectual ideas regarding theology or social change.

But I contend that King's failure to refer directly to the black church as the chief source for his theological perspective does not mean that it is not, in fact, the chief source. What then is the evidence for my claim regarding the primacy of the black church in Martin King's theology? It is difficult to answer this question, because we are accustomed to looking for evidence in printed sources and also from people who knew him personally. While the evidence for my claim does not necessarily contradict what King said about himself or what others say about him, it is not primarily dependent upon their testimonies. My evidence is indirect, and it can only be understood by people who believe that there is an interplay between their social context and the ideas they promote.

To contend that King's graduate teachers and the books he read in graduate school accounted for the whole of his theological perspective is to discount completely his early home and church context and thereby suggest that he arrived at Crozer Seminary and Boston University with a blank mind. Even if we do not hold with [German philosopher] Karl Marx's contention that "consciousness is from the beginning a social product," we cannot claim the opposite, that is, that "life is determined by consciousness," and still appropriately account for the whole of a person's perspective. We must say with Marx "that circumstances make men just as much as men make circumstances." If circumstances are relevant in the assessment of a person's ideas and actions, we must then inquire about Martin King's circumstances so that we can understand properly the distinctive contribution of his theology. . . .

KING'S THEOLOGICAL PERSPECTIVE

What were the circumstances that determined the perspective of King's theology and politics? The most significant circumstances that shaped King's theology, in my judgment, were the oppression of black people and the liberating message of the black church. These two realities—the oppression of blacks and the black church's liberating message of the Gospel—provided King with the intellectual challenge to develop a theology that was Christian and also relevant for the social and political needs of black people. That was why he entered the ministry while a student at Morehouse and later accepted a call to be pastor of Dexter Avenue Baptist Church in Montgomery, rather than seeking a teaching post at a white seminary or university. In fact, King turned down many teaching offers at major white universities and seminaries, and he also refused several invitations to pastor white churches, because of his primary commitment to the black church and its message of liberation for black people.

The black church was also the context out of which Martin King accepted the call to be the leader of the Montgomery Bus Boycott. After his success in Montgomery, King founded the Southern Christian Leadership Conference (SCLC) which received its support primarily from black preachers and their churches. In order to keep his identity firmly tied to the black church as he served as the president of SCLC, he became the co-pastor of Ebenezer Baptist Church in Atlanta. Martin King's close ties with the black church in preference over the alternatives indicate that his primary commitment was to that community. Anyone, therefore, who wishes to understand his life and thought must make the black church the primary source for the analysis.

THE BLACK CHURCH AS A SOURCE OF RENEWAL

The best way of deciding what was primary for King's life and thought is to ask, "What tradition did he turn to in moments of crisis during his ministry?" Where one turns when one's back is up against the wall and when everything seems hopeless will tell us far more about our theology than what is often printed in articles and books. When King encountered the harsh contradictions of white violence and when he had run out of rational alternatives on how best to defeat it non-violently, where did he turn for insight, courage and hope that things can and will be otherwise? Did he turn to Brightman, DeWolf, Niebuhr, or Gandhi? Of course not. None of these intellectual resources were useful to him in the context of crisis.

In moments of crisis when despair was about to destroy the possibility of making a new future for the poor, King turned to the faith contained in the tradition of the black church. Whether one speaks of Montgomery, Albany, Birmingham, Selma, or Chicago, the crises arising from his struggle to implement justice never produced despair in his theological and political consciousness. The reason is not found in his intellectual grasp and exposition of white liberal theology but in the faith and life of the black church. With the resources of this religious tradition, he had a foundation that could sustain him in his struggle for justice. Had not his people been struggling for freedom for over three hundred and fifty years, and despite many disappointments and apparent defeats? Does not the faith of the black church empower black Christians to "keep on keeping on" even though the odds might be against them?

This is the context for understanding the often heard faith claim, "I ain't no ways tired." This affirmation of faith is not derived from the faith of middle class blacks or whites and their capitalistic orientation. Rather this faith is derived from the meeting of God in the pains and struggles of poor blacks who refuse to accept despair as the logical consequence of their oppression, because they firmly believe that "God can make a way out of no way."

It was Martin King's identity with the tradition of this black faith that enabled him to overcome crisis moments during his fight for justice. While he was not always sure how to make this faith intellectually convincing to his friends and supporters in the white community, he knew that his own people were already aware of the inability of white concepts to explain the certainty of black faith. That was why it was so easy for him to get a little carried away when speaking in a black church. Their enthusiastic responses to his sermons on justice and non-violence, saying "amen," "right-on," "speak the truth," let him know that they were in solidarity with him, and that they would follow him wherever he led them. They had already demonstrated their presence with him in Montgomery, Birmingham, and Selma. Furthermore, King also knew that their belief in him was in no way dependent upon his theological perspective as defined by white theological resources. Black people followed King, because he embodied in word and deed the faith of the black church which has always claimed that oppression and the Gospel of Jesus do not go together. . . .

The Tradition of the Black Church

What was the main content of King's thought which he derived from the black church tradition? This question is not easy to answer because the black church has not done much systematic reflection in the area of theology. Our theologies have been presented in the forms of sermons, songs, prayers, testimonies, and stories of slavery and oppression. In these sources we have given our views of God and the world, and how each may be understood in relation to our struggle for freedom. We did not write essays on Christian doctrine because our descendants came as slaves from Africa and not as free people from Europe. Many blacks were prevented from learning to read and write either by the circumstances of our birth or by the legal restrictions defined by the Government. Therefore, we had to do theology in other forms than rational reflections. We sang and preached our theology in worship and other sacred contexts. The central meaning disclosed in these non-rational sources is found in both their *form* and *content* and is identical with *freedom* and *hope.*

The influence of the black church and its central theme of freedom and hope can be seen in the language of King's speaking and writing. Everything he said and wrote sounds like a black sermon and not rational reflection. To be sure, King finished first in his class at Crozer and also wrote a Ph.D. dissertation at Boston on [theologians] Henry Nelson Wieman's and Paul Tillich's conceptions of God. But it is significant to note that he did not adopt the style of theological presentation from any of his white theological mentors. He may have referred to white theologians and philosophers when he needed to explain his views to a white public, but the style of his presentation was unmistakably from the tradition of black preaching.

Like his predecessors and contemporaries in the black church, King preached his theology, because the theme of freedom and hope had to be reflected in the movement and rhythm of his voice, if he expected a black congregation to take his message seriously. The eschatological hope of freedom is not only an idea to be analyzed in the conceptual language of white theologians and philosophers. It is primarily an event to be experienced when God's word of freedom breaks into the lives of the gathered community through the vehicle of the sermon's oration. No one understood the relationship between style and meaning in the context of the black church any better than Martin King.

In the black church, the meaning is found not primarily in the intellectual content of the spoken word but in the *way* the word is spoken and its effect upon those who hear it. That was why King could speak on [Greek philosopher] Plato, [medieval church father] Augustine, or even Boston Personalism [philosophy King studied at Boston University], about which most blacks know nothing and care even less, and still move the congregation to tears and shouts of praise, even though they did not understand the content of his discourse. What they understood was the appropriate tone and movement of his speech which the people believe is the instrument for the coming presence of God's spirit, thereby empowering them with the hope for freedom. The people believe that freedom is coming because a foretaste of it is given in the sermon event itself. When King spoke of his dream at the 1963 March on Washington, and when he spoke the night before his assassination in Memphis of his hope that we will reach the Promised Land, black people did not believe him because of the cogency of his logic but rather because of the spirit of empowerment generated by the style of his sermon oration. The people believed him because they contended that they experienced in their hearts the Spirit of God's liberating presence.

I think style is important in doing theology, and I try to reflect it in my own theology. How can black theology claim to be derived from the black community if it does not reflect in its style the language of the people? If black people do not recognize themselves in the language of theology, how can theology really claim blackness as its identity? For any theology to be truly black, its blackness must be expressed in the form in which it is written. This point was impressed on my own theological consciousness by the black critics of my early books, *Black Theology and Black Power* (1969) and *A Black Theology of Liberation* (1970). With the publication of *The Spirituals and the Blues* (1972), *God of the Oppressed* (1975), *My Soul Looks Back* (1982), and other subsequent writings, I have tried to incorporate not only the *content* of liberation in theology but also in the very form of the language itself. Martin King has been helpful in the accomplishment of this task.

The Impact of King's India Trip

Coretta Scott King

Coretta Scott King recalls that in March of 1959 she and Martin traveled to India to learn more about the teachings of Gandhi. Coretta writes that Martin stressed the fact that he was not traveling as a tourist; instead, he said, "To India I come as a pilgrim." During his meetings with Prime Minister Jawaharlal Nehru, Martin compared Gandhi's struggle for freedom with that of black Americans struggling for civil rights. Coretta remembers the meaningful discussions Martin had with Nehru concerning the power and methodology of nonviolence. Martin concluded that violence bequeaths bitterness while nonviolence offers the possibility for eventual friendship. Nehru, however, disagreed with some of Gandhi's revolutionary tactics and visions for the country's future.

Coretta writes that Martin was particularly impressed with the spiritual qualities of Gandhi's followers. He gained a deeper insight into the Gandhian principles of *satyagraha*, the soul force that is central to the teachings of Gandhi's nonviolence. Coretta concludes that Martin's trip through India had a tremendous impact on him: He gained an appreciation for the power of patience, he dedicated himself to living a simple life, he confirmed his desire to be more like Gandhi spiritually, and he committed himself wholeheartedly to the cause of nonviolence.

Coretta Scott King is the widow of Martin Luther King Jr. She has won numerous awards that include the Annual Brotherhood Award, the Dag Hammarskjöld Award, and the Women of Conscience Award, National Council of Women. She contributes to magazines like *Good Housekeeping*, *Ebony*, and *Theology Today*.

For nearly a year Martin had had an invitation from the Gandhi Peace Foundation to make a speaking tour of India to meet their leaders, including Prime Minister Jawaharlal Nehru. Since we had neither time nor money, we postponed the trip. Now it was made possible by a grant of five thousand dollars from a devoted friend, Libby Holman Reynolds, through the Christopher Reynolds Foundation, to the Friends Service Committee.

Early in March, 1959, Martin and I, accompanied by [King biographer] Professor Lawrence D. Reddick, flew to India. Our plane was supposed to land in New Delhi, but due to some difficulty we were diverted to Bombay, where we arrived the night of March 9. Thus, our first sight of India, so eagerly anticipated, was a shock to us. The city was beautiful from the air, with a bright necklace of lights encircling the fine harbor. But as we drove in from the airport through narrow, odorous streets, we saw thousands of people dressed in rags sleeping on the sidewalks or huddled in doorways, lying wherever they could find space. We were appalled. When we asked why hundreds and thousands of people were stretched out on the dirty pavements, we were told that they had no other place to sleep; they had no homes. They carried everything they owned with them, wrapped up in a rag or a newspaper. It was very hard for us to understand or accept this. The sight of emaciated human beings wearing only a dirty loincloth, picking through garbage cans both angered and depressed my husband. Colonialism was responsible. Never, even in Africa, had we seen such abject, despairing poverty.

IMPRESSIONS OF INDIA

As we drove up to the luxurious Taj Mahal Hotel, a man with a child in his arms came up to the airport bus. He couldn't speak English, but he opened his mouth and pointed to it, and then he pointed to the child, making it plain he was starving. Before we had left the United States our sponsor had told us not to give money to beggars because the government was trying to discourage this sort of thing. Martin soon disobeyed these instructions and gave all the money he could to the forlorn humans who beseeched us.

Later, when we returned to America, Martin talked many times about these sad sights. He spoke of our great surplus of grain and the cost of storing it, and he said, "I know where we could store it free of charge, in the wrinkled stomachs of starving people in Asia and Africa."

MEETING WITH PRIME MINISTER NEHRU

The next day we flew on to New Delhi. At the airport Martin told the reporters, "To other countries, I may go as a tourist, but to India I come as a pilgrim."

That very first evening we were invited to dinner at Prime Minister Nehru's house. We were thrilled and excited at the prospect of meeting Nehru, the political leader of the Independence Movement. The Prime Minister's residence was a huge classic sandstone house which had been built by the British at the height of the Empire. We drove through high wrought-iron gates guarded by sentries, and around a drive between fine lawns and beds of brilliant flowers.

Nehru, looking very elegant in his long, fitted, white coat with a rose pinned on it, greeted us in the spacious hall. He took us up a broad flight of stairs into a formal sitting room, where we met his daughter, Indira Gandhi, who is now the Prime Minister. She was quietly charming, a gracious hostess. Of course, Nehru was grace and courtesy itself, and he seemed genuinely glad to meet my husband.

At dinner Nehru talked with Martin, comparing the Indian struggle for freedom with that of the American Negro for civil rights. They also discussed the method of nonviolence in our struggle. Nehru stressed the importance of the use of nonviolence. He commended my husband for the leadership he had given in this direction. Martin said to him, "I've read so much about Gandhi and the success of the nonviolent movement here that I wanted to come and see for myself."

Martin commented on the fact that British-Indian friendship had been possible even between people who had represented a colonial power and those who had been its subjects. He felt that this was because the Indians had used nonviolence to achieve their independence instead of bequeathing a legacy of bitterness that violence would have engendered.

As they talked about Gandhi, Nehru said, "You know I did not always agree with him."

NEHRU'S VIEWS ON GANDHI

We knew this from our reading. Also our Indian friends who came to Montgomery had told us about the policy battles between Nehru and Gandhi. Gandhi was completely dedicated to nonviolence, while Nehru was inclined to accept it as a useful revolutionary technique. Gandhi did not wish to thrust India into a modern technological society; Nehru felt that India could not survive without becoming industrialized.

But their quarrel was not simple. Both men realized the complexities of using nonviolence as a technique of the masses. Nehru had written most logically of the dangers in *Toward Freedom:*

"Were a remote village and a mob of excited peasants in an out-of-the-way place going to put an end, for some time at least, to our national struggle for freedom? If this was the inevitable consequence of a sporadic act of violence, then surely there was something lacking in the philosophy and technique of a nonviolent struggle. For it seemed to us to be impossible to guarantee against the occurrence of some such untoward incident. Must we train the three hundred and odd millions of India in the theory and practice of nonviolent action before we could go forward? And, even so, how many of us could say that under extreme provocation from the police we would be able to remain perfectly peaceful?"

Then, Gandhi himself never saw nonviolence as a retreat from confrontation, as an avoidance of risk. He wrote in *An Autobiography:*

"I do believe that when there is only a choice between cowardice and violence, I would advise violence. . . . I would rather have India resort to arms in order to defend her honor than that she should in a cowardly manner become or remain a helpless victim to her own dishonor. But I believe that nonviolence is infinitely superior to violence, forgiveness is more manly than punishment."

My husband and the Prime Minister talked about these matters for about four hours. I listened carefully, but I am not sure I would have been so politely still if our meeting had taken place later in the trip. For example, I certainly would have talked about the women of India, had I realized how much progress they had made with the coming of Independence. As we traveled through the land, we were greatly impressed by the part women played in the political life of India, far more than in our own country. We knew that Gandhi had involved the women of India in the struggle for independence and that many of them had gone to jail like the men. Gandhi also worked to liberate women from the bondage of Hindu and Muslim traditions.

MARTIN WITNESSES THE LEGACY OF GANDHI

The next morning my husband and I went to lay a wreath on the shrine of the Raj Ghat, where Gandhi's body had been cremated. Then we met with other officials who had been leaders in the fight for freedom. Among them were the first President of India, Rajendra Prasad, who lived in the two-block-long palace with a golden dome that had been the viceroy's house; and Vice-President Sarvepalli Radhakrishnan, the philosopher-politician. Of all the people we met in New Delhi, we most enjoyed listening to him. He talked about his philosophy of life and, in a way, he reminded me of Mordecai Johnson [President of Howard University], who had first inspired Martin's interest in Gandhian ideals. When we left, Martin said that our first twenty-four hours in India had been like meeting George Washington, Thomas Jefferson, and James Madison in a single day.

In the days to come, we met many other Indians who had been disciples of Gandhi. Some of them still dressed as he had, in coarse, handwoven khaki cloth robes. Gandhi had vowed poverty, and he rejected the materialism of Western civilization. One of the things that presented a paradox for us was that certain of these men still dressed in that simple way, while at the same time they lived in the great houses the British had built, and, in their many luxuries, copied their former masters. It was difficult for us to resolve this conflict. We understood that people who have been oppressed often have the need to live luxuriously as a sort of compensation; we hoped that someday they might strike a balance. However, when we left New Delhi, we did find many people who lived in true Gandhian simplicity.

We loved the Indian people for the warmth and the spiritual quality they possessed. An especially interesting experience was our visit with the saintly Vinoba Bhave, who was walking through India, as Gandhi had, preaching his idealistic doctrine of *sarvodaya*, or a spiritual, decentralized socialism.

We found Bhave and his followers camped in a big meadow dotted with tents. They were cooking on open fires while the children ran about playing. While we were there, they struck camp and started walking up the dusty road. Martin and I walked with Bhave, listening to him talk. He believed that people would be better off if they had no government, because government corrupts, and the more organization you have, the more corrupt people become. I think

Martin felt that Bhave's views, while truly idealistic, were too impractical for implementation. However, he was impressed by Bhave's argument that it *was* possible for a nation to totally disarm unilaterally; and if that were done by a country like India, it would have a profound moral effect on the whole world.

TRAVELING THROUGH INDIA

In the course of our travels we visited many places that Gandhi had made so memorable by his presence that they had become shrines. Gandhigram (Gandhi Village), in southern India, was a training center, almost like a school, with many young people. We were fortunate enough to attend a religious service conducted as Gandhi had done when he was alive. Before several hundred people sitting cross-legged on the ground in off-white robes, prayers were read from Hindu, Muslim, Christian, Jewish, and Buddhist holy books.

Most of the people we met were dedicated Gandhians, and in our talks with them we gained a deeper insight into the principles of *satyagraha*, or soul force, which was the basic concept of Gandhi's nonviolent movement.

By way of contrast, we went to a cattle show with the Maharaja of Mysore. He was a pleasant, charming, enlightened man who was progressive in his thinking, even if regressive in the opulence of his manner of living. At the fair he was cheered by the crowd and appeared very popular. We could not help feeling that as maharajas go, he was one of the good ones.

Martin made speeches all over India, always emphasizing his debt to Gandhian thinking. Most of the time, I sang on the same program; the Indians loved the Negro spirituals. And wherever we went we met the officials of the various states. Some of them seemed to us good men and idealists. Others appeared to have been corrupted by power, like politicians all over the world. Though such as these disturbed us, because of our idealistic attitude toward India, we then asked ourselves, "Why should Indians be different from humanity everywhere?"

IMPACT OF THE TRIP ON MARTIN

With all its terrible contrasts of rich and poor, its materialists and idealists, philosophers and self-seekers, the Indian experience had a terrific impact on Martin's mind. One thing he learned was patience. It had taken nearly half a century for the Indian people to gain their independence. Many of their leaders had been imprisoned for ten years or longer, whereas ours had stayed in jail only a few days or weeks. Somehow in America we had felt the gains would come fast, and we were certainly not prepared to wait passively for freedom. The Indians, influenced by Eastern philosophy, did not have our sense of urgency; but we learned from them that the long struggle for freedom required endurance and even more suffering than we had already known.

KING'S FASCINATION WITH GANDHIAN PHILOSOPHY

In his 1960 article "How My Mind Has Changed,"
written for the magazine Christian Century, *Martin*
Luther King Jr. recounts his excitement as he discovered the
writings of Mahatma Gandhi.

Then I came upon the life and teachings of Mahatma Gandhi. As I read his works I became deeply fascinated by his campaigns of nonviolent resistance. The whole Gandhian concept of *satyagraha* (*satya* is truth which equals love, and *graha* is force; *satyagraha* thus means truth-force or love-force) was profoundly significant to me. As I delved deeper into the philosophy of Gandhi my skepticism concerning the power of love gradually diminished, and I came to see for the first time that the Christian doctrine of love operating through the Gandhian method of nonviolence was one of the most potent weapons available to oppressed people in their struggle for freedom.

Martin returned from India more devoted than ever to Gandhian ideals of nonviolence and simplicity of living. He constantly pondered how to apply them in America. His great problem was the enormous difference between the mechanized complexity of our way of living and theirs. He even considered the idea of changing his style of dress to a simpler one, but he decided that since his main purpose was to attract people to the Cause, unusual dress might even tend to alienate followers. Dress was really a superficial form rather than the spiritual quality he was aiming for.

He was more determined than ever to live as simply as possible. He felt, as in India, that much of the corruption in our society stems from the desire to acquire material things—houses and land and cars. Martin would have preferred to have none of these things. He finally said to me, "You know, a man who dedicates himself to a cause doesn't need a family."

I was not hurt by this statement. I realized that it did not mean he loved me and the children less, but that he was giving his life to the Movement and felt he therefore could not do as much for his family as he might in other circumstances. He saw a conflict between duty and love that prevented his giving himself utterly to the Cause. But I knew that, being the kind of man he was, Martin needed us. He functioned better with a wife and children because he needed the warmth we gave him, and from the standpoint of the cause, having us gave him a kind of humanness which brought him closer to the mass of the people.

The influence of India was so strong that Martin's conscience continually questioned whether he was being really nonviolent and really ascetic. He realized that in our civilization a man who has to travel a lot will do his job much more efficiently with a car; he could not function without having a place to live, and would have grave difficulties without a telephone. He finally decided that in the conditions prevailing in America, we had to have certain things, and that he must strive to be more like Gandhi spiritually.

His struggle with these problems was not unlike the struggle of Gandhi himself, who had written:

"How was one to treat alike insulting, insolent, and corrupt officials, co-workers of yesterday raising meaningless opposition, and men who had always been good to one? How was one to divest oneself of all possessions? Was not the body itself possession enough? Were not wife and children possessions? Was I to destroy all the cupboards of books I had? Was I to give up all I had and follow Him? Straight came the answer: I could not follow Him unless I gave up all I had. . . ."

Martin never took on the pretentious qualities of the leader of a large movement, nor did he ever feel the need to have people at his beck and call, as happens to so many men who rise in the world. When our staff people tried to make him a person of importance who should have all sorts of attention paid him, he refused to allow it. He would much rather drive a Ford car than a Cadillac. I remember when he was coming back from the Birmingham jail, our staff members were very excited and thought that he should have a real hero's welcome. It was even suggested that we use a motorcade of Cadillacs.

When I told Martin about this, he said, "Now, what would I look like coming back from jail in a Cadillac? You just drive our car to the airport, and I'll drive you home."

But it was very difficult for Martin to keep from being worshiped by the black masses. It was a great temptation to them, because they had never had the opportunity to acclaim a great leader of their own before. They felt that nothing was too good for Dr. King, that he should ride in Cadillacs behind motorcycles and have every sort of pomp and tribute usually paid to the great leaders of mankind.

You see, they thought of him as the outstanding person of their race in the world. He was, to many of them, the President of the Negroes.

CHAPTER 2

King's Social and Political Ideology

King's Philosophical Roots

L.D. Reddick

L.D. Reddick suggests that Martin Luther King Jr. was influenced philosophically by three major figures: Jesus, Henry David Thoreau, and Mohandas K. Gandhi. For King, Jesus' Sermon on the Mount was particularly important because it provided King with the core components of his nonviolent philosophy: love, humility, self-criticism, and forgiveness.

Reddick argues that King was shaped by Henry David Thoreau's arguments that one's individual conscience is above any man-made law. In his essay "Civil Disobedience," Thoreau maintained that to exercise one's individual conscience is the highest social duty.

Like Thoreau, Gandhi asked his followers in India to obey their individual consciences as he mobilized them against imperialist Britain. Gandhi, like King, preached plain living, kindness, the cause of brotherhood, and love. Reddick asserts that both King and Gandhi were men of gentleness but fierce determination. Both mobilized their people to social action using self-discipline and the renunciation of vindictiveness.

L.D. Reddick was a professor of Afro-American history at Temple University, Philadelphia. He is the author of many books that include *Library Sources for Negro Studies* and *Worth Fighting For: The History of the Negro in the United States During the Civil War and Reconstruction*. He has contributed many articles to professional journals.

Three of King's heroes—Jesus, Thoreau and Gandhi—supply the philosophical roots for his own theory of nonviolent social change. This is the concept that pervaded the Montgomery mass movement and that has subsequently spread far and wide over the South and elsewhere.

Excerpted from *Crusader Without Violence: A Biography of Martin Luther King Jr.*, by L.D. Reddick. Copyright ©1959 by Lawrence Dunbar Reddick, renewed ©1987 by Lawrence Dunbar Reddick. Reprinted by permission of HarperCollins Publishers, Inc.

King is reluctant to list Jesus Christ as a hero, for he thinks of him not only as a natural, that is, historical, personality but also as supernatural. The appeal of Jesus for King is best expressed in the "Sermon on the Mount." "This is," King declares, "a wonderful statement of the practical solution of the major problems that man must face in any generation. In it, answers to life's great questions are given in terms of the love ethic."

This relatively short sermon (St. Matthew, Chapters 5–7) is the classic summary of the philosophy of Jesus, the very essence of Christianity. Though it is perhaps departed from more often than adhered to in our acquisitive society, it is the conscience of Western man. It contains the Beatitudes, the Golden Rule and the Lord's Prayer—all in support of humility, self-criticism, forgiveness and the renunciation of material gain. These are all prime elements of King's nonviolent movement:

> Blessed are the meek . . . the merciful . . . the peacemakers . . . they which are persecuted. . . . Ye are the salt of the earth . . . the light of the world. . . . Whosoever is angry with his brother . . . shall be in danger of the judgment. . . . Agree with thine adversary quickly. . . . If thy right hand offend thee. . . . Whosoever shall smite thee on thy right cheek, turn to him the other also. . . . Love your enemies, bless them that curse you, do good to them that hate you, and pray for them which despitefully use you, and persecute you. . . . Seek ye first the kingdom of God, and his righteousness; and all these things shall be added unto you. . . . Judge not, that ye be not judged. . . . And why beholdest thou the mote that is in thy brother's eye, but considerest not the beam that is in thine own eye? . . . Beware of false prophets, which come to you in sheep's clothing, but inwardly they are ravening wolves. . . . Every good tree bringeth forth good fruit. . . . Thy kingdom come. Thy will be done in earth, as it is in heaven.

These are living truths for the Montgomery bus boycotters.

Henry David Thoreau, in King's opinion, is one of the most neglected of American idealists. He lived out most of his life (1817–1862) in or near his native Concord, Massachusetts. Yet his influence went around the world and Gandhi paid homage to him as the guide to his own thought and campaigns of civil disobedience.

Thoreau was not a reformer. His great concern was not in changing the conduct of other men but in freeing himself from the obligations and conventions of the social order so that he could do what he really wanted to do and what he thought was right. Of himself he said, "I wished to live deliberately, to front only the essential facts of life and see if I could learn what it had to teach and not, when I came to die, discover that I had not lived."

So, Thoreau withdrew to the fringes of the community. He never married and worked only enough to support his bare physical needs. He saved his time and energy for himself. He loved nature, spending hours in the fields and forests and streams. Most of his writings are those of an inspired amateur naturalist. Thoreau labored to bring man into harmony with nature.

But Thoreau did not withdraw from human society altogether and thus found himself involved in the great Negro question of his day. He was not an Abolitionist in the sense that he sought to influence other men mainly by his individual example. Nevertheless, his essays on "Slavery and Massachusetts" and "John Brown's Body" rank among the best thinking—and feeling—of his time on what we would call today "race relations." His essay "On Civil Disobedience" has been a textbook for many others besides Gandhi.

In "Slavery and Massachusetts," written in 1854, at the height of the antislavery controversy, Thoreau made it plain that a Northern, nonslaveholding state was guilty along with the slaveholding South for this crime of human bondage. That is to say, Massachusetts was passive; it tacitly assented and even actively returned fugitive slaves to the South. If a judge in Massachusetts ruled against a runaway bondsman who sought haven in the "free North," Thoreau contended that "only they are guiltless who commit the crime of contempt of such a court."

"The law will never make men free," he went on; "it is men who have got to make the law free." Sadly he concluded, "The majority of men in the North and the South and East and West are not men of principle."

Five years later, when John Brown electrified the nation with his attempt at Harper's Ferry to lead slaves in an insurrection for their freedom, Thoreau came out of retirement, as it were, and spoke on the burning issue at Concord's Town Hall, October 30, 1859. Henry S. Canby, a Thoreau biographer who does not altogether approve of the speech, concedes that it "belongs among the great orations in the history of the Republic."

Thoreau said: "Many, no doubt, are well disposed, but

sluggish by constitution and by habit, and they cannot conceive of a man who is actuated by higher motives than they are. Accordingly, they pronounced this man insane, for they know that *they* could never act as he does, as long as they are themselves."

And

> [John Brown] did not recognize unjust human laws, but resisted them as he was bid. No man in America has ever stood up so persistently and effectively for the dignity of human nature, knowing himself for a man, and the equal of any and all governments. In that sense he was the most American of us all.

Thoreau endorsed John Brown's use of force against "evil": "It was his peculiar doctrine that a man has a perfect right to interfere by force with the slaveholder, in order to rescue the slave. I agree with him." Again Thoreau says, if government "requires you to be an agent of injustice to another, then, I say, break the law." He recalls John Brown's statement:

> I want you to understand that I respect the rights of the poorest and weakest of colored people, oppressed by the slave power, just as much as I do those of the most wealthy and powerful.

Thoreau then goes on to quote one of John Brown's most famous lines:

> You may dispose of me very easily. I am nearly disposed of now; but this question is still to be settled—this Negro question, I mean; the end of that is not yet.

Thoreau was arrested and jailed for not paying the annual poll tax for six years. He remained in prison for just one night, his aunt paying his fine and tax without his consent. On his brief stay there, Thoreau wrote:

> I did not for a moment feel confined, and the walls seemed a great waste of stone and mortar. . . . They plainly did not know how to treat me, but behaved like persons who are underbred. In every threat and in every compliment there was a blunder; for they thought that my chief desire was to stand on the other side of that stone wall. I could not but smile to see how industriously they locked the door on my meditations, which followed them out again without let or hindrance, and *they* were really all that was dangerous.

Mrs. Rosa Parks, who initiated the Montgomery bus boycott, could understand this when she was in jail.

Thoreau, for all his well-known gentleness with birds and flowers and children, did not disapprove of violence when it came to what he felt was injustice. The nonviolent principle in Gandhi and King does not come from Thoreau, only the element of *non-co-operation with evil.* This is clearly set forth in Thoreau's most famous essay of all, "On Civil Disobedience."

Thoreau agreed with Thomas Jefferson that "that government is best which governs least." He really preferred, ideally, no government at all but was practical about it. "I asked for, not at once no government, but *at once* a better government."

Thoreau placed individual conscience at the summit of social duty. "The only obligation which I have a right to assume is to do at any time what I think right." Or again, "O for a man, who is a *man,* and, as my neighbor says, has a bone in his back which you cannot pass your hand through!"

One passage that the leaders of the Montgomery boycott seemed to take literally was the observation that "Under a government which imprisons any unjustly, the true place for a just man is also prison." When some ninety-odd leaders of Montgomery were indicted for their part in the boycott, instead of running and hiding, they willingly came forth and submitted themselves to arrest.

Logically, there was always a contradiction in Thoreau for King and his followers, because if they could disregard Jim Crow laws that they felt were wrong, could not white Southerners also defy federal laws that they thought were wrong?

So the boycotters had to adapt Thoreau to their own conditions. They accepted federal laws—and the United States Supreme Court's interpretation of these laws; but resisted state and local laws that were contrary to federal laws. Negroes in the Montgomery movement applied civil disobedience to what was actually a Southern defiance of the highest law of the nation. In contrast, Thoreau placed individual conscience above *any* man-made law. On this ground a conscientious white segregationist, who challenged the United States Supreme Court, was as right in Thoreau's principle as Martin Luther King.

But would a sincere segregationist dare quote Thoreau? How far would he get? Even the reading of Thoreau, if done with an open mind, would bring segregationists and anti-segregationists together on many points.

Mohandas K. Gandhi, unlike Thoreau, was a mass leader. He read "Civil Disobedience" in the midst of the struggle of East Indians in South Africa against discrimination and segregation. Thoreau never made use of his own theories, save in his individual rebellion, while Gandhi devoted his life to the liberation of multitudes, first in South Africa, then in his native India.

Under Gandhi's leadership—and following his example—the Indian masses would deliberately break laws they considered unjust, invite arrest and accept blows from the police or military without fleeing or striking back.

More than any other personality, Gandhi mobilized India for its struggle against imperialism, and he used methods that were certain of victory in world opinion. His was the appeal to conscience. Accordingly, the motives as well as the devices of the foreign rulers were exposed. Imperialist Britain lost her moral prestige during the Indian struggle for independence.

Gandhi appealed to the ordinary people with symbols that they understood: prayer, fasting, the famous salt march to the sea in 1930, and the boycott of British goods and British honors. With such methods, the nonviolent resisters required more self-discipline than the military force and more courage then those who would fight back. Gandhi made it plain that nonviolence is not a refuge for the fearful: "Where there is a choice between cowardice and violence, I would choose violence."

In the large, Gandhi was interested in something more than merely putting his opponent in a morally weak position. The Mahatma's main point was to activate his own followers to higher standards of conduct and living. "Desirelessness" was the core of his teachings—renunciation of the world's materialism and vanity. "Satyagraha"—soul force—Gandhi said, "is the vindication of truth not by infliction of suffering on the opponent but on one's self." "Turn the searchlight inward," he urged, "perhaps the fault is partly yours. Adjudicate, negotiate, arbitrate, otherwise one interreligious brawl or one race riot will immediately create fuel for another, and one war will generate the venoms, fears and military designs which make a second and third more likely."

In all of his gentle directness Gandhi drove the point home: the impulses to anger and retaliation, the appetites to indulgence and false pride must be conquered. Plain living, personal kindness, sacrifice—love—these are the essentials of the good life.

The only cause for which Gandhi would ask men to lay down their lives was the cause of brotherhood.

Withal, Gandhi alone did not free India. He worked concurrently with other leaders and, above all, in harmony with the progressive historical forces of his day. Gandhi did not try to do everything himself. He was aware of his limitations and was most pleased when he could inspire or encourage others to do what he personally might be unable to do well.

Gandhi was a man of great determination, despite his soft spokenness. He threatened to fast himself to death when it appeared that drastic measures had to be taken, forcing certain of the Indian leaders to accept the untouchables. Gandhi knew that this agreement was but a start toward wiping out India's great internal problem of caste. This, he reminded his countrymen, could not be blamed on the British. He felt certain that once a start had been made by removing the religious and social sanctions to caste segregation that the subsequent industrialization and urbanization of India would complete the job of social integration.

For all of his influence and sagacity, Gandhi could not prevent the partition of India. When the day of freedom came in 1947, two "nations"—Pakistan and India—were born.

And so likewise, Martin Luther King knows that nonviolence is not the only element in the struggle of Southern Negroes for equality. Neither is the American South of the mid-1950's Southern Asia. Nor are American Negroes a majority ruled by outsiders. All this is to say that the situation of Martin Luther King's South is vastly different from that of Gandhi's India. Nevertheless, the Gandhian philosophy and technique have a great application to the needs of the Negro masses, making America's nonconformist tradition as symbolized by Thoreau socially useful. Moreover, Gandhianism fits in with the strong Christian traditions of the Negro people and mobilizes them to social action under self-discipline. Above all, in not being vindictive, they leave a way open for the opponent to stop being an opponent.

As [American historian] Chester Bowles has written of the Montgomery movement:

> It is difficult to judge prospect for this program on a nationwide scale. Gandhi was not only a spiritual leader of depth, dedication and courage but also a political genius. In America much will depend on the ability of Negro leaders to develop similar conviction and skill under pressure. Even more will depend on the number, raw courage and dedication of their followers.

Gandhi himself once said that perhaps through American Negroes the message of nonviolence might be delivered to America and the world. "This," Bowles adds, "will take a miracle of greatness. . . . But we Americans are living in an age of miracles and we are capable of greatness."

The teachings of the Great Three—Jesus, Thoreau and Gandhi—have been brought together by the Montgomery movement. This new synthesis is known simply as a "philosophy of love." It is not just a theory; for almost a year, despite the sharpest provocation, the bus strikers demonstrated in practice that there is an alternative to the conflict and killing that we usually associate with social progress.

The boycotters withstood assaults by the state (local), the press (local), racist organizations, gangs and terrorists. At the same time, the boycotters were supported—often fitfully but supported nonetheless—by the state (national), the press (national) and various equalitarian and humanitarian organizations and groups and individual idealists (but no terrorists).

Without the help of the "outside world" the boycotters never would have won. But it was the philosophy of love that gave the Negro masses their inner strength to endure their travail and the compassion of their "enemies." Symbolically, they did learn to love [a local Montgomery segregationist, Sam] Engelhardt while hating what he stood for.

"Love" is a much-used and abused word. King has attempted to clarify its meaning for the Montgomery movement:

> We must distinguish between levels of love. . . . *Eros* is a very interesting type of love. *Plato* talks about it a great deal in his dialogue. It is romantic love, and we must admit that there is something selfish about romantic love. You love your lover because there is something about your lover that attracts you. That is *Eros*. . . . Then there is *Philia*, another kind of love that we have for personal friends. That is not the type of love we talk about when we say "love your oppressor and love your enemy.". . . *Agape* is understanding good will for all men. It is the love of God working in man. It is a type of love that loves a person that does an evil deed while hating the deed that the person does. That is the love that we are talking about—a transforming, creative sort of love—and that is the love that we place at the center of our movement.

King's Philosophy of Nonviolence

Hanes Walton Jr.

Hanes Walton Jr. asserts that Martin Luther King Jr. believed that society can move forward only when pressure and tension work to disturb and disrupt the status quo. King insisted that this pressure must be moral and, as a result, nonviolent.

According to Walton, it is King's conviction that nonviolence disarms the opponent, exposes his moral weakness, and affects his conscience, while, at the same time, it provides the nonviolent initiators self-respect, strength, devotion, and dignity. For King nonviolence attacks evil directly rather than assaulting the evildoer. Hence, the nonviolent resister can avoid the resentments and hatred that are an inherent part of violence. Nonviolence emanates from the soul and is rooted in a love ethic. Walton argues that King's love ethic is similar to a Greek form of love called *agape*. *Agape* is a dispassionate, redemptive love that springs from underlying forces of good that tie all people in the human family together.

Dr. King preached that a nonviolent, righteous individual must refuse to cooperate with an evil system like segregation. But when one uses nonviolence as civil disobedience, one must accept the penalty of the unjust law.

Hanes Walton Jr. is a professor of political science at Atlanta University. His writings include *Black Politics: A Theoretical and Structural Analysis* and *The Poetry of Black Politics.* He has contributed over sixty articles to national periodicals.

The phenomena of political and social change are, in King's philosophy, tied to his idea of the dialectic: "The dialectical process . . . helped me to see that growth comes through struggle." Progress comes through a struggle that begins

Excerpted from *The Political Philosophy of Martin Luther King Jr.*, by Hanes Walton Jr. Copyright ©1981 by Hanes Walton Jr. Reproduced with the permission of Greenwood Publishing Group, Inc., Westport, Conn.

with a confrontation between what is and what ought to be, through the experience of what he termed "creative tension," a nonviolent tension that he considered necessary for growth. An absence of tension, in his view, means stagnation and complacency. For the simple reason that human progress is not automatic or inevitable, it will not come about without a struggle, with pressure exerted on the status quo.

A glance at human history, King believed, reveals that the pursuit of justice and equality requires not only continual exertion, concern, and dedicated individuals, but sacrifice, suffering, and struggle. Time, together with perseverance, becomes a powerful force for motion and social progress. As he saw it, no privileged group would give up its position without resisting strongly. Creative suffering, on the part of those attacking the privileged, helps also to transform the social situation. Every attempt to change the status quo should be moral; hence, nonviolence should be the method employed. Moreover, the struggle implicit in any effort toward social progress, if it is to succeed, must be unified with God. Only with the tireless efforts of men in unison with God is triumph assured.

EFFECTIVENESS OF NONVIOLENCE

Within this framework of assumption and beliefs, nonviolent civil disobedience fitted as no other form of political action could have. It furnished the "arms" for all of King's political tactics; the means for keeping the government "stirred to life," and it was morally right and obligatory. More than a philosophical posture, nonviolence was for him a way of life, one that men adopt out of recognition of the sheer morality of its claim. As a rule, King held, if a person is willing to use nonviolence as a technique, he is likely to adopt it later as a way of life.

King firmly believed that as a method of civil disobedience, nonviolent resistance and direct action is the most potent weapon available to oppressed people in their struggle for freedom and human dignity. It is a way of disarming the opponent, exposing his moral weaknesses, undermining his morale, and, at the same time, affecting his conscience. It paralyzes and confuses the power structure against which it is directed, while it endows its initiators with a new sense of self-respect, duty, strength, devotion, courage, and dignity. To employ the method of nonviolence, one must be very strong spiritually; spiritual strength is the opposite of the shirking passivity associated with cowardice. Strictly speaking, nonviolence does not defeat the opponent, but tries to win his friendship and understanding.

Also characteristic of nonviolence, according to King, is that it attacks evil itself, rather than the evildoer. A nonviolent person resisting the evils of racial injustice can see that the basic tension is not between the races, but "between justice and injustice, between the force of light and the force of darkness." Through the willing acceptance of suffering without retaliation the nonviolent resister attempts to overcome by the power of his persistent love the intransigence of the oppressor. Violence and punishment must be tolerated by the peaceful resister, for, though he may hate the deed, he must love the perpetrator of that deed.

As King interpreted it, nonviolent resistance derives from the conviction that justice abounds in the universe, and that this justice works on the side of the nonviolent resister. He has, therefore, a deep faith in the future outcome of his struggle for justice since he carries with him the awareness that he has "cosmic companionship." In sum, King's nonviolence sought simultaneously to: resist; defeat an unjust system; attack evil but not the evildoer; make suffering a virtue; love rather than hate; and create faith in God and the future. And, for him, the techniques of nonviolence offered every possible moral and ethical way, both internally and externally, to achieve these ends.

It was King's great hope that blacks would, as they plunged deeper into the quest for freedom, come ever closer to the philosophy of nonviolence. For blacks especially, in his view, have a mission as well as an obligation to work "passionately and unrelentingly for first-class citizenship," without, of course, resorting to violence to achieve this end. Just as passivity on the part of blacks would earn for them increased disrespect, contempt, and be interpreted as proof of their inferiority, so would violence leave future generations a heritage of racial bitterness and meaningless chaos. Whereas, with nonviolent techniques passionately and unrelentingly applied, it would be possible for blacks to remain in the South and work for full status as citizens. They would also thereby absolve themselves from the perpetuation of hate, malice, and involvement with the forces of evil. With a nonviolent foundation, King conceived that the black struggle in the South could also serve as a model for oppressed people everywhere. Blacks could then enlist to their side men of good will from all parts of the world, because nonviolence addresses itself to the conscience of men, not to racial groups or individuals.

NONVIOLENCE AS A WAY OF LIFE

By overcoming the personal feelings of resentment which might otherwise be expressed in retaliation and hatred, the nonviolent resister develops an internal strength and discipline that is not of the body but of the soul. Those qualities, in other words, assumed to convert the oppressor to a greater sense of respect and justice for his "fellow in God." The soul-force of nonviolent resistance, King claimed, affects the adversary unconsciously and in a way far greater than any conscious effect. Thus, in reality then, nonviolence is potentially the most active force in the world. It has the additional advantage of being self-activating and independent of any outside physical force.

For King, there could be no question of defeat. For what is obtained by love is retained for all time; whereas what is obtained through hatred becomes a burden, for it breeds more hatred. In a nonviolent struggle there are no casualties. The victory is complete because the method used is not coercive. To be nonviolent is to be God-like. Thus, to use nonviolence in any struggle against injustice is to do the will of God and to be His representative as well. In King's words:

> Nonviolence is a powerful and just weapon. It is a weapon unique in history, which cuts without wounding and ennobles the man who wields it. It is a sword that heals. Both a practical and a moral answer to the Negro's cry for justice, nonviolent direct action proved that it could win victories without losing wars.

However, merely to accept the concept of nonviolence is, according to King, not enough. The "love ethic" brings nonviolence into another dimension and makes of it a way of life. King readily saw that many people would accept nonviolence in certain situations as the most practical method, but he felt that it was necessary for them also to follow the love ethic "which becomes a force of personality integration." The love of which he spoke was not a sentimental or affectionate emotion, but understanding and redemptive good will.

KING'S DEFINITION OF LOVE

To clarify the nature of the love he had in mind, King compared the three Greek words for love: eros, philia, and agape. Eros refers to romantic or aesthetic love; philia is a reciprocal love, the kind that may exist between close friends; agape is a dispassionate, redemptive love that embraces all men. Agape is an overflowing love "which seeks nothing in return, it is the love of God operating in the human heart." On this level of love, man can love his enemies while yet hating their actions. "It is a love in which the individual seeks not his own good, but the good of his neighbor." Nondiscriminating, seeking the best in every man, agape springs from the need of every person to belong to the best of the human family. The highest principle, for King, was love, for only through a certain kind of love, agape, would there be the constant willingness to sacrifice in the interest of mutuality; the willingness to forgive, over and over again, as many times as necessary; and the possibility of restoring the broken fragments of community. Because King felt that segregation had greatly distorted the white man's personality and scarred his soul, he needed the love of black people to repair these damages which only love could cure.

In the final analysis then, agape, for King means "a recognition of the fact that all life is interrelated." On another level, this interrelationship of all humanity implies union within a single process of harmony and brotherhood that persists regardless of the acts of individual men who may work against it. "To the degree that I harm my brother no matter what he is doing to me, to that extent I am harming myself." To love, King felt, is to resist injustice, to meet the needs of your brother, to restore community, and to be God-like.

THE LOVE ETHIC AND CIVIL DISOBEDIENCE

But how does this nonviolent love ethic become a political motivation directed toward changing the status quo? The hierarchy of a citizen's loyalties is explicitly stated by King:

> Your highest loyalty is to God, and not to the mores or folkways, the state or the nation or any man-made institution. If any earthly institution or custom conflicts with God's will, it is your Christian duty to oppose it. You must never allow the transitory, evanescent demands of man-made institutions to take precedence over the eternal demands of the almighty God.

A righteous man, therefore, to be true to his conscience and true to God, has no alternative but to refuse to cooperate with a system judged to be evil. And, since his oppressor may not recognize the nature and extent of his own injustice if it is accepted without protest, the obligation to act forcefully on the side of good is mandatory.

Segregation, for example, was viewed by King as not only politically, economically, and socially unsound, but as morally wrong because it has the deeper effect of distorting the soul and damaging the personality. Refusal to cooperate with a segregated system can take various forms of nonviolent civil disobedience, which, if accomplished in the spirit of the love ethic, work to right existing wrongs while, at the same time, are in harmony with the direction of human progress and the community of men. On a practical level, nonviolent civil action can breathe life into civil rights legislation granted Negroes on paper but absent in reality; thus proving, according to King, an ideal and unique way for the Negro to attain social justice and equality.

Again, within the framework of democracy, where the legal means to redress grievances has been perverted, nonviolent civil disobedience proves itself to be the only practical and moral way to gain permanent change. In King's mind there was an equal moral responsibility to obey just laws as there was to disobey unjust ones. The difference between the two lay in the latter's being out of harmony with eternal, natural law, or the law of God. "I would agree with Saint Augustine that 'an unjust law is no just law' at all." Attempting to give a concrete example of just and unjust laws, King explained:

> An unjust law is a code that a numerical or powerful majority group compels a minority group to obey but does not make it binding on itself. This is *difference* made legal. By the same token, a just law is a code that a majority compels a minority to follow and that it is willing to follow itself. This is sameness made legal.

Giving still more explicit expression to this definition, King went even further when he stated that "A law is unjust if it is inflicted on a minority . . . that has been denied the right to vote and had no part in enacting or devising the law." In other words, when a minority is excluded from the total democratic process, as the Negroes in Alabama and Mississippi were, then the laws of these states cannot be considered just. "Any law enacted under such circumstances cannot be considered democratically structured." Further, a law may be just on the surface and unjust in its application. An example of this would be denying Negroes the right to use a parade permit as a way of maintaining segregation. This would be a situation calling for acts of nonviolent protest.

King made an added distinction between civil disobedience and uncivil disobedience. The former was represented by those who sat-in, the latter by the rabid segregationist who defies, evades, or circumvents those laws he considers inimical to his personal prejudices. Unwilling to accept the penalty for his defiance of the law, his violation ends in anarchy and a show of utter disrespect for the law. The nonviolent student protester, on the other hand, willingly accepts the penalty for a law he disobeys because his conscience tells him that it is unjust. By his actions, his willingness to remain in jail until the law is changed, the student shows his respect for the law. King stressed the importance of disobeying unjust laws with a willingness to accept whatever penalty the law then imposes, so that the public would then come to reexamine the law in question and decide whether it was uplifting or degrading.

In sum, while disobedience is in itself destructive and antisocial, obedience to an immoral law is even worse and should always be opposed. A law, to be worthy of obedience, must be moral and democratically formulated. In extreme cases in a democracy, if a citizen cannot obtain the repeal of an immoral law through constitutional means, he should disobey the law as an act of conscience and willingly accept the penalty for having done so. Nonviolent civil disobedience, in King's view, was an effort to reconcile the demands of freedom and law, justice and democratic process, this world and that to come.

King's Dream of the Beloved Community

Ira G. Zepp Jr.

Ira G. Zepp Jr. writes that Dr. King's vision of a beloved community was his primary organizing principle of activism. For King the beloved community was defined simply as an integrated society where brotherhood is a reality. At one point King referred to the idea of a beloved community as "the cornerstone of my faith." It was King's goal to transform the world community into a beloved community where brotherhood and God transcend all divisions of nationality, religion, and race.

Zepp argues that at the core of King's concept of the beloved community are two fundamental components: interrelatedness and integration. According to Zepp, King believed that people are tied together, interrelated and bound to a single destiny. Hence, what affects one person affects all people indirectly. Moreover, humanity's interrelatedness makes everyone dependent on meaningful relationships with others.

Zepp maintains that King's belief in the beloved community requires society to move beyond desegregation and embrace integration. According to King, an integrated society offers more than equal opportunities; it is built on relationships created by love and spiritual oneness. Finally, the beloved community is egalitarian; the gap between poverty and wealth is bridged and no one does without the necessities of life.

Ira G. Zepp Jr. is a United Methodist minister and a professor of religion at Western Maryland College, Westminster. He is the author of several books, including *The Social Vision of Martin Luther King, Jr.*

King's devotion to the realization of the beloved community was his primary goal. It was the organizing principle of his

Excerpted from *The Social Vision of Martin Luther King Jr.*, by Ira G. Zepp Jr. (Brooklyn: Carlson, 1989). Copyright ©1971, 1989 by Ira G. Zepp Jr. Reprinted with permission.

life and around which all of his thought and activity centered. His writings and his involvement in the civil rights struggle were illustrations of and footnotes to this fundamental preoccupation. . . .

The concept of the beloved community can be traced from those early formative addresses delivered by King in 1955–56. In one of his first published articles, "We Are Still Walking," he said, reflecting [theologian Walter] Rauschenbusch, "We are striving for the removal of all barriers that divide and alienate mankind, whether racial, economic, or psychological." In "Facing the Challenge of a New Age," King stated that the bus boycott was not an end in itself. The real purpose of the Montgomery campaign was healing; its "end is reconciliation; the end is redemption; the end is the creation of the beloved community."

Toward the end of *Stride Toward Freedom*, published in 1958, King discusses the relationship of nonviolence to the goal of "genuine . . . interpersonal living." Then he concludes, "Only through nonviolence can this goal be attained, for the aftermath of nonviolence is reconciliation and the creation of the beloved community." In a sermon, "Loving Your Enemies," King calls upon his hearers to follow the "impractical" method of love. Communities have been wrecked when they followed the "practical" methods of violence, hatred, and vengeance. The "obligation to love" remains with us. "While abhorring segregation, we shall love the segregationist. This is the only way to create the beloved community." Again in 1962 in an address, "The Ethical Demands of Integration," King emphasized the importance of community. For him, the "most creative turn of events" in man's long history was when he gave up his stone axe to cooperate with his neighbor.

> That seemingly elementary decision set in motion what we know now as civilization. At the heart of all that civilization has meant and developed is "community"—the mutually cooperative and voluntary venture of man to assume a semblance of responsibility for his brother.

In the *Playboy* interview of 1964 (published in January 1965), King persists in his claim that all Americans have "got to live together. We've got to find a way to reconcile ourselves to living in community, one group with the other." He continues, "It is the keystone of my faith in the future that we will someday achieve a thoroughly integrated society."

King posits two alternatives for American society in the title of his next-to-last book, *Where Do We Go From Here: Chaos or Community?* In this book King speaks of the necessity of an international community. He sees the world as a "large house" and since we all now live in one house, we must "transform this world-wide neighborhood into a world-wide brotherhood. Together we must learn to live as brothers or together we will be forced to perish as fools." The latter note of world perspective is repeated in *The Trumpet of Conscience* and there is here also a renewed stress, found in the early addresses, on the eradication of barriers of all kinds. "Our loyalties must transcend our race, our tribe, our class, and our nation. . . ." This is reminiscent of Rauschenbusch, who asserted that the Christian God is:

> a barrier of barriers from the first. All who have a distinctively Christian experience of God are committed to the expansion of human fellowship and to the overthrow of barriers.

The Kingdom of God for Rauschenbusch ultimately transcends all divisions of nationality, religion, and race. . . .

KING'S VIEW OF THE HUMAN FAMILY

Integral to King's understanding of community was his conception of the "solidarity of the human family." A phrase he used innumerable times, as late as March 31, 1968, was "We are tied together in the single garment of destiny, caught in an inescapable network of mutuality."

To support his belief that "whatever affects one directly affects all indirectly," he repeatedly uses in his writings the oft-quoted observation of [English Poet] John Donne, "no man is an island, entire of itself." There is an "interrelated structure of reality." This structure means that we are dependent on each other. What we have and are we owe to many people who have preceded us. "Whether we realize it or not, each of us is eternally 'in the red.' We are everlasting debtors to known and unknown men and women." This element of debt and implied gratitude destroys an unhealthy self-sufficiency in men which isolates them as individuals and then destroys community.

Secondly, this "structure" means that we need each other for personal fulfillment. Our individual maturity and personal growth cannot take place apart from meaningful relationships with other persons. The interrelated, interdependent character of life means that "I" cannot reach fulfillment without

"Thou." "The self cannot be self without other selves." These fulfilled selves constitute the real human community.

The third implication of this "structure" and its most serious one is the corporate effect of injustice and immorality summed up in one of King's favorite lines, "Injustice anywhere is a threat to justice everywhere." This observation is ultimately King's argument against the "outside agitator" ploy used by many southerners against people (even Atlanta-born King himself) who came into their state to intervene in local affairs.

King understood that the denial of constitutional rights to anyone potentially violated the rights of all citizens. The victims of electric cattle prods and biting police dogs were the entire national community. Discrimination against ten per cent of our population weakens the whole society. South Africa and the southern United States were mutually affected by discrimination in each area. The poverty and racial issues are not merely sectional problems; they are American problems. By the same token, the liberation of black men means the full freedom for the white man. King took seriously the indivisibility of our country and the indivisibility of life. So he contends:

> In a real sense, all life is interrelated. The agony of the poor impoverishes the rich; the betterment of the poor enriches the rich. We are inevitably our brother's keeper because we are our brother's brother. Whatever affects one directly affects all indirectly.

KING'S BELIEF IN MUTUALITY

In a letter to fellow clergymen written in 1963 from a Birmingham, Alabama, jail cell, King expresses his belief that any particular injustice is a threat to justice everywhere.

Moreover, I am cognizant of the interrelatedness of all communities and states. I cannot sit idly by in Atlanta and not be concerned about what happens in Birmingham. Injustice anywhere is a threat to justice everywhere. We are caught in an inescapable network of mutuality, tied in a single garment of destiny. Whatever affects one directly affects all indirectly. Never again can we afford to live with the narrow, provincial "outside agitator" idea. Anyone who lives in the United States can never be considered an outsider anywhere in this country.

Martin Luther King Jr., *I Have a Dream: Writings and Speeches that Changed the World.* New York: HarperCollins, 1992.

This is what King means by being "tied together in a garment of mutuality" and this reinforces his Donne reference:
"and therefore never send to know for whom the bell tolls; it
tolls for thee." Because of this solidaristic understanding of
life, King saw the civil rights movement contributing "infinitely more to the nation than the eradication of racial injustice. It will have enlarged the concept of brotherhood to a
vision of total interrelatedness." That is to say, our society
will be approaching the ideal of the beloved community.
That human life is initially and ultimately social was be-
queathed to King by Rauschenbusch's strong emphasis on
the solidarity of life and [American philosopher Edgar S.]
Brightman's contention that all life was social.

INTEGRATION AND THE BELOVED COMMUNITY

In a Southern Christian Leadership Conference (SCLC)
Newsletter in 1957, shortly after the new civil rights organization was formed, King described its purpose and goal.

> The ultimate aim of SCLC is to foster and create the "beloved
> community" in America where brotherhood is a reality. . . .
> SCLC works for integration. Our ultimate goal is genuine in-
> tergroup and interpersonal living-*integration.*

An integrated society where "brotherhood is a reality" suc-
cinctly summarizes King's understanding of the beloved
community. To appreciate the positive meaning King at-
taches to integration, one must review how he distinguishes
segregation, desegregation, and integration.

Segregation is "prohibitive," denying the Negro equal access to schools, parks, restaurants, and libraries. Desegregation is "eliminative and negative"—it merely removes the legal prohibitions. Integration, on the other hand, is more
far-reaching than desegregation; it is more "creative" in that
"integration is the positive acceptance of desegregation and
the welcomed participation of Negroes into the total range of
human activities. . . ."

It is clear to King that a desegregated society is not an integrated society. In that desegregation makes available public facilities and services to all people, it usually precedes integration. But there is no necessary nor automatic shift from
desegregation to integration. The latter is "much more subtle and internal, for it involves attitudes: the mutual acceptance of individuals and groups."

Integration, as King understood it, is a matter of personal

relationships created by love; thus an integrated society cannot be legislated. Once segregationist laws have been stricken from the books, Negroes and whites will have to relate to each other across these nonrational, invisible psychological barriers which have traditionally separated them in our society. King hoped our society would eventually be "stricken gloriously and incurably color-blind." King's high expectation for integration is seen in the following statement.

> It (desegregation) gives us a society where men are physically desegregated and spiritually segregated, where elbows are together and hearts are apart. It gives us special togetherness and spiritual apartness. It leaves us with a stagnant equality of sameness rather than a constructive equality of oneness.

Integration meant primarily for King "black and white together." Chapter six in *Why We Can't Wait* is entitled "Black and White Together" and a significant verse of the civil rights hymn "We Shall Overcome" contains the same words. But integration for King was broader than simply racial equality.

KING'S VIEW OF JUSTICE

King never sought black supremacy to transplant white supremacy. His search was for brotherhood. King was not interested in black justice as opposed to white justice. He was interested in justice for all. He hoped for a day when Negro newspapers and Negro churches would become American newspapers and Christian churches. As a result of commitment to solving the problem of racial hatred and oppression

> the sense of brotherhood springs as a practical necessity, and once this happens, there is revealed the vision of a society of brotherhood. We seek new ways of human beings living together, free from the spiritual deformation of race hatred—and free also from the deformation of war and economic injustice. And this vision does not belong to Negroes alone. It is the yearning of mankind.

In his address to the Prayer Pilgrimage in Washington, D.C. in May of 1957, King unequivocally states:

> We must not become victimized with a philosophy of black supremacy. God is not interested in merely freeing black men, brown men and yellow men; God is interested in freeing the whole human race. We must work with determination to create a society in which all men will love together as brothers and respect the dignity and worth of human personality.

And the elimination of the unjust system will permit each

person to develop his unique potential. The presence of freedom for all will "create a moral balance in society which will allow all men, Negro and white, to rise to higher levels of self-completion." Some specific indications of what the beloved community will be like are found in the "Dream Speech" of August 1963. These indications point to King's overriding concern for integration.

> . . . sons of former slaves and the sons of former slave owners will be able to sit down together at the table of brotherhood.

> The injustice and oppression of the state of Mississippi "will be transformed into an oasis of freedom and justice."

> . . . my four little children will one day live in a nation where they will not be judged by the color of their skin but by the content of their character.

Even the state of Alabama will be transformed so that

> little black boys and black girls will be able to join hands with little white boys and white girls and walk together as sisters and brothers.

But it is not simply black and white joining hands—

> . . . all of God's children, black men and white men, Jews and Gentiles, Protestants and Catholics, will be able to join hands. . . .

KING'S EGALITARIANISM

The beloved community, however, is not completely constitutive of the subtle, internal, spiritual relationships between people embodied in the rhetoric of the "Dream Speech." King evidenced impatience with the meaninglessness of "human dignity" and "brotherhood" if these words and phrases were not concretely expressed in the transformation of society. Every man must now have food and the material necessities of life for his body as well as education and dignity.

> Let us be dissatisfied until rat-infested, vermin-filled slums will be a thing of a dark past and every family will have a decent sanitary house in which to live. Let us be dissatisfied until the empty stomachs of Mississippi are filled and idle industries of Appalachia are revitalized. . . . Let us be dissatisfied until our brother of the Third World—Asia, Africa and Latin America—will no longer be the victim of imperialist exploitation, but will be lifted from the long night of poverty, illiteracy, and disease.

This comment made in 1968 is an enlargement upon, yet an echo of an early and consistent concern of King's, namely, an egalitarian, socialist approach to wealth. In 1956, he chastised America for "taking necessities from the masses to give luxuries to the classes." To bridge the gap between poverty and wealth was to be a goal of America. King continues his admonition.

> You can use your powerful economic resources to wipe poverty from the face of the earth. God never intended for one group of people to live in superfluous inordinate wealth, while others lived in abject deadening poverty.

The beloved community would be an expression of God's intention that no one was meant to be without the necessities of life. It is for this reason that King, in the last two years of his life, began to advocate the creation of jobs and a guaranteed annual minimum income. He sensed that the civil rights struggle had not seriously dealt with the economic problems of the Negro. In early 1968, when he was interpreting the meaning of the Poor People's Campaign, he said, while referring to the Negro

> I am speaking of all the poor, I am not only concerned about the black poor; I am concerned about poverty among my Mexican-American brothers; I am concerned about poverty among my Puerto Rican brothers; I am concerned about poverty among my Indian brothers; I am concerned about poverty among my Appalachian white brothers, and I wish they would realize that we are struggling against poverty for everybody and would join in a movement to get rid of poverty.

King could not envision a human community apart from the alleviation of economic inequity. [American theologian] Harvey Cox says that King has here combined two traditionally biblical concerns—the "holiness of the poor" and the "blessed community." In King's movement, the Negro became the embodiment of "the poor" and "integration" now points to the vision of the holy community.

> It is also essential to notice that the two elements, the holy outcast *and* the blessed community, must go together. Without the vision of restored community, the holiness ascribed to the poor would fall far short of politics and result in a mere perpetuation of charity and service activities.

King's vision of the beloved community included all races, all classes, all religions, all ethnic groups, and, ultimately, all nations. The community transcended economic, social, political, and cultural lines.

King's Political and Social Radicalism

Adam Fairclough

Although Martin Luther King Jr. is often portrayed as a leader who worked within the political mainstream, Adam Fairclough argues that King's political views harbored deep political radicalism and an overriding distrust of American capitalism. Fairclough writes that King was influenced by the ideology of German political philosopher Karl Marx. While in school, King was impressed by Marx's ideas, and later, as a young preacher, he was influenced by the founders of the Southern Christian Leadership Conference, who had ties with socialist organizations. At first, Fairclough reasons, King approached civil rights by appealing to idealism and Christian principles. Eventually, however, two factors worked to radicalize his political thought. First, he came to realize that racism was not just a social aberration, but rather a deeply ingrained dedication to class privilege and economic stratification. King ultimately felt that the American economic structure must be reordered. The second factor to radicalize King was the Vietnam War. Although King was against the war for moral reasons, he was also opposed to it because it was another manifestation of oppression used to bolster American capitalist interests.

Fairclough concludes that King believed that behind the ills of racism, economic exploitation, and militarism was the American capitalist notion that profits and property rights are more important than people. During the last two years of his life, King advocated democratic socialism built on economic justice and the uplifting of the economically downtrodden.

Adam Fairclough is a professor of modern American history at the University of Leeds, England. He contributes to

Excerpted from Adam Fairclough, "Was Martin Luther King a Marxist?" in *Martin Luther King Jr.: Civil Rights Leader, Theologian, Orator*, vol. 2, edited by David J. Garrow (Brooklyn: Carlson, 1989). Reprinted with permission.

history journals and is the author of *Race and Democracy: The Civil Rights Struggle in Louisiana.*

Martin Luther King, Jr., has seldom figured in the Left's pantheon of Socialist heroes. To many of his contemporaries he seemed a typical product of the 'black bourgeoisie': a middle-class preacher from a middle-class family who pursued middle-class goals. Although an eloquent and courageous crusader for racial justice, his ultimate vision—as expressed for example in his famous 'I Have A Dream' oration—seemed to be the integration of the Negro into the existing structure of society; capitalism was not at issue. When he talked about the need for cleanliness, godliness and thrift, he sounded like [American educator] Booker T. Washington, that epitome of bourgeois values who, at the turn of the century, had exhorted blacks to pull themselves up by their own bootstraps. King's own admiration for Washington, whom many blacks viewed as an arch 'Uncle Tom', was widely-known and openly advertised. By the mid-1960s, at the height of his fame and success, King struck many of his contemporaries as an essentially conservative figure. He was always 'amenable to compromise', wrote one commentator, 'with the white bourgeois political and economic Establishment'. Lawrence Reddick, King's friend and biographer, had anticipated such verdicts years earlier. 'Neither by experience nor reading is King a political radical', he wrote in 1959. 'There is not a Marxist bone in his body.' True, King adopted a much more radical stance during the last two years of his life, but he never seemed to wander very far from the political mainstream. To the student radicals of the 'New Left', as well as to the angry advocates of 'Black Power', King remained a staid, unexciting figure, the ineffectual exponent of an outdated brand of liberalism.

It seems scarcely credible, then, that King was, as the Federal Bureau of Investigation maintained, a self-confessed Marxist. Did the FBI's ubiquitous wiretaps really record the civil rights leader saying, 'I am a Marxist', and that he would profess this publicly but for the knowledge that it would destroy his position? In view of the notorious conservatism of the FBI, which branded the mildest of social critics 'subversive', this allegation might be dismissed as a paranoid fantasy, or perhaps a product of the racism that permeated the Bureau under its chief, J. Edgar Hoover. Hoover's own loathing for King, and his malevolent campaign to destroy him, have been thoroughly documented in Congressional investigations and a recent book by [King scholar] David J. Garrow.

Yet the FBI's perception of King as a radical threat to American institutions was not as far-fetched as it may seem, for King did, in fact, express admiration for Marx and argue that the United States should move towards Socialism. King's placid exterior, his orotund manner, and his sober clerical mien tended to disguise his deep political radicalism. In addition, he expressed his political beliefs far more frankly and explicitly in private than he did in public. Only recently, when Mrs Coretta King allowed researches access to the records of the Southern Christian Leadership Conference (the organization that her husband headed) has the real scope of King's radicalism become apparent. By 1966 he had become a passionate enemy of Western capitalism and an advocate, in his own words, of 'democratic socialism'.

KING'S EXPOSURE TO MARXIST IDEOLOGY

King's attraction to socialism pre-dated his career as a civil rights leader. In a student essay, he spoke of his anti-capitalist feelings. At Crozer Theological Seminary, he read *Capital, The Communist Manifesto*, and some interpretive works on the thinking of Marx and [Russian Communist leader Vladimir] Lenin. Although he rejected the materialist conception of reality, King was clearly enamoured by much of what he read. The *Communist Manifesto*, he later wrote, 'was written by men aflame with a passion for social justice.' Marx had raised 'basic questions', and 'in so far as he pointed to weaknesses of traditional capitalism, contributed to the growth of a definite self-consciousness in the masses, and challenged the social conscience of the Christian churches, I responded with a definite "yes".' Later, as a doctoral student at Boston University, King read and admired the writings of Reinhold Niebuhr, who combined Christian ethics with a Marxian analysis of history and society, and whose seminal work, *Moral Man and Immoral Society*, had a profound and continuing impact on him. King's radical views while a student did not please his conservative father: as 'Daddy' King later wrote, 'Politically, he . . . seemed to be drifting away from the bases of capitalism and Western democracy that I felt very strongly about. There were some sharp exchanges; I may even have raised my voice a few times.'

In December 1955 King was thrust into a position of leadership that he had neither sought nor wanted. Elected to serve as president of the Montgomery Improvement Association, a group formed to boycott the segregated buses in Montgomery, Alabama, King soon became the internationally-recognized symbol of the emerging civil rights movement. When black clergymen from across the South met to found a new civil rights organization, the Southern Christian Leadership Conference (SCLC), they automatically chose King to act as president. Interestingly, they decided to include the word 'Christian' in their name partly to avoid being labelled as a 'Red' organization.

Nevertheless, the three New Yorkers—two blacks and one white—who organized SCLC on King's behalf were all firmly on the Left. Bayard Rustin, Ella Baker and Stanley Levison were much older than King; their political involvement went back to the 1930s. Rustin had joined the Communist Youth League before the war but, like so many others, broke with the party over its subservience to Moscow. He subsequently worked for various pacifist organizations, and helped set up the first London-to-Aldermaston march against nuclear weapons. He also tried, without much success, to popularize Gandhian civil disobedience as a means of fighting racial discrimination. He remained a Socialist, however, and had the long-term goal of moving blacks into a radicalized labour movement. Ella Baker lacked Rustin's interest in pacifism, but otherwise moved in the same political milieu. 'I had been friendly with people who were in the Communist Party and all the rest of the left forces', she would recall. Levison's political allegiance was more ambiguous. Ostensibly a liberal Democrat, he had been active in such groups as the businessman's committee for the re-election of Roosevelt (1944) and the American Jewish Congress. But he was also close to leading members of the beleaguered Communist Party and may have, in the early 1950s, offered them financial advice and assistance. Baker simply remembered that he, too, 'had come out of the New York left'. All three recognized that mass civil disobedience, especially in the context of the American South, was a tactic that had far-reaching potential. Excited by the Montgomery bus boycott—an entirely spontaneous protest—they offered the inexperienced King help and advice, and constructed SCLC as a vehicle for mass action throughout the South. Interestingly, Baker soon fell out with King because, in part, she deemed him insufficiently radical. Rustin and Levison, on the other hand, worked with him until his death in 1968, acting as unofficial advisers and behind-the-scenes organizers.

Because of his association with these two, the FBI depicted King, from 1963 until his death, as either a conscious 'fellow traveller', or, at best, a naive dupe. Levison, the Bureau asserted, was a particularly subversive influence: a man who manipulated King in the interests of the Communist Party. Years after King's death, Levison, who was white, attributed this canard to the FBI's 'racist contempt for the intellect of the black man. No one with a modicum of sense . . . could have concluded that a man with the force of intellect and fierce independence that Martin King had could have been dominated by anybody. . . . And if there had been any domination in the relationship, the greater probability was that he would influence or perhaps dominate me.' Levison raised funds for SCLC, helped King with his speeches and writings, and proffered common-sense advice that remained, in David Garrow's words, 'wholly innocuous'. Rustin assisted King in similar ways and, far from being a dangerous radical, drifted steadily to the right, eventually attaching himself to the Johnson-Humphrey wing of the Democratic party.

With his religious cast of mind, King tended to reject political ideology. Interested first and foremost in combating racism, he accepted assistance from whatever quarter it came. As for his staff, all he asked was they they accept nonviolence—as a tactic if not a philosophy—and be fully committed to the civil rights movement. On rare occasions, however, he succumbed to political pressure, and he distanced himself from both Rustin and Levison for a time because of their allegedly 'tainted' political pasts. In the case of Levison the pressure came from the White House itself. Later, King reproached himself for moral cowardice, and reestablished a close relationship with both of them. 'There's nothing to hide,' he told Levison. 'And if anybody wants to make anything of it, let them try.' By 1965, King had concluded that 'anti-communism' provided a handy cloak for opposition to social progress. By making continual allegations about 'communist infiltration' of the civil rights movement, he charged, J. Edgar Hoover aided and abetted the 'Southern racists and the extreme right-wing element.' Radicalism among blacks grew out of 'impatience with the slow pace of establishing justice.' America's fear of communism, he concluded, was 'morbid', 'irrational' and 'obsessive'.

KING'S RADICALIZATION

Until 1965, King's radicalism was more intellectual than emotional. He had approached the struggle for racial justice in a non-ideological way, hoping to overcome bigotry and prejudice through an appeal to idealism and Christian principles. Perhaps because his parents had shielded him from the worst effects of racial oppression, he viewed racism as a Southern anachronism which would, in the course of a decade or two, wither away and die. After that, he believed, blacks would have to 'work desperately to improve their own conditions and their own standards. . . . The Negro will have to engage in a sort of Operation Boot-strap.' By 1966, however, he categorically rejected the idea of piecemeal reform within the existing socio-economic structure: a massive redistribution of wealth, not self-help, was the most urgent necessity.

Two factors hastened this process of radicalization: King's belated realization that racism was endemic in American society; and his horror of America's military role in Vietnam. When he took SCLC North, to Chicago, he had to abandon his assumption that racism outside the South was a secondary, residual phenomenon. When blacks demanded an end to discrimination in housing, education and jobs, white support for the civil rights movement melted away. Routine police brutality pushed back frustration to the boiling-point, yet government, both federal and local, responded to the eruption of rioting with repression rather than root and branch reform. By the end of 1966 King's optimism had been shattered. Only 'a minority of whites,' he wrote, 'genuinely want authentic equality'. To black audiences, and to his staff, he put it more bluntly: 'the vast majority of white Americans are racists'.

More and more, King saw racism as an instrument of class privilege, a means of dividing the working-class by giving whites marginal economic advantages and encouraging their psychological pretensions to superiority. Both black and white labour was thus more easily exploited and cheapened. With his top aid James Bevel, King viewed the black ghettos as 'internal colonies', a segregated market where goods and services were deliberately restricted in order to boost the profits of the capitalists who provided them. At an SCLC retreat in November 1966, he warned that demanding an end to the ghetto meant 'getting on dangerous ground because you are messing with folk then. You are messing with Wall Street. You are messing with the captains of industry'. He told his staff not to be afraid of the word 'socialism', for 'something is wrong with capitalism' and 'the Movement must address itself to the restructuring of the whole of American society'. Sweden, he pointed out, had 'grappled with the problem of more equitable distribution of wealth'; it had free health care, and no slums, poverty or unemployment. Institutional racism could only be eliminated through a radical redistribution of economic power; 'privileged groups will have to give up some of their billions'. America, too, he argued, 'must move toward a Democratic Socialism'.

THE VIETNAM WAR AS AN ACT OF SUPPRESSION

The war in Vietnam reinforced King's disenchantment with American capitalism. His opposition to the war has often been interpreted as a purely moral concern, an expression of his dogmatic commitment to non-violence. Not so: he did not take a politically agnostic position, but roundly condemned the United States as the aggressor. Time and again he insisted that Ho Chi Minh was leading a popular nationalist revolt against a corrupt dictatorship, and that the United States had taken the wrong side. Again, King expressed his views more plainly and frankly when talking to black audiences, to friends, and to his own staff. During an SCLC retreat in May 1967, he left his staff in no doubt about his admiration for Ho Chi Minh—nor his utter contempt for the rulers of South Vietnam. He scornfully dismissed the notion that the South was being 'invaded' by the North: 'the Vietcong came into being in the South as a movement to resist the oppression of Diem'. Besides, he argued, the division of Vietnam had been imposed from without: 'how can somebody invade himself?' When America supported the South, it was 'as if the French and the British had come over here during the Civil War to fight with the Confederacy'. Speaking to an SCLC-sponsored conference of black ministers in early 1968, he cited the recent Tet offensive as conclusive proof that 'the vast majority of the people in Vietnam are sympathetic with the Vietcong. That is a fact'.

King did not see America's involvement in Vietnam as an isolated aberration, but as part of a wider 'pattern of suppression' that embraced Africa and Latin America in addition to Southeast Asia. America bolstered the racist regimes in South Africa and Rhodesia; American arms and personnel helped to fight rebels and guerrillas in Venezuela, Guatemala, Colombia, and Peru. Why, he asked, had 'the Western nations that initiated so much of the revolutionary spirit of the modern world' become 'the arch anti-revolutionaries' of the twentieth century? Ultimately, he believed, the answer lay in the very nature of Western capitalism: 'individual capitalists of the West' invested 'huge sums of money in Asia, Africa and South America, only to take the profits out with no concern for the social betterment of the countries'; multinational cartels stripped underdeveloped nations of their resources 'while turning over a small rebate to a few members of a corrupt aristocracy'. The historic freedom accorded to capital in the United States had made government the servant of private profit:

> A nation that will keep people in slavery for 244 years will 'thingify' them, make them things. Therefore they will exploit them, and poor people generally, economically. And a nation that will exploit economically will have to have foreign investments . . . and will have to use its military might to protect them.

This 'need to maintain social stability for our investments' explained the alliance with the landed gentry in Latin America; the support for colonial and white settler regimes in Africa; and the sponsorship of puppet dictators in Southeast Asia. The United States had become the world's foremost neo-colonial power.

THE LINK BETWEEN RACISM AND CAPITALISM

During the last two years of his life, King became convinced that capitalism was the common denominator that linked racism, economic exploitation and militarism. These 'triple evils' of the modern era were 'incapable of being conquered' when 'profit motives and property rights are considered more important than people'. If hostility to capitalism coloured his writings and speeches so strongly, could he, then, be described as a 'Marxist'? In private, King readily acknowledged his intellectual debt to Marx and commended his critique of capitalism. Yet he always coupled such praise with qualifications. King, echoing the conventional definitions of the day, associated Marxism with the rejection of spiritual values, a shallow economic determinism, and the absolute supremacy of the state. All this he emphatically rejected. He summed up his feelings about Marx, both positive and negative, in a talk to the SCLC staff in 1966:

> I always look at Marx with a yes and a no. And there were some things that Karl Marx did that were very good. Some very good things. If you read him, you can see that this man had a great passion for social justice. . . . [But] Karl Marx got messed up, first because he didn't stick with that Jesus that he had read about; but secondly because he didn't even stick with [German philosopher Georg] Hegel.

As always, King then went on to talk about Jesus as his primary inspiration:

> Now this is where I leave Brother Marx and move on toward the Kingdom [of Brotherhood]. . . . I am simply saying that God never intended for some of his children to live in inordinate superfluous wealth while others live in abject, deadening poverty.

That King should have stated 'I am a Marxist', without these qualifications and in such bald terms, is, in the opinion of this writer, unlikely in the extreme. His hostility to excessive materialism, and his concern for the poor and the oppressed, owed more to the Social Gospel than to Marxist ideology.

KING'S OPPOSITION TO CAPITALISM

Regardless of the influences that helped shape his political analysis, King made no bones about his radical opposition to American capitalism. 'For years,' he told one reporter, 'I labored with the idea of reforming the existing institutions of the society, a little change here, a little change there. Now I feel quite differently. I think you've got to have a reconstruction of the entire society.' He did not openly advocate 'socialism', but talked instead of a 'synthesis' between capitalism and communism; a 'socially conscious democracy which reconciles the truths of individualism and collectivism'. As he admitted in private, however, such definitions were really euphemisms for democratic socialism. In public, the best he could hope for was to encourage questioning and doubt. 'Why are there 40 million poor people in America?' he asked at the SCLC convention in August 1967:

> When you begin to ask that question, you are raising questions about the economic system, about a broader distribution of wealth. When you ask that question, you begin to ques-

tion the capitalistic economy. And I'm simply saying that more and more, we've got to begin to ask questions about the whole society. We are called upon to help the discouraged beggars in life's market place. But one day we must come to see that an edifice which produces beggars needs restructuring. . . . You see, my friends, when you deal with this, you begin to ask the question, 'Who owns the oil?' You begin to ask the question, 'Who owns the iron ore?'

King clearly found the gap between his own deepening radicalism and the political unsophistication of his followers frustrating. He hoped that black clergymen could, through education and training, be oriented toward his own radical values, enabling them to occupy the vanguard in a struggle for economic justice just as they had been in the forefront of the civil rights movement in the South. 'We must develop their psyche', he told a planning meeting of SCLC's Ministers Leadership Training Program. 'Something is wrong with capitalism as it now stands in the United States. We are not interested in being integrated into *this* value structure . . . a radical redistribution of power must take place.' As Louis Lomax wrote, this vision of the clergy was, perhaps, 'the most ethereal dream he ever entertained'.

KING ATTACKS POVERTY

In his 1967 book, Where Do We Go from Here: Chaos or Community? *King expresses his loathing of widespread poverty in America.*

The curse of poverty has no justification in our age. It is socially as cruel and blind as the practice of cannibalism at the dawn of civilization, when men ate each other because they had not yet learned to take food from the soil or to consume the abundant animal life around them. The time has come for us to civilize ourselves by the total, direct, and immediate abolition of poverty.

By the end of 1967, King believed that he had found a more viable alternative: an interracial alliance of the poor. His last major project, the 'Poor People's Campaign', was an attempt to translate this concept into political reality. America, he argued, already had 'socialism for the rich'; if the government could hand out massive subsidies to affluent farmers, giant corporations and wealthy individuals, then it could guarantee jobs and a decent income for all. He did not define his goal as 'socialism'; instead, he called it 'poor people's power'. King proposed to lead thousands of the poor to Washington where, if necessary, they would engage in mass civil disobedience in order to stimulate government action. 'We will be confronting the very government, and the very federal machinery that has often come [to] our aid', he warned his staff. Many old allies and supporters were aghast at the plan. His old friend Bayard Rustin publicly opposed it. Even colleagues in SCLC had grave doubts. King nevertheless showed every intention of going ahead. In the midst of the preparations for the campaign he went to Memphis to support striking sanitation workers in their fight for union recognition. 'In a sense', he told a reporter shortly before his assassination there, 'you could say we are engaged in a class struggle, yes'.

Civil Rights and the Vietnam War

James A. Colaiaco

James A. Colaiaco argues that in the last year and a half of his life Martin Luther King Jr. radicalized his position on civil rights by linking it with other controversial issues haunting the nation. King claimed that race hatred, ghetto riots, and the Vietnam War all grew from a pervading moral sickness in America. This sickness was a manifestation of America's dependence on three cultural forces: racism, materialism, and militarism. As a result, King became one of the most prominent spokespersons against the war in Vietnam, suggesting that America desperately needed to realign its values.

According to Colaiaco, King's stand on the Vietnam War alienated many supporters of the civil rights movement. Some black leaders saw his stand on the war as a tactical error that would weaken their struggle for equal rights. King's radical stance was severely criticized in the press; some national writers claimed that King had fallen under the Communist influence. Colaiaco maintains, however, that King's position was perfectly consistent with the civil rights leader's moral imperatives against violence.

James A. Colaiaco is a humanities teacher at Dalton School, New York City. He is the author of *Martin Luther King, Jr.: Apostle of Militant Nonviolence*. He also contributes articles to numerous history journals.

During the final year and a half of his life, King challenged the nation to undertake radical reforms. Stiffening white resistance to black equality, in addition to the spreading ghetto riot and the escalating Vietnam conflict, had created the greatest crisis in America since the Civil War. King saw these developments as symptoms of a moral sickness afflicting the nation that could be remedied only by radical changes in its political, social and economic structure. In an interview with journalist David Halberstam in 1967, he explained his recent political transformation: 'For years I labored with the idea of reforming the existing institutions of society, a little change here, a little change there. Now I feel quite differently. I think you've got to have a reconstruction of the entire society, a revolution of values'. King spoke of the possible nationalization of certain industries, a guaranteed annual income, a review of foreign investments and programmes to revitalize the cities. In the ensuing months, King would promote radical proposals such as these while the broad coalition of support he had depended upon in the past continued to dwindle. The Chicago campaign and the 'white backlash' clearly revealed that racism was not confined to the South, but was deeply ingrained in all aspects of American life. 'Most Americans', King lamented, 'are unconscious racists'.

KING'S OPPOSITION TO THE VIETNAM WAR

The Vietnam War was to a great extent responsible for King's radical stand. By 1967, Vietnam had supplanted civil rights as the major issue confronting the nation, and hundreds of young activists were diverted from the black freedom struggle to protests against the war. Refusing to ignore what he regarded as an injustice and the most serious threat to world peace, King emerged as one of the most prominent spokesmen of the anti-war movement. Though he had publicly opposed the war since 1965, he delivered his first speech devoted entirely to Vietnam at a conference in Los Angeles sponsored by *The Nation* on 25 February 1967. Attacking American foreign policy as 'supporting a new form of colonialism', he argued that 'we are presently moving down a dead-end road that can only lead to national disaster'. He concluded: 'We must combine the fervor of the civil rights movement with the peace movement. We must demonstrate, teach, and preach until the very foundations of our nation are shaken'. At a rally in the Chicago Coliseum on 25 March, King repeated his call to unite the civil rights and peace movements. Within a week, his stand was approved by the directors of SCLC, who condemned the war as 'morally and politically unjust'. In an interview on 2 April with John Herbers of the *New York Times*, King said that if the war continued to escalate, 'it may be necessary to engage in civil disobedience to further arouse the conscience of the nation'.

King's most famous denunciation of the war occurred at Riverside Church in New York City on 4 April 1967, when he was the principal speaker at a convocation sponsored by Clergy and Laymen Concerned About Vietnam. Delivered to a crowd of 3000, King's speech was widely covered by the news media. 'A time comes when silence is betrayal', he began. Alleging that the war was symptomatic of a 'malady within the American spirit', King pulled no punches, charging that the United States government was 'the greatest purveyor of violence in the world today'. He then surveyed the background to the war: the proclamation of Vietnamese independence under the leadership of Ho Chi Minh in 1945; the refusal of the United States to either recognize Vietnam's independence or support its war against French colonialism; the United States' endorsement of the repressive regime of 'one of the most vicious modern dictators', Premier Diem in South Vietnam and the failure of the United States to honour the 1954 Geneva accords, conspiring with Diem to prevent an election that would have established Ho Chi Minh as leader of a united Vietnam. After the fall of Diem, increasing numbers of American troops buttressed a series of corrupt military dictatorships in South Vietnam, encountering staunch resistance from the insurgent National Liberation Front or Viet Cong. Pointing to the devastating effect of the war upon the Vietnamese people—the destruction of their land, villages and families—King observed: 'They must see Americans as strange liberators'.

To end the tragic war and bring justice to a victimized people, King proposed that the United States declare a unilateral cease-fire, halt the bombing of Vietnam, recognize the right of the National Liberation Front to participate in peace talks and in any future Vietnamese government and establish a date for the withdrawal of all foreign troops from Vietnam, consistent with the Geneva accords. 'Somehow this madness must cease', King implored. 'We must stop now. . . . I speak as an American to the leaders of my own nation. The great initiative in this war is ours. The initiative to stop it must be ours'.

KING'S CRITICISM OF AMERICAN FOREIGN POLICIES

Expanding his indictment of American foreign policy beyond Vietnam, King charged that the United States was 'on the wrong side of a world revolution' against exploitation and oppression in Asia, Africa and South America. The nation was more interested in protecting its foreign investments than in promoting international peace and justice. If America did not radically alter its policies, taking the side of justice, he warned, humanity would continue headlong into war and destruction. In a world threatened by nuclear holocaust, King believed that the decision had to be made: either 'nonviolent coexistence or violent co-annihilation'. He explained that before America could take an international role in defeating the triple evils of 'racism, materialism, and militarism', the nation had to undergo a 'radical revolution of values', substituting a 'person-oriented' society for a 'thing-oriented' society. Such a revolution would undermine the appeal of communism, which he regarded as a symptom of the failure of capitalism. The best defence against communism, King proclaimed, is not violent warfare, but the removal of the poverty and injustice which provide fertile ground for its development.

Later that April, King again criticized America's involvement in the war. At a press conference, he supported those whose conscience opposed military service. 'Honestly, if I had to confront this problem,' he confessed, 'I would be a conscientious objector'. On 15 April, King was in New York City as the principal speaker for the 'Spring Mobilization to End the War in Vietnam', organized by SCLC's James Bevel, in which over 125 000 demonstrators marched from Central Park to the United Nations Plaza. Among the participants were Dr Benjamin Spock, Harry Belafonte, Stokely Carmichael and Floyd McKissick. At the conclusion of the protest, King inspired the huge crowd, attacking the war in a condensed version of his Riverside Church speech. Meanwhile, his wife Coretta, a pacifist since college and a member of the Women's International League for Peace and Freedom, spoke to 60 000 people at an anti-war rally in San Francisco. In November 1967, King had an opportunity to re-state his arguments in a radio speech recorded for the Canadian Broadcasting Corporation, and later published as part of his book, *The Trumpet of Conscience.*

THE EFFECTS OF KING'S RADICAL POSITION

King's opposition to the war alienated many supporters of civil rights. In 1967, the majority of Americans, white and black, approved of the war. In fact, according to a Harris poll, only 25 per cent of all black Americans favoured King's anti-war stand. Even civil rights leaders rebuked King. Roy Wilkens of the NAACP and Whitney Young of the National Urban League accused him publicly of hindering the cause of racial justice. On 12 April, the National Association for the Advancement of Colored People (NAACP) adopted a resolution declaring: 'To attempt to merge the civil rights movement with the peace movement . . . is, in our judgment, a serious tactical mistake. It will serve the cause neither of civil rights nor of peace'. Prominent black Americans, including Massachusetts Senator Edward Brooke, Ralph Bunche of the United Nations and former athlete Jackie Robinson, concurred. But King was relentless. What his critics regarded as two separate issues, racism at home and the war abroad, he considered inseparable. 'I have worked too long now', he said in a television interview on 28 July 1967, 'and too hard to get rid of segregation in public accommodations to turn back to the point of segregating my moral concern. Justice is indivisible'.

King was also severely criticized by the national press. The *Washington Post* condemned the Riverside Church speech as 'a grave injury' to the civil rights struggle and concluded that King had 'diminished his usefulness to his cause, to his country, and to his people'. A *Life* magazine editorial, entitled 'Dr. King's Disservice to His Cause', contended that King had exceeded his personal right to dissent by proposing a peace plan that was tantamount to 'abject surrender' in Vietnam. A *New York Times* editorial echoed the prevailing criticism, alleging that King's speech was 'a fusing of two public problems that are distinct and separate', and was therefore 'a disservice to both'. In an article for *Reader's Digest*, 'Martin Luther King's Tragic Decision', black journalist Carl Rowan argued that the Riverside Church speech 'put a new strain and new burdens on the civil rights movement'. To the disadvantage of millions of impoverished black Americans, Rowan charged, King had not only lost the support of his friends in Congress, but he had also become '*persona non grata* to Lyndon Johnson'. Rowan, convinced that King had fallen under Communist influence, also maintained that Americans of all races regarded as 'utterly irresponsible' King's urging young blacks to resist the draft. 'It is a tragic irony', Rowan concluded, 'that there should be any doubt about the Negro's loyalty to his country—especially doubt created by Martin Luther

King, who has helped as much as any one man to make America truly the Negro's country, too'.

But King remained true to his moral conviction that injustice anywhere is a threat to justice everywhere. He could not advocate nonviolence and civil rights at home and ignore violence and injustice abroad in Vietnam or any other country, especially when America was involved. A recipient of the Nobel Peace Prize, he felt a moral imperative to resist violence and speak out for the victims of poverty and injustice throughout the world.

CHAPTER 3

King's Role in the Civil Rights Movement

King's Rise to Prominence in Montgomery

Stephan Thernstrom and Abigail Thernstrom

When Rosa Parks was arrested for not giving up her seat to a white man on a Montgomery, Alabama, bus, authorities hoped to intimidate all blacks in the city. Stephan and Abigail Thernstrom write that few Americans realized then that Rosa Parks's action would begin a determined mass movement and, at the same time, bring forth Martin Luther King Jr. as a national civil rights celebrity.

The authors report that at the time of Rosa Parks's defiant action black leadership in Montgomery was unfocused and at times indifferent. Nevertheless, the chairman of the local office of the National Association for the Advancement of Colored People (NAACP) printed flyers calling for a citywide bus boycott. Church leaders supported the action and appointed Martin Luther King Jr. to carry out the boycott. Stephan and Abigail Thernstrom report that King proved to be a charismatic and passionate leader whose call for justice inspired Montgomery blacks. King introduced his call for nonviolent resistance soon after his home was bombed, the authors argue, because he understood then how disastrous armed revolt would be for America's black citizens. After 381 days the Montgomery boycott ended when a federal judge intervened and ruled that Montgomery's city bus segregation was unconstitutional.

The Thernstroms assert that with his actions in Montgomery, King became a national celebrity. It was at Montgomery that King began his role as the single most important asset in the civil rights movement.

Stephan Thernstrom is a history professor at Harvard University, Boston. He is the author of several books, including *A History of the American People, Vols. 1 & 2*. Abigail Thernstrom is a senior fellow at the Manhattan Institute in New York City. She contributes to numerous periodicals and is the author of *Whose Votes Count?: Affirmative Action and Minority Voting Rights.*

Although white defenders of "the southern way of life" had formidable power and few scruples about using it, by the 1950s they no longer held all the cards. Ever since blacks were driven from the polls and subjected to Jim Crow laws at the turn of the century, the voice of African Americans in the South had been ruthlessly silenced. The occasional rebels who dared to complain of racial injustice were easily squelched. The system seemed impervious to pressures for change from within. John Dollard's *Caste and Class in a Southern Town* made the pattern of black-white relations in Indianola, Mississippi, look strikingly similar to the caste system of traditional India, a system which had lasted thousands of years. Dollard suggested that the forces that ensured white supremacy and black subordination in the South were so deeply rooted that change could happen only at a glacial pace, if at all. It was inconceivable to Dollard, and indeed to almost all American social scientists in those years, that within two decades tens and tens of thousands of southern black people would rise up in resistance.

The Defiance of Rosa Parks

Dollard's book would not have provided a reader anything that would have proved very useful in understanding the chain of events that began unfolding in the Alabama state capital, Montgomery, on 1 December 1955. Rosa Parks, a forty-two-year-old black woman, boarded a bus after finishing work as a seamstress in a downtown department store. She took a seat that—according to the local segregation ordinance—could be used by a black person only when no white passenger wanted it. It was neither in the front (reserved for whites) nor in the back (assigned to blacks), but in the "no-man's-land" middle, where blacks could sit when all the whites had already been seated. If additional whites boarded the bus, however, blacks who had ventured forward into no-man's-land were required to surrender their places and stand in the rear aisle.

After a white man boarded the bus on that December

evening and found no vacant seat in the front section reserved for whites, the driver turned to Rosa Parks and the
other three black passengers seated in the row just behind
the white section and asked them to get up and move to the
rear, where there was standing room only.

Three of the four blacks seated in the row that the driver
ordered cleared did comply with his demand, but Mrs. Parks
refused, and the driver had her arrested for violating the
segregation ordinance. Contrary to legend, Rosa Parks was
not an ordinary, anonymous working woman who ran afoul
of the law one day simply because she happened to feel too
tired to give up her seat. Although her defiance of the driver's orders on that particular day was apparently not
planned, she was a veteran political activist who had often
been involved in discussions of how the segregation ordinances might be challenged. She had been the secretary of
the Montgomery chapter of the NAACP [National Association
for the Advancement of Colored People] for a dozen years,
secretary of the statewide Alabama State Conference of
NAACP branches, and an active member of the Women's Political Council, a group organized after the Montgomery
League of Women Voters refused to admit black women as
members. In fact, December 1, 1955, was not the first time
that Montgomery blacks had chosen to defy Jim Crow rules
on the buses. Mrs. Parks herself had objected to giving up
her seat to a white several times before, although in the past
she had been kicked off the bus rather than arrested. The
driver who removed her on one of those earlier occasions
was the same one who finally had her arrested.

MOBILIZATION OF THE AFRICAN-AMERICAN COMMUNITY

The arrest of Rosa Parks was designed to send a clear message to other blacks who might be tempted to disobey when
ordered to turn over their seats to whites. The news that Mrs.
Parks was behind bars (a dangerous place for a southern
black person to be), did not have its intended effect, however.
In one of those fascinating and mysterious moments in history, the system of social control that had worked effectively
for many decades suddenly broke down. Instead of intimi-
dating Montgomery's African Americans into compliance
with the law once again, the arrest of Rosa Parks was the
catalyst for a defiant, determined, and disciplined mass
movement.

The leaders of the multitude of churches and civic organizations in black Montgomery had not displayed much unity in the past. Just a few months before the arrest of Mrs. Parks, an effort to form a "Citizens Coordinating Committee" that would bring the city's black leadership together had collapsed as a result of what a dismayed newcomer to the community called "crippling factionalism." The Montgomery black community "was marked by divided leadership, indifference, and complacency." It was an inauspicious setting for the extraordinary action soon to follow. But the chairman of the local branch of the NAACP, trade union leader E.D. Nixon, helped to persuade Mrs. Parks to fight the case in court. And the Women's Political Council, led by faculty members at the local black college, quickly printed fifty thousand flyers announcing a boycott of all Montgomery's buses on December 5.

Montgomery's black community could never have been mobilized behind the boycott of municipal buses without the backing of most of the African-American churches, traditionally the chief source of leadership for the group. In the past black clerics had often been criticized for stressing the otherworldly consolations of religion, overlooking social injustice in the here and now. Whatever the merits of that charge in previous circumstances, it was not one that could be made this time around. In 1955, Montgomery's African-American ministers showed themselves eager to demonstrate that religion could be a powerful force for social change.

King's Leadership Appointment

Among the black clergymen who joined in the debate on how to respond to the jailing of Rosa Parks was a twenty-six-year-old graduate of the Boston University Divinity School who had recently taken up the pulpit at the Dexter Avenue Baptist Church—the Reverend Martin Luther King, Jr. When an organization to carry out the bus boycott was formed—the Montgomery Improvement Association—King was named its head. He was a newcomer to Montgomery, but that seeming liability was in fact an asset. He had not been in town long enough to have made many friends—or many enemies.

Under King's leadership, what started as a one-day gesture of protest against the mistreatment of black people on local buses became a major long-term commitment, supported by almost the entire black community, which accounted for 37 percent of the city's population and about three-fourths of its regular bus patrons. When the initial boycott produced no response from local authorities, the Montgomery Improvement Association pledged (from its position of extraordinary strength) that it would continue until black passengers were assured of better treatment. The sight of empty buses rolling through black neighborhoods led one woman to remark gleefully that the buses that went by her door were "as naked as can be." Car pools were organized to take care of those in desperate need of a ride, but most of the boycotters simply walked to their destinations. The Montgomery police did their best to put the car pools out of business by arresting drivers for petty, sometimes altogether imaginary, traffic violations. King himself was hauled off to jail on one occasion for allegedly driving at thirty miles an hour in a twenty-five-mile-an-hour zone. But these efforts at harassment were ineffective.

At a mass meeting called to decide whether to continue the boycott, King warned whites that a new day was dawning—that blacks would no longer tolerate being treated as second-class citizens. And he told his fellow blacks that change would never come unless they had the courage to stand up for their rights, regardless of the cost. "We are here this evening," he declared,

> to say to those who have mistreated us so long that we are tired—tired of being segregated and humiliated; tired of being kicked about by the brutal feet of oppression. We had no alternative but to protest. For many years we have shown amazing patience. . . . But we come here tonight to be saved from that patience that makes us patient with anything less than freedom and justice.

Although this was a radical and unflinching challenge to the principle of white supremacy, the concrete changes the organizers of the boycott sought at the outset were remarkably modest. King spoke passionately of the need to obtain "justice on the buses of this city," but by "justice" he did not mean an entirely desegregated bus system. The principal demand of the boycotters at this point was only that Montgomery adopt the somewhat milder form of segregation that was used on the buses in Mobile, Alabama. In Mobile your race determined where you were allowed to sit when you first boarded, but no African American was required to move after having settled into a seat.

The boycott began, then, as a call for better treatment within the framework of "separate but equal." Its organizers launched no principled attack against the whole notion of assigning seats on a bus on the basis of race. In fact, it could even be argued that their demands, by making the system seem a bit more fair, would have given the segregation some additional life. That is precisely why the NAACP refused at first to help with Mrs. Parks's appeal. The organization would not intervene in a case that seemed to be "asking merely for more polite segregation."

The mildness of the initial demands is particularly striking in light of the fact that by December 1955 the principle of segregation in public facilities was being challenged across the South in a variety of ways. *Brown v. Board of Education of Topeka, Kansas*, after all, had recently sounded the death knell for state-imposed segregation in public education, and its basic message—separate is not equal—could not be confined to schooling. Thus, a week after its 17 May decision, the Court made clear the applicability of *Brown* to a case involving the admission of black patrons to a theatrical performance. Other decisions quickly followed giving blacks access to public beaches and bathhouses, municipal golf courses, and other facilities. Furthermore, just six days before Rosa Parks defied the Montgomery ordinance, the Interstate Commerce Commission, endorsing arguments made by the NAACP, had outlawed racial segregation on all trains and buses traveling across state lines, and in the waiting rooms of the stations they used. Given this trend, the initial demands in Montgomery were remarkably moderate and restrained. It was a "lowest common denominator" strategy. To unite the previously fragmented black community, the movement would push only those demands that hardly anyone could object to.

ESCALATION OF THE PROTEST

The protest escalated into a fight for the complete abolition of bus segregation only after two months of futile negotiations with city authorities made their intransigence all too clear. The bus company itself might have welcomed a settlement; with 75 percent of its patrons walking to work, it was running in the red. Privately owned, it was dedicated not to the cause of segregation but to its financial bottom line. (Similarly, the railroad involved in the *Plessy v. Ferguson*

(1896) case [upholding segregation] opposed segregation; it was a costly nuisance forced upon the company by the politicians.) But the politicians didn't care about the company's balance sheet. They cared about votes—that is, white votes. And whites, with few exceptions, had no sympathy for black demands. In fact, the mayor, all three members of the city commission, and several other public officials belonged to the local chapter of the Citizens' Council, whose membership quickly reached 12,000, more than a quarter of Montgomery's adult white population. Not surprisingly, these officials were determined not to give an inch.

The possibility of reaching a negotiated settlement vanished altogether after a grand jury issued criminal indictments against no fewer than eighty-nine of Montgomery's black citizens (twenty-four of them ministers) for conspiring to boycott in violation of a 1921 statute. But again, the attempt at repression only strengthened the protest effort. For the first time, the Montgomery story became front-page news in several national newspapers, which in turn increased the flow of outside contributions to the movement.

Once it was agreed that the objective was to abolish segregation, not to make it a little more comfortable, the NAACP's lawyers were happy to do the necessary legal work. Shifting the struggle into a federal courtroom was a momentous and revealing development. Southerners had always insisted that they were capable of resolving racial conflict without the interference of outsiders—judges, in this instance. But the surge of white rage that led to the mushrooming of Citizens' Councils poisoned the political climate; the South, in fact, did not have the capacity to save itself.

KING'S INTRODUCTION OF NONVIOLENT PROTEST

It was during the Montgomery boycott that Martin Luther King first articulated the principle of nonviolent resistance so integral to the success of the civil rights movement. And yet it is important to recall that King was not fully committed to nonviolence when the Montgomery struggle began. Although he had been attracted to Gandhian ideas in his student days, in 1955 he apparently believed that "the only way we could solve our problem of segregation was an armed revolt." Painfully aware that black men who defied southern racial mores could expect to be the victims of violence, he had armed guards to protect his residence, and kept a gun at home.

King became a convinced advocate of nonviolence only after experiencing violence directed against his wife and infant daughter. On January 30, 1956, just a few hours after the Montgomery Improvement Association decided to sue the city in federal court, a stick of dynamite exploded on his front porch. No one was hurt, but a furious crowd of blacks, many of them armed, quickly gathered outside the house. King, who had been off at a meeting, arrived on the scene to hear one of his supporters tell a policeman, "You got your .38 and I got mine, so let's battle it out." The incident drove home the obvious point that "an armed revolt" would mean blacks pitted against a white population that outnumbered them ten to one. Rejecting violence as an instrument not only gave civil rights advocates the moral high ground; it was a pragmatic necessity. King calmed the angry crowd that night by warning that "he who lives by the sword will perish by the sword"; "love your enemies," "meet hate with love," he urged. He disarmed his own guards and got rid of his gun.

The boycott finally came to an end after 381 days, but not because either side had lost its will to fight. In June 1956 a three-judge federal panel ruled that the racial segregation of Montgomery's buses was unconstitutional, and in November the Supreme Court affirmed the decision. The boycott officially continued until December 21, 1956, when the court order took effect and King and other supporters of the movement, black and white, boarded a bus and occupied the front seats.

The rage that the boycott had stirred up did not suddenly evaporate with the legal decision. Two days after integrated buses started running, in the middle of the night, someone fired a shotgun through King's front door. A few days later snipers fired upon three buses. More than a dozen prominent blacks had their cars splashed with acid. In early January 1957 four black churches and the homes of both [black community leader] Ralph Abernathy and Robert Graetz (the leading local white minister in the Montgomery Improvement Association) were bombed. Two men were eventually arrested and tried for the bombings. But despite overwhelming physical evidence and their own confessions, a jury refused to convict them.

KING'S RISE TO NATIONAL PROMINENCE

Montgomery's blacks had won a great victory, of course. But the victory could not be credited to the boycott. The courts would have rendered precisely the same verdict even if there had been no mass protest movement. From one perspective, a boycott in Baton Rouge, Louisiana, three years earlier had been much more successful. The city held out only ten days, and then decided to adopt a Mobile-style, first-come first-served segregation plan. But the Montgomery protest was of far greater historical significance. Not only did it achieve real desegregation; it started a movement that, in King's words, "would gain national recognition; whose echoes would ring in the ears of people of every nation; a movement that would astound the oppressor, and bring new hope to the oppressed."

Montgomery was where King happened to live, and that, too, heightened the boycott's significance. His charismatic presence and exceptional oratorical skills were vital in keeping the spirits of his followers in Montgomery high enough to continue their sacrifices month after month; that it endured so long made the Montgomery struggle much more dramatic and newsworthy than the brief spasm of protest in Baton Rouge. Most important, his personal magnetism and radiance made for intensive coverage in the national and international press. In 1956, *Time, Life,* and *Newsweek* tripled their coverage of civil rights topics, with most of the rise in the number of articles due to the Montgomery protest. The media's fascination with King was greater than a number of other movement leaders thought justified. He had become a national celebrity, the subject of a cover story in *Time* and the focus of a long article in *The New York Times Magazine.* He went on *Meet the Press,* only the second African American ever to appear as a guest on that show. Every move he made thereafter generated publicity. His ability to keep the press corps following him, to make headline news, to fill churches and lecture halls, and to inspire contributors made him the civil rights movement's most important single asset until his assassination a dozen years later.

As the news of what was happening in Montgomery spread, donations came in from as far away as India and Japan. But the bulk of the money came from church groups around the United States, particularly black churches. African Americans throughout the land were inspired to see so many of their brethren refusing to be "kicked about by the brutal feet of oppression," enduring great personal hardship in hopes of obtaining racial justice. "There is a new Negro in the South," King declared, "with a new sense of dignity and destiny."

The Failure of King's Albany Campaign

John A. Salmond

In 1961 the young people of Albany, Georgia, used voter registration, picketing, sit-ins at lunch counters, and demonstrations to protest local segregation practices. John A. Salmond suggests that the white authorities of Albany worked diligently to avoid mistreating the protestors in order to evade the media coverage that accompanies violence. The protests weakened and the older black leadership in Albany called on Martin Luther King Jr. to give their campaign a boost.

Salmond argues that King swept into the action before he understood the subtleties of the conflict and the deep divisions between established black leaders and younger protestors, who wanted to keep the demonstration local. King was arrested and told to return in February of 1962 to stand trial. According to Salmond, King was found guilty and jailed, but the authorities, who wanted to avoid trouble, released him after only two days.

Salmond maintains that Albany was by all accounts a failure; little was accomplished and King lost prestige, particularly among young protestors. However, the experience provided King with valuable lessons. He realized that he must carefully plan his campaigns, solidify black leadership, and escalate the visibility of the protest in order to involve national attention and, subsequently, bring federal intervention.

John A. Salmond is professor of American history at La Trobe University in Melbourne, Australia. He has written four books, including *Miss Lucy of the CIO* and *A Southern Rebel*.

Martin Luther King went to jail in Georgia in 1961 and 1962, in Albany, in the southwest part of the state. Charles Sher-

Excerpted from *"My Mind Set on Freedom": A History of the Civil Rights Movement, 1954–1968*, by John A. Salmond. Copyright ©1997 by John A. Salmond. Reprinted by permission of Ivan R. Dee, Publisher.

rod, SNCC's [Student Nonviolent Coordinating Committee] first field secretary, just twenty-two years of age, had been encouraged to establish a voter registration project there. In Albany he found an enthusiastic group of young blacks, anxious for a wide-ranging confrontation, and a rather skeptical black community leadership, most of them deeply involved with the NAACP [National Association for the Advancement of Colored People]. Sherrod decided to ignore the older group and work exclusively with the town's high school and college students. Their citywide campaign began in November 1961. For more than a year thousands of young blacks marched in Albany, picketed local stores, sat-in at lunch counters, and demonstrated at the local voter registration office in a massive assault on segregation. More than a thousand of them were jailed as a consequence, yet nothing changed. By the end of 1962 Albany was still a completely segregated city, one in which only a few blacks could vote. Why had the campaign failed so badly?

THE STRATEGY OF WHITE AUTHORITIES

One reason was because its organizers, perhaps naively, had expected the federal government to move decisively whenever federal laws were broken, as they clearly had been throughout the long [civil rights] campaign. The Kennedys [President John F. and Attorney General Robert], however, were not of a mind to do so, provided local officials could maintain the peace with a minimum of violence. Here the chief of police, Laurie Pritchett, was pivotal. He was no stereotypical Southern racist cop but a highly intelligent man who had studied King's writings, among other things, and who knew how important national media attention was in keeping pressure on localities. Nothing excited the media more than white violence against peaceful demonstrators. Indeed, King's philosophy depended on such images to elicit white sympathy and support. Pritchett therefore determined that there would be no violence in Albany. Demonstrators would be arrested, of course, and jails would be filled, but there would be no mistreatment of prisoners. In particular there would be no mobs, no repeats of Little Rock [where whites violently protested school desegregation]. Anyone practicing or even advocating violence against the demonstrators would be promptly punished, that Pritchett made quite clear. He always seemed to be one step ahead of the

SNCC activities; he always seemed to know their plans. Worried, Sherrod assumed his phone was tapped, but actually the police chief relied mainly on reports from adult members of the black community itself.

Eventually a truce was effected between the young activists and senior members of Albany's black professional community, lead by osteopath William G. Anderson, who began to support the mass action campaign. It did not seem to do much good. Four hundred and seventy-one demonstrators were jailed on December 6, many of them held in neighboring counties, yet the city officials showed no sign of negotiating. In this context Dr. Anderson, realizing that the SNCC people had bitten off much more than they could chew, decided to seek assistance from King and his SCLC [Southern Christian Leadership Conference]. King agreed to come briefly to Albany upon receipt of a formal invitation. On Thursday, December 14, therefore, Anderson sent him a telegram which simply read, "We urge you to come and join the Albany movement." Sherrod and his SNCC companions had had no part in the decision.

KING'S ARREST IN ALBANY

King, [community leader Reverend Ralph] Abernathy, and [executive director of SCLC, Wyatt T.] Walker arrived late the next day. Their plans were simply to address two mass meetings in the evening, stay overnight, and return to Atlanta in the morning. King made what had become a standard speech for him, but the people of Albany, hearing it for the first time, responded rapturously. Indeed, their intensity surprised King. It reminded him of the first weeks of the Montgomery boycott, he later commented. At the meeting's conclusion Anderson told the crowd that, as no settlement with the city had yet been reached, there would be mass demonstrations the next day. Publicly he asked King to join them. King and his colleagues had neither wanted nor prepared for this. They had been in town only a few hours and had but an imperfect grasp of the local issues and leadership rivalries. Still, King knew he had no choice. To leave town now would be to desert the cause.

At 4 p.m. on Saturday, December 16, King and Anderson led more than 250 marchers toward city hall. After several blocks, Pritchett and his officers barricaded the road and ordered them to disperse or be arrested for parading without a permit. They refused to move and were thus taken into custody, with bond set at $200. King and Anderson refused to make bail, vowing to stay in jail until the city started down the road to desegregation. Abernathy did accept bond so that he could return to Atlanta to rally support for the movement in which SCLC had suddenly and unexpectedly become deeply involved.

The arrests brought tensions in the black community into the open. Those who had opposed King's involvement made public statements emphasizing the movement's local nature and discounting the need for outside support. Yet at the same time Abernathy, back in Atlanta, was making plans for a national pilgrimage of civil rights supporters to Albany. From

---

KING'S MISTAKE IN THE ALBANY CAMPAIGN

In a January 1965 Playboy *interview, King candidly discusses the mistakes that he made in his 1962 civil rights campaign in Albany, Georgia.*

PLAYBOY: Do you feel you've been guilty of any comparable errors in judgment since then?

KING: Yes, I do—in Albany, Georgia, in 1962. If I had that to do again, I would guide the community's Negro leadership differently than I did. The mistake I made there was to protest against segregation generally rather than against a single and distinct facet of it. Our protest was so vague that we got nothing, and the people were left very depressed and in despair. It would have been much better to have concentrated upon integrating the buses or the lunch counters. One victory of this kind would have been symbolic, would have galvanized support and boosted morale. But I don't mean that our work in Albany ended in failure. The Negro people there straightened up their bent backs; you can't ride a man's back unless it's bent. Also, thousands of Negroes registered to vote who never had voted before, and because of the expanded Negro vote in the next election for governor of Georgia— which pitted a moderate candidate against a rabid segregationist—Georgia elected its first governor who had pledged to respect and enforce the law impartially. And what we learned from our mistakes in Albany helped our later campaigns in other cities to be more effective. We have never since scattered our efforts in a general attack on segregation, but have focused upon specific, symbolic objectives.

"*Playboy* Interview: Martin Luther King, Jr." *Playboy* (January 1965): 117ff.

his jail cell King explained that while he had never intended to do more than make a speech, he was now involved for the duration. He expected to spend Christmas in jail, he said, indeed he promised to do so, and he hoped thousands would join him. Clearly the Albany movement was in danger of unraveling because of these deep internal tensions between those who wished to keep the movement local and those who wished to make Albany a national symbol.

King and Anderson were brought to Albany on Monday for trial. Before the proceedings, the local leadership group announced they had reached verbal agreement with the city on certain issues relating to the arrests, and with vague promises of reform to come. King and Anderson therefore signed their bonds, and despite King's promise they were soon out of jail. King was glad to be out of Albany altogether. Nevertheless, the experience, especially the broken promise, cost him dearly in prestige. Moreover he would have to return to Albany to face trial in the new year.

KING'S RETURN TO ALBANY

Albany city officials, however, had no real intention of making any accommodation with the movement, and thus the demonstrations and the arrests continued into 1962. On February 27 King and Abernathy returned to the city to stand trial for their December arrests. After two hours the judge recessed the proceedings, announcing he would reach a verdict within sixty days. King quietly returned to Atlanta as Albany remained unsettled, its white leaders intransigent, its black community deeply divided. The verdict, announced on July 10, was scarcely unexpected. Judge Durden found both King and Abernathy guilty, sentencing them to forty-five days in jail or a fine of $178. Both chose imprisonment—for King a distasteful imperative, given growing SNCC criticism of his seeming unwillingness to put his body on the line, especially after his early release the previous December. Chief Pritchett was deeply unhappy with this development. The Albany movement was sputtering to a halt; King's presence in jail might well revive it. The city's leadership moved quickly. After only two days Pritchett told both prisoners that an "unknown negro" had paid their fines and they were free to go. Unhappily King and Abernathy left, first the jail, and soon the city, knowing that the "unknown negro" did not exist and that the city's white leadership probably secured their release. There seemed little point in remaining after a federal judge issued an order preventing further demonstrations in Albany. King would never defy such an order, and, despite his pledge to remain there till the city capitulated, he soon returned to Atlanta. Anderson announced that there would be no more mass protests, and that the movement would turn its attention to voter registration.

THE LESSON OF ALBANY

SCLC's first involvement in a mass action campaign had failed, and King had lost prestige as a result, especially with the young activists of SNCC. But it had taught him some valuable lessons. Albany, located in rural Georgia, and without a moderate white business community inclined to negotiate, was the wrong choice for a mass action campaign. SCLC had involved itself summarily, without careful planning and without understanding the complexities and divisions of the local black community. Chief Pritchett had played a crucial role. By keeping the white mob at bay and by instructing his officers to treat demonstrators gently, even when arresting them, he had successfully prevented the massive disorder that might have provoked federal action. King understood as never before how crucial federal action was to the cause of black freedom. This would never be achieved through changing the hearts and minds of Southern whites, nor through peaceful protests. Legislation was the key, civil rights legislation that would compel the South to treat blacks equally, and this could only come once a national consensus for such action had been created. A far greater crisis than Albany was needed to achieve this, one in which massive white violence would ensure federal intervention. From the ashes of defeat in Albany, then, came the seeds of victory in Birmingham the following year.

Birmingham and the Children's Crusade

Stephen B. Oates

Stephen B. Oates argues that King's use of children in the Birmingham protests was a monumental decision for the civil rights movement. King knew that he would receive criticism for involving children, but he also understood that it might shock the city authorities into negotiations. Oates writes that on May 2, 1963, approximately 1,000 children marched; over 900 were arrested. Undaunted, 2,500 youngsters protested the next day. This time, with the press watching, police and firemen brutally sprayed the children with high-pressure hoses and attacked them with police dogs. Oates reports that over 250 were arrested and many were injured, some seriously.

Oates recounts that the press and public opinion condemned the police action. President Kennedy said publicly that what he saw on television sickened him. He subsequently sent Burke Marshall, Assistant Attorney General for Civil Rights, to Birmingham to seek a settlement. In response, King staged even a larger demonstration, a prayer pilgrimage in front of the Birmingham Jail. This time the police and firemen refused to turn on the 3,000 children who had kneeled down in prayer. Oates writes that when King saw this he felt "the pride and the *power* of nonviolence." Outraged, segregationists bombed the house of A.D. King, Martin's brother, who lived and preached in Birmingham. Although A.D. was not hurt, blacks were outraged, and rioting broke out in downtown Birmingham. The next day King went to the streets to restore order and President Kennedy ordered 3,000 federal troops into Birmingham.

Ultimately, city commissioners were replaced, and the Birmingham segregation ordinances were rescinded. According to Oates, the campaign taught blacks that they could work together to overcome fear and bring about posi-

Excerpted from *Let the Trumpet Sound: The Life of Martin Luther King Jr.*, by Stephen B. Oates. Copyright ©1982, 1994 by Stephen B. Oates. Reprinted by permission of HarperCollins Publishers, Inc.

tive change. For King, Birmingham proved that nonviolence works.

Stephen B. Oates is a biographer and historian. He has
published many books and contributed historical essays to
periodicals like *American Heritage,* the *Nation,* and the
New York Times.

By the end of [the last week of April, four weeks after King
formally began the Birmingham campaign], demonstrations
had all but stopped, and [civil rights strategist Andrew]
Young and [protest organizer Wyatt] Walker said the situation was desperate. "We needed more troops," Walker recalled. "We had scraped the bottom of the barrel of adults
who would go [to jail]. . . . We needed some new something."
Out of spirited SCLC strategy sessions came a portentous decision. King's young lieutenants—[James] Bevel, [Bernard]
Lee, Dorothy Cotton, and others—had been out working in
the city's Negro colleges and high schools spreading King's
nonviolent message, and several college students had become involved in the campaign. Now, though, his staff would
actively recruit high-school students to fill up their depleted
ranks. King conceded that this would be controversial, but
"we needed this dramatic new dimension."

What happened next made movement history. At the urging of King's young aides, hundreds of high-school students
swarmed into SCLC [Southern Christian Leadership Confer-
ence] workshops at the churches, all raring to march. But so
did hundreds of their little brothers and sisters from the
grade schools. "We had a terrible time trying to keep them
out," Lee said. But the youngsters kept coming back, begging
Bevel and Lee to let them march and go to jail with the big
kids. Finally, Bevel went to King with an idea: why not
launch a "D Day" when hundreds of school children of all
ages would get arrested and imprisoned?

KING'S DECISION TO ALLOW
SCHOOLCHILDREN TO DEMONSTRATE

King gave this careful thought. Sending children into the
streets was bound to provoke hostile criticism. Yet it might
be the very thing he needed to revive the campaign and
shock the city's business leaders to the bargaining table.
Schoolchildren didn't hold jobs, so whites couldn't threaten

them with economic reprisals as they did their elders. Thousands of demonstrating youngsters would tie up downtown Birmingham, and their arrests would cause a colossal overload of juvenile courts. With the children, King might literally be able to fill up the jails.

True, there were high risks involved. Some of the children might get hurt—or worse. But Negro children were maimed every day of their lives in the segregated South. If an incessant torture could be ended by a single climactic confrontation, he thought it worth the risk. Also, "our family life will be born anew if we fight together." And, too, the spectacle of schoolchildren marching for their freedom might awaken the entire country. "I hope to subpoena the conscience of the nation to the judgment seat of morality," he had said of his campaign. And here seemed a dramatic and symbolic way to do it.

THE CHILDREN'S MARCH

And so he agreed to let the children march. In a staff meeting on May 1, he decided that the next day would be D Day—the start of a children's crusade to save the soul of Birmingham once and for all.

The next day more than 1,000 excited youngsters—some only six years old—thronged Sixteenth Street Baptist, King's "church command post," as *Time* called it. From here, adults and special march marshals led the children downtown two abreast, column after column, singing and clapping in holiday merriment. When [Public Safety Commissioner T. Eugene] Bull Connor saw all those "little niggers" demonstrating in his town, he charged about in a rage, commanding his men to lock them all up. As the police set about making arrests, the children delighted in confusing them: a decoy group would lead them astray while the main column would proceed to its downtown target. In one demonstration, a gruff cop confronted an eight-year-old walking with her mother. "What do you want?" the policeman asked. She looked him straight in the eye. "Fee-dom," she said.

In all, the police arrested more than 900 young people that day and had to bring in school buses to cart them all to jail. One police captain was deeply troubled by that sight. "Evans," he told another officer, "ten or fifteen years from now, we will look back on all this and we will say, 'How stupid can you be?'"

King and his lieutenants all rejoiced in the day's success. "Oh man," Walker exclaimed, "it's a great time to be alive." King himself had seen the encounter between the cop and the little girl. "It was beautiful!" He recalled what an old woman had said about her involvement in the Montgomery bus boycott: "I'm doing it for my children and for my grandchildren." Seven years later, King mused, "the children and grandchildren were doing it for themselves." As he expected, many newsmen deplored his "using" the children in this fashion. But he wanted to know where these writers had been "during the centuries when our segregated social system had been misusing and abusing Negro children."

Meanwhile his aides were drumming up an even larger children's march for the next day. "I want everybody to listen to me," Bevel told a rally of prospective young volunteers. "You get an education in jail, too. In the schools you've been going to, they haven't taught you to be proud of yourselves and they haven't taught you good history—they haven't taught you the price of freedom. . . . As long as one Negro kid is in jail, we all want to be in jail. If everybody in town would be arrested, everybody would be free, wouldn't they?"

That message worked like magic. The next day some 2,500 youngsters turned out to march, so revved up that King and his staff could scarcely restrain them. "Yesterday was D Day in Birmingham," King said happily. "Today will be Double D Day." He admonished his young followers, "Don't get tired. Don't get bitter. Are you tired?" "No!" they screamed back. Then off they went with their adult leaders, heading toward town with signs that read "FREEDOM."

As King and his men coordinated the marching columns, he could see the first one bearing down on a line of police and firemen, deployed by Bull Connor to block off the route downtown. A crowd of Negro bystanders had gathered under the tall elms in nearby Kelly Ingram Park, and they surged forward when the students reached Connor's barricade, shouting, "We want freedom!" It was a muggy afternoon, and the firemen stood sweating in dun-colored slickers, pointing high-powered firehoses at the marchers. And there was Bull Connor, a cigar in his mouth and a sweaty straw hat on his head, giving orders to his men. Several cops had German police dogs, which growled and strained at their leashes. When the demonstrators refused to return to the church, Connor bellowed, "Let 'em have it." With scores of reporters and TV cameramen recording what happened, the firemen turned on their hoses, which exploded with a noise like machine-gun fire and sent columns of water crashing into children and adults alike, knocking them down, ripping their clothes, smashing them against the sides of buildings, sweeping them back into the street, driving them crying and bloodied into the park. When Negro bystanders hurled bricks and bottles in retaliation, Connor unleashed the dogs. They charged into the Negroes' ranks with fangs bared, lunging wildly at running children and biting three severely. In a cacophony of snarling dogs and screaming people, the march column disintegrated and children and adults all fled back to the church. "Look at those niggers run," Connor sneered. When the carnage ended at three that afternoon, a great many people had been injured and 250 arrested. "God bless America," said a reporter in disgust.

RESPONSE TO THE CHILDREN'S CRUSADE

King too was revolted. If what had happened that day didn't rouse the moral conscience of the nation, then it had no moral conscience. With eyes blazing, he told a thousand followers that night that they were going on despite the dogs and fire hoses. They were going on because they had started a fire in Birmingham that water could not put out. They were going on because they loved America and loved democracy. And they were going to remain nonviolent. "Don't worry about your children who are in jail," he cried. "The eyes of the world are on Birmingham."

And they were indeed, as papers the next day carried front-page reports and photographs of Birmingham's day of infamy. Millions of readers in America—and millions overseas—stared at pictures of police dogs lunging at young marchers, of firemen raking them with jet streams, of club-wielding cops pinning a Negro woman to the ground. And television news brought similar macabre sights into millions of living rooms. Abroad, African and European journals universally condemned such police brutality. At home, a storm of indignation broke over the land, as newspapers and politicians and labor and religious leaders all excoriated Bull Connor and the city of Birmingham. In Washington, Senator Wayne Morse of Oregon declared that Birmingham "would disgrace the Union of South Africa." President Kennedy told an irate group of Americans for Democratic

Action that what he saw in the papers made him "sick," but that there was nothing he could legally do to restrain Connor. Like his brother, the President regretted the timing of King's campaign. Yet he was not asking for patience. "I can well understand why the Negroes of Birmingham are tired of being asked to be patient." That same day, May 4, Burke Marshall, Robert Kennedy's Assistant Attorney General for Civil Rights, flew to Birmingham to seek a settlement.

With the nation and the world looking on, King escalated the pressure in the streets of Birmingham. Each day the demonstrations grew larger and more dramatic, as grade schoolers and high schoolers, parents and children, old and young together, marched and sang toward freedom's land. Again the firemen sprayed them with hoses, again Connor brought out his dogs and even added an armored car to his motorized forces. When someone in a building threw a little plaster on some officers, Director of Public Safety Al Lingo, itching to bring in his state troopers, ranted at a Birmingham cop, "I'd shoot them god-damn son-bitches, that's what I'd do."

And so it went in embattled Birmingham, as the police chased after elusive columns of children and the firemen pulled and grunted at their hoses. But the children baffled them, springing up first here, then there, then somewhere else, waving their signs "WE WANT FREEDOM." And when the police finally got them subdued and into the buses and paddy wagons, they shouted at the tops of their lungs on the way to jail, "WE WANT FREEDOM! WE WANT FREEDOM! WE WANT FREEDOM!" Then playfully, "*Every*body wants freedom! Bull Connor wants freedom! Our mayor wants freedom! The driver wants freedom!"

And over the noise of Birmingham, over the songs and the sirens, the cries and the clash of battle, sounded the haunting voice of Martin Luther King: "We must say to our white brothers all over the South who try to keep us down: We will match your capacity to inflict suffering with our capacity to endure suffering. We will meet your physical force with soul force. We will not hate you. And yet we cannot in all good conscience obey your evil laws. Do to us what you will. Threaten our children and we will still love you. . . . Say that we're too low, that we're too degraded, yet we will still love you. Bomb our homes and go by our churches early in the morning and bomb them if you please, and we will still love you. We will wear you down by our capacity to suffer. In winning the victory, we will not only win our freedom. We will so appeal to your heart and your conscience that we will win you in the process."

THE CHILDREN'S PRAYER PILGRIMAGE

On Sunday, May 5 [1963], occurred the largest demonstration so far, as Reverend Charles Billups and other Birmingham ministers led more than 3,000 young people on a prayer pilgrimage to Birmingham jail, singing "I Want Jesus to Walk with Me" as they moved. King and his aides were in the streets that day, orchestrating operations with walkie-talkies, and King saw Billups's column approach the police barricade, the ministers and the children ready to pit their bodies against Connor's dogs, fire hoses, and armored car. King saw the column halt and then kneel in prayer, all the while Connor repeatedly ordered them to turn back. But the Negroes continued their prayer, calling up to God in rising exaltation, then singing, then praying again. Suddenly Billups stood and confronted the police. "We're not turning back. We haven't done anything wrong. All we want is our freedom. . . . How do you feel doing these things? . . . Bring on your dogs. Beat us up. Turn on your hoses. We're not going to retreat." Then he started forward, followed by the other ministers and the children. Connor whirled about and yelled, "Turn on the hoses." His men just stood there. "Damnit! Turn on the hoses!" But as the blacks marched through their ranks, the firemen and cops fell back "as though hypnotized." Some of the firemen were crying. The Negroes continued their journey unimpeded, prayed for their imprisoned comrades in front of the jail, then headed back to the Negro section singing "I Got Freedom Over My Head."

"You would have to say that the hand of God moved in that demonstration," said one Negro. "For the people who went through the line without being caned or kicked or beaten," said another, "well, it did something to them. They had experienced nonviolence in its truest form." King agreed. "It was one of the most fantastic events of the Birmingham story. I saw there, I felt there, for the first time, the pride and the *power* of nonviolence."

By Monday, May 6, more than 3,000 Negroes were in jail in Birmingham—the largest number ever imprisoned at one time in the history of the movement—and some 4,000 more were still parading and picketing. In one demonstration, the police intercepted 500 youngsters and simply dispersed them without arrests. There was no place to jail them. "The activities which have taken place in Birmingham over the last few days to my mind mark the nonviolent movement's coming of age," said King. "This is the first time in the history of our struggle that we have been able literally to fill the jails. In a real sense this is the fulfillment of a dream, for I have always felt that if we could fill the jails in our witness for freedom, it would be a magnificent expression of the determination of the Negro and a marvelous way to lay the whole issue before the conscience of the local and national community. And I think in a real sense this Birmingham movement is one of the most inspiring developments in the whole nonviolent struggle."

With the jails full, with Birmingham roundly condemned in the court of world opinion and her economy hurting from the racial crisis, business leaders agreed at last to start serious negotiations with King's forces. Dave Dellinger, a notable pacifist who covered Birmingham for *Liberation,* attributed the breakthrough to King's use of the children, because it forced white people to look at something they had hidden from themselves: the impact of segregation and racism on Negro youngsters. Dellinger contended that the spectacle tortured the conscience of the white moderate—the South's "silent integrationist"—and that it got to hardened segregationists, too, that even they recoiled from the sight of a police dog lunging at a child. By exposing that kind of evil, King had indeed opened the boil of segregation to the medicine of air and light, as he had phrased it in "Letter from Birmingham jail." In that respect, the decision to enlist the children, as Abernathy said, "was an act of wisdom, divinely inspired.". . .

RIOTING IN BIRMINGHAM

Late that Saturday night [May 11, 1963], King received a desperate phone call from Birmingham. It was his brother A.D., who lived and preached there and who had been active in the demonstrations. Vengeful whites—probably Klansmen—had bombed A.D.'s house and dynamited the Gaston Motel, too, in an obvious attempt to kill King and his lieutenants. Yes, A.D. and his family were safe, but several people had been injured at Gaston's. And Negroes were now rioting in retaliation. Over the phone, King could hear the pandemonium in the streets—shouts, the sound of breaking glass, the awful dogs again. Marauding blacks had already stabbed a cop and set a taxi and two stores ablaze. "Let the whole fucking city burn," some raged. "This'll show those white motherfuckers." With fires glowing against the night, Lingo's state troopers stormed into the Negro district and started beating people at random with billy clubs and gun butts. A.D. said that movement leaders were in the streets, too, trying to disperse the rioters before somebody got killed. Over the phone, King heard a chorus of voices rising above the din, and he got tears in his eyes. Led by SCLC's Dorothy Cotton, a group of Negroes were singing "We Shall Overcome."

The next day King rushed back to Birmingham and took to the streets himself to preach nonviolence and forestall further rioting. Clearly the bombs last night were the work of demonic men who wanted to destroy the accord [between city leaders and blacks, reached May 10, to desegregate the city] and plunge the city into a bloodbath. And the Kennedys thought so too. On Sunday evening, the President announced to the nation that he would not let extremists imperil the pact in Birmingham. He ordered 3,000 federal troops into a position near the city and made plans to federalize the Alabama National Guard. That, King said later, put an abrupt end to the bombings.

King was deeply disappointed that violence had marred his long and arduous campaign. But he stood firmly behind the accord with Birmingham's business leaders. "This won't destroy the agreements," he and his associates declared; "this kind of thing didn't come from the men we were dealing with." "Whatever happens from here on, Birmingham will never be the same again."

RESULTS OF THE CAMPAIGN

And Birmingham never was the same again. Though recalcitrant city officials fought bitterly against the accord, the forces of reason won out in the end. On May 23, the Alabama Supreme Court ruled that Bull Connor and the other two city commissioners were out of office and that [Birmingham mayor, Albert] Boutwell's was the legal city government. One of the dethroned commissioners ranted about King— "This nigger has got the backing of the Attorney General and the White House"—and warned of the horrors of race mixing. But when Boutwell's government took over, it rescinded Birmingham's segregation ordinances and under strong Negro pressure eventually desegregated public facilities, including the library, municipal golf courses, public buildings, and finally even the schools themselves. Although initially interpreting the Birmingham accord as narrowly as possible, local merchants at last removed "WHITE" and "COLORED" signs on drinking fountains and restrooms, opened downtown lunch counters to Birmingham's long-suffering Negroes, and even hired some in hitherto whites-only positions. And if these were small breaches in the fortress of segregation, as some contended, King and most local Negroes thought them extraordinary achievements, given the power of the fortress.

But the greatest accomplishment of the campaign was its positive impact on local Negroes. As in Montgomery and Albany, they had learned for the first time that they could work together against the most determined opposition whites could muster. And this strengthened "the backbone of Negroes all down the line," said a local black, "whether he was middle class or no class." Indeed, as Dave Dellinger of *Liberation* pointed out, Birmingham was "a turning point in the civil-rights struggle" because of "the extent to which the whole community became involved." Not long after the campaign, Dellinger found Birmingham Negroes "so permeated by the sense of fulfillment and well-being . . . that there is practically no room left for fear and hate. They have learned that they can stand up to brutality without compromise."

For King himself, the Birmingham campaign was indisputable proof that nonviolent direct action could work, proof that he and his organization could mobilize people in masses and win a resounding victory for love and racial justice. In the eyes of his fellow Negroes, he now became the top black leader in the country. A *Newsweek* poll of Negro opinion indicated that 95 percent of black leaders and 88 percent of ordinary Negroes regarded King as their most successful spokesman, ranking him ahead of Jackie Robinson, James Meredith, Roy Wilkins, Thurgood Marshall, and Ralph Bunche. Though Atlanta student Julian Bond griped that King had "sold the concept that one man will come to your town and save you," most Negroes sampled praised him effusively for his willingness "to fight for his brother under any condition," as a black construction worker put it. "King's magic touch with the masses of Negroes remains," wrote a journalist in the *Saturday Evening Post.* "What they see is a powerful crusader for equality who does something instead of just talking, who sticks lighted matches to the status quo," and who "endows this American struggle with qualities of messianic mission."

After Birmingham, Negro Congressman Adam Clayton Powell proclaimed King "probably the greatest human being in the United States today." Glenn Smiley of the Fellowship of Reconciliation agreed. "In my book he's the best and freshest thing that ever happened in America, not just in Negro life, but in American life."

The March on Washington: A Landmark in the Struggle for Freedom

James A. Colaiaco

James Colaiaco writes that the August 28, 1963, March on Washington was the largest demonstration in the history of civil rights. Its goal was to show support for the pending Civil Rights Bill. At a strategy meeting with King and other black leaders prior to the march, President John F. Kennedy had argued that the planned march was poorly timed and would turn violent. Violence, Kennedy reasoned, would provide Congress a justification to vote against the bill. King and the other march organizers stated bluntly that the protest could not be aborted. Colaiaco maintains that black leaders worked hard to keep the march moderate and, to this end, made a passionate appeal for support from white liberals, churches, and labor unions.

More than 250,000 people, including over 75,000 whites, showed up in front of the Lincoln Memorial to hear the march speakers. Colaiaco writes that King's speech was the highlight of the afternoon. He moved the crowd by outlining his dream for an America that provided freedom and equality to all citizens. As millions watched on television, King asked all Americans to fulfill the promise of democracy by ending segregation and racial injustice.

Colaiaco argues that the March on Washington was one of the finest days for nonviolent civil rights protest. Both King and Kennedy believed that the march mobilized support for the Civil Rights Bill. However, Colaiaco affirms that many young and militant blacks echoed the charge by Malcolm X that the march was a sellout to a racist system. Nevertheless, Colaiaco concludes that most Americans saw the march as a significant step forward to improve racial relations in America.

Excerpted from *Martin Luther King Jr.: Apostle of Militant Nonviolence*, by James A. Colaiaco. Copyright ©1988 by James A. Colaiaco. Reprinted with permission from St. Martin's Press, Inc.

James A. Colaiaco is a humanities teacher at Dalton School, New York City. He is the author of *Martin Luther King, Jr.: Apostle of Militant Nonviolence* and a contributor to numerous history journals.

The wave of nonviolent protests throughout the summer of 1963 reached a dramatic climax with the 'March on Washington for Jobs and Freedom' on 28 August, the largest demonstration in the history of civil rights. The March was conceived by A. Philip Randolph, whose proposal for a similar demonstration in 1941 had prompted President Franklin D. Roosevelt to desegregate the nation's defence plants and to institute the Fair Employment Practices Commission. On 30 May 1957, Randolph had been instrumental in organizing the Prayer Pilgrimage to Washington, in which some 37 000 demonstrators listened to King's eloquent speech calling upon Congress to pass legislation guaranteeing black Americans the right to vote. In 1963, capitalizing upon the national moral outrage aroused by the Birmingham campaign, a March on Washington was planned by black leaders to show mass support for the pending Civil Rights Bill.

KING'S MEETING WITH PRESIDENT JOHN F. KENNEDY

On 22 June, President Kennedy met at the White House with the 'Big Six' of the civil rights movement: King, Randolph, Roy Wilkens of the NAACP [National Association for the Advancement of Colored People], James Farmer of CORE [Congress of Racial Equality], John Lewis of SNCC [Student Nonviolent Coordinating Committee] and Whitney Young of the National Urban League. Also present were Vice President Johnson, Attorney General Robert Kennedy, United Automobile Workers president Walter Reuther and millionaire Stephen Currier, president of the Taconic Foundation. The purpose of the meeting was to discuss the pending Civil Rights Bill and the proposed March on Washington. The President expressed concern that the March was poorly-timed and would be counter-productive. Originally, there had been plans to disrupt the Capitol with massive civil disobedience. But Kennedy warned: 'We want success in Congress, not just a big show at the Capitol'. The President feared that if the March were to become violent, it would be perceived by Congress as a threat, and provide a justification for those who were opposed to the bill. 'Some of these people are looking for an excuse to be against us; and I don't want to give any of them a chance to say "Yes, I'm for the bill, but I am damned if I will vote for it at the point of a gun."'

Although Wilkens shared the President's fears, Randolph nevertheless insisted that it was too late to cancel the March. 'The Negroes are already in the streets', he told the President. 'It is very likely impossible to get them off'. In response to Kennedy's contention that the March was ill-timed, King said: 'Frankly, I have never engaged in any direct-action movement which did not seem ill-timed. Some people thought Birmingham ill-timed'. King also maintained that the March would provide a nonviolent means for blacks throughout the country to channel their legitimate discontent. James Farmer added that black leaders would be in a difficult position if the bill were defeated in Congress after the March was called off. Embittered blacks might resort to violence. By the end of the meeting, President Kennedy, realizing that the March on Washington could not be stopped, had no alternative but to use his influence to ensure that it would not be disruptive.

Elaborate preparations preceded the Washington demonstration. [Civil rights leader] Bayard Rustin was appointed national organizer. Under the directorship of Stephen Currier, the United Civil Rights Leadership Council was set up to coordinate plans for the March. In order to attract sympathy for the Civil Rights Bill, black leaders decided to work with the Kennedy Administration to make it a moderate demonstration. Plans for massive civil disobedience to disrupt Capitol Hill were put aside, and an attempt was made to gain the support of white liberals and church and labour groups throughout the nation. The March would be confined to a mass demonstration in front of the Lincoln Memorial, a site chosen for its symbolic significance. With a push from Kennedy, the civil rights movement had joined the democratic coalition, and the March on Washington had become respectable. On 17 July, the President said that the forthcoming demonstration was within 'the great tradition' of peaceful assembly for 'redress of grievances'.

THE PEACEFUL DEMONSTRATION

They came by the thousands to Washington on 28 August. Far exceeding original expectations, an estimated 250 000 demonstrators, including at least 75 000 whites, arrived in the nation's capital by aeroplane, train, bus and car. They gathered for a peaceful parade from the Washington Monument to the Lincoln Memorial. After being entertained by celebrities, the huge crowd listened to a number of speakers, presented by Randolph: Reverend Eugene Carson Blake of the United Council of Churches, Walter Reuther of the UAW, John Lewis of SNCC, Floyd McKissick of CORE, Whitney Young of the Urban League, Matthew Ahmann of the National Catholic Conference, Roy Wilkens of the NAACP, Rabbi Joachim Prinz of the United Jewish Council and, finally, Martin Luther King, Jr., president of the Southern Christian Leadership Conference. In keeping with the spirit of moderation that characterized the demonstration, John Lewis had been pressured by March leaders, especially Randolph, to revise the first version of his speech because it was considered too critical of the Kennedy Administration.

The highlight of the day was the speech of King. Introduced by Randolph as 'the moral leader of our nation', the crowd roared as he approached the rostrum. The previous night, King had worked diligently for hours on the speech, with some assistance from his staff. He decided to begin by calling the nation's attention to the persisting American Dilemma, and to conclude by stating his dream of an America that provided freedom and equality to all citizens, regardless of race. Standing in the shadow of the Lincoln Memorial, King addressed the crowd and the millions of people witnessing the historic event on television or radio.

King reminded his audience that a century ago, President Abraham Lincoln signed the Emancipation Proclamation. Though this historic document originally gave great hope to millions of slaves, the black American was still not free in the twentieth century. The thousands of demonstrators had come to Washington that day, King said, to dramatize this condition and to compel the nation to fulfil its promise. 'When the architects of our republic wrote the magnificent words of the Constitution and the Declaration of Independence', King proclaimed, 'they were signing a promissory note to which every American was to fall heir . . . the promise that all men, yes, black men as well as white men, would be guaranteed the unalienable rights of life, liberty, and the pursuit of happiness'. The crowd shouted in approval as King proceeded to point out that the nation continued to deny the blessings of democracy to black Americans. Now is the time, he insisted, to fulfil the promise of democracy by ending segregation and racial injustice. Black Americans would wait no longer to be granted full citizenship rights. After urging blacks to employ nonviolence in their struggle for justice, 'meeting physical force with soul force', King stopped reading his prepared speech, and began to speak extemporaneously. Borrowing phrases from the Declaration of Independence, the Bible and the patriotic hymn, 'My Country 'Tis Of Thee', he revealed to the nation his dream, 'a dream deeply rooted in the American dream', that all Americans, regardless of race, would one day live together in freedom, justice, equality and brotherhood. As the crowd roared, King concluded with the words of the Negro spiritual: 'Free at last. Free at last. Thank God Almighty, we are free at last'.

The 'I Have a Dream' speech, the most inspiring of his career, etched the image of King as a dreamer indelibly on the national consciousness. But King was not a mere dreamer. He dedicated his life to moving masses of blacks to take practical steps to attain their rights as American citizens. In pursuit of his ideals, King was indefatigable. *Time* magazine reported that in 1963 alone he travelled some 275 000 miles and made more than 350 speeches throughout the United States.

THE POWER OF THE DEMONSTRATION

Many regarded the March on Washington as the finest moment of the nonviolent civil rights movement, anticipating a bright new day for the black American. Millions watched the event live on television, and it was transmitted internationally via telestar satellite. The evil of Southern racism had been dramatized to the entire world. Journalist David Halberstam described the March as a 'great televised morality play'. According to *New York Times* reporter Russell Baker: 'No one could remember an invading army quite as gentle as the two hundred thousand civil-rights marchers who occupied Washington today'. James Baldwin later epitomized the prevailing optimism among blacks: 'That day, for a moment', he reflected, 'it almost seemed that we stood on a height, and could see our inheritance. Perhaps we could make the kingdom real, perhaps the beloved community would not forever remain that dream one dreamed in agony'. Immediately following the demonstration, March leaders met with President Kennedy, who later issued a public state-ment praising the 'deep fervor and quiet dignity' that had characterized the protest. The President concluded: 'The na-tion can properly be proud of the demonstration that has oc-curred here today'.

The impact on Congress is difficult to measure. As Senator Hubert Humphrey observed: 'All this hasn't changed any votes on the civil-rights bill, but it's a good thing for Washington and the nation and the world'. New York Senator Jacob Javits said that the March 'may or may not change the votes of any mem-ber of Congress, but it will certainly establish a mood for the coming civil rights Congressional battle'. King believed that the March mobilized national support for the Civil Rights Bill. The Washington demonstration, he said, 'has already done a great deal to create a coalition of concern about the status of civil rights in this country. It has aroused the conscience of millions of people to work for this legislation'.

CRITICISM OF THE MARCH

Amid the chorus of enthusiasm, there were some discordant voices. Malcolm X attacked the March as 'the Farce on Washington', accusing its leaders of selling out to the racist system. In his well-known 'Message to the Grass Roots' speech, Malcolm explained that, as originally conceived, the black masses were going to protest the inevitable Southern filibuster of the Civil Rights Bill:

> They were going to march on Washington, march on the Sen-ate, march on the White House, march on the Congress, and tie it up, bring it to a halt, not let the government proceed. . . . It was a grass roots revolution out there in the street. . . . When they found out that this black steamroller was going to come down on the capital, they called in Wilkens, they called in Randolph, they called in these national Negro leaders that you respect and told them, "Call it off". Kennedy said, "Look, you are letting this thing go too far". And old Tom said, "Boss, I can't stop it, because I didn't start it". . . . And that old shrewd fox, he said, "If you all aren't in it, I'll put you in it. I'll put you at the head of it. I'll endorse it. I'll welcome it. I'll help it. I'll join it".

Malcolm's denunciation reflected the sentiments of many young black militants. Cleveland Sellers recorded the further disillusionment of SNCC as a result of the March—the shift in strategy from disruption and confrontation, the censoring of John Lewis's speech and the 'take-over' by the white liberal establishment. SNCC's James Forman also expressed resentment: 'We were beginning to see the whole process by which fancy productions like the March on Washington tended to "psych off" local protest and make people feel they had accomplished something—changed something, somehow—when, in fact, nothing had been changed'.

IMPACT OF THE MARCH

Despite the criticisms of SNCC and others, the March on Washington was a landmark in the black freedom struggle. No demonstration, Bayard Rustin wrote a decade later, 'has influenced the course of social legislation and determined the shape of institutional reform to the degree that the March did'. Just as President Kennedy realized that he could not prevent the March, black leaders realized that the March had to be moderate in order to receive support for the Civil Rights Bill from white liberals, and civic, church and labour groups throughout the nation. This coalition, galvanized by militant nonviolent direct action in Birmingham and throughout the South in 1963, was essential for the defeat of *de jure* [by rights] segregation. To most observers, passage of the Civil Rights Act of 1964 signified that the nation had taken a giant stride toward resolving the American Dilemma.

The Memphis Campaign and King's Assassination

Lionel Lokos

At the outset, the Memphis sanitation strike of 1968 did not attract much attention. According to Lionel Lokos, even King's planned appearance did not seem extraordinary. The demands of the thirteen hundred garbage collectors were typical requests for improvements in their benefits and a desire to have their union recognized officially. Lokos argues that the issues were soon put aside and the strike became a racial issue with whites supporting Mayor Henry Loeb's refusal to recognize the union and blacks supporting the workers, who were mostly black. To make matters worse, the governor of Tennessee announced he was planning to have the National Guard hold riot training exercises in predominantly black areas in the state's major cities.

Lokos writes that King's first march in Memphis resulted in violence when a group of marchers smashed store windows. Loeb immediately called for National Guard troops to restore order. Lokos maintains that the rioting not only embarrassed King but also created the impression he might be unable to keep order in the upcoming planned march on Washington, D.C. King returned to Memphis to prepare for a second march, one that would remain nonviolent. However, before the march could happen, King was shot to death standing on a motel balcony. In the days following the April 4, 1968, murder, riots exploded in over one hundred American cities.

Lionel Lokos is a radio and television copywriter. He is the author of *Hysteria 1964: The Fear Campaign Against Barry Goldwater* and *The New Racism: Reverse Discrimination in America.*

Excerpted from *House Divided: The Life and Legacy of Martin Luther King,* by Lionel Lokos. Copyright ©1968 by Arlington House, New Rochelle, New York. Reprinted by permission of Arlington House, a division of Random House, Inc.

In and out of government—in white and Negro neighbor-hoods—the talk, the exhilaration, the fears revolved around and around the march on Washington—Part 2—with Martin Luther King in one corner, and the Congress of the United States in the other. And given King's awesome string of victories in the years gone by, no one pretended for a moment that the contenders were not evenly matched.

Newspaper article after article fed the public's voracious appetite for any and all details about the forthcoming march. Anything else seemed superfluous. A garbage strike? Well yes, there had been a sanitationmen's strike in New York City—and now there was one in Memphis. And King was going to Memphis. But then, King was always going somewhere. And almost that perfunctorily, the public shifted its attention from garbage collections in a Tennessee city to the massive civil rights confrontation that would soon blitz Washington, D.C.

MEMPHIS SANITATION STRIKE ISSUES

Under normal circumstances, there would have been nothing in the strike of the Memphis sanitationmen to absorb the public interest very long. The basic details could hardly have been more prosaic. It all started a week and a half before King's speech in Carnegie Hall—on February 12—when 1,300 garbage collectors and sanitation workers went out on strike. Their demands were: 1) recognition of Local 1733 as bargaining representative of the sanitation men; 2) establishment of grievance procedures; 3) payroll deduction of union dues; 4) "fair" provisions for promotions; 5) health, hospital, and life insurance; 6) a uniform pension program; 7) sick leave, vacation, and overtime pay; 8) a wage increase.

Mayor Henry Loeb had said flatly that he would not recognize the union (which had been chartered two-and-a-half years before) and would not permit a union dues checkoff. And this apparently was the crux of the controversy. The city garbagemen were making $1.70 an hour, but wages were almost incidental to the question of union recognition. The city had offered, and the workers were ready to accept, a 10-cent raise immediately, and five cents more an hour in July.

So far, this could have sounded like a perfectly straightforward union dispute, interlaced with serious policy problems about the right of civil service workers to strike against a city and withhold essential services necessary for the health and well-being of its citizens. But soon these valid and legitimate issues were shunted aside and the racial issue became paramount. Most of the strikers were Negroes, the Mayor would not recognize their union, and the entire matter escalated into a full-blown civil rights issue. It was no longer labor versus management, but black versus white.

RACIAL POLARIZATION

The Memphis chapter of the NAACP [National Association for the Advancement of Colored People] estimated that 98 per cent of the Negro vote went against Mayor Loeb in the 1967 election in which he won a second term. Inevitably the sanitationmen's strike evolved into a polarization of support for and against the mayor along substantially rigid racial lines.

This same polarization was the reflex reaction to Tennessee Governor Buford Ellington's preparations for the Long Hot Summer. In early March, the Governor announced his determination to allow a National Guard riot training exercise in which troops would be concentrated in the state's four metropolitan areas. He stood his ground in the face of furious charges by Negro leaders that it would heighten racial tensions and might even lead to civil disturbances. They indignantly cited the report that the Guardsmen would go through anti-riot drills in the North Nashville Negro section, including the campuses of the predominantly Negro Fisk University and the state-operated Agricultural and Industrial University. A year before, this had been the scene of three nights of rioting in which policemen and students were injured and a number of buildings were destroyed by fire. The Governor replied that there was "nothing to be excited about," and denounced critics for spreading false rumors about the operation. He said there had never been any intention to assemble troops in the Negro section, but acknowledged that the exercise was aimed at preparing the Guard to combat civil disorder that might occur in the summer. Perhaps he had the ghastly Newark and Detroit riots in mind when he emphatically declared, "We are going to take advantage of all the training we can get in this area." As for his critics, he grimly noted, "There are people who would like to see riots, and they are not all in the North Nashville area. Martin Luther King is training 3,000 people to start riots, and when we say we are going to train the Guard to protect the lives of people and their property, there is a big hullabaloo about it." Governor Ellington said he had planned to invite newsmen to travel with the troops and witness the exercises.

PROTEST VIOLENCE

Three weeks later, 4,000 of these troops were called up by Governor Ellington at the request of Mayor Loeb. A total of 8,000 more troops were placed on alert. What had begun as a massive protest march in support of the sanitationmen, led through downtown Memphis by Martin Luther King, had been accompanied by violence in which a group of Negro youths smashed windows and looted stores. Negro students, prevented by the police from leaving high school to join the march, hurled missiles at the officers. The youths dashed along, shattering store windows with sticks. In all, 155 stores had their windows smashed, with about 35 per cent of their window displays rifled. Forty-one persons were arrested on looting charges. A number were beaten and gassed, a 16-year-old boy was killed, and 60 were injured. Mayor Loeb said he called for the National Guard "two minutes" after the first window was broken on Beale Street. President Johnson offered federal assistance if Memphis needed it, and said, "We will not let violence and lawlessness take over the country."

Charges were made that the police had lost their heads, launching a full-scale offensive instead of moving in and arresting the 30 to 70 teen-agers actually involved. But Mayor Loeb was convinced that firmness was the deciding factor in containing the disorders. The mayor's convictions seemed borne out by the tragedy that was only a week away. Certainly in the frightening days that lay ahead, riots swept many of its sister cities, but Memphis remained relatively quiet by comparison.

KING'S PREPARATION FOR A SECOND MARCH

At the first sign of trouble, King was whisked away from the march. The front-page photo of him in the Memphis march shows him stunned—dazed—by the violence. That the rioting was a tremendous embarrassment to King was all too evident, in view of the many doubts and misgivings that had been raised about the potential for violence in the forthcoming march on Washington. To reassure the doubters, King was practically compelled to promise to return to Memphis "as quickly as possible" to stage a "massive" march without disorder. This is a fact that has already been lost sight of by far too many Americans—that Martin Luther King was back in Memphis that fateful day preparing for a second march, because of the Negro violence which had marred the first procession.

At first, King had scheduled this second march for Friday, April 5, but he put it off until Monday, April 8, in order to give union men from across the country time to come to Memphis and join in the protest. He expected about 5,000 marchers to come in from other cities. Tensions were running high in the city, and Mayor Loeb instructed City Attorney Frank Gianotti to seek an injunction in United States District Court forbidding the march. After hearing the arguments on April 3, United States District Court Judge Bailey Brown issued a temporary restraining order forbidding King to hold that march on Monday. The order was not only against King but also on all persons under his authority and those acting in concert with him. King angrily called the order "illegal and unconstitutional" and said that there was a "real possibility" that he would not obey it. King said he would first attempt to have the restraining order set aside in the courts. He said his lawyers would go into Federal Court the following day in an effort to have the order dissolved. "Beyond that," King declared, "it is a matter of conscience. It will be on the basis of my conscience saying that we have a moral right and responsibility to march." He recalled that he had been "forced" to defy court orders in the past, and cited as a case in point his week in jail in Alabama the preceding year for having defied a court injunction in Birmingham back in 1963. This is a second fact which must be remembered—that Martin Luther King was in the middle of planning a demonstration which would flout a court injunction, issued to avoid precisely the kind of violence that ended his life.

On the evening of April 3, King addressed a cheering crowd of 2,000 supporters. He had flown in from Atlanta to Memphis, and told them that his flight had been delayed because of a baggage search that airlines officials said resulted from threats to him. In King's words:

> And then I got into Memphis. And some began to say the threats—or talk about the threats that were out. Or what would happen to me from some of our sick white brothers. Well, I don't know what will happen now. We've got some difficult days ahead. But it really doesn't matter with me now.

Because I've been to the mountain top. I won't mind. Like anybody, I would like to live a long life. Longevity has its place. But I'm not concerned about that now. I just want to do God's will. And He's allowed me to go up to the mountain. And I've looked over, and I've seen the promised land. I may not get there with you, but I want you to know tonight that we as a people will get to the promised land. So I'm happy tonight. I'm not worried about anything. I'm not fearing any man. Mine eyes have seen the glory of the coming of the Lord.

. . . On the morning of April 4, Memphis Police Director Frank Holloman was in Federal Court, in support of the temporary restraining order against the march granted by Judge Brown the day before. Holloman said that the Negro community was so worked up that another mass demonstration in Memphis could "be worse than Watts or worse than Detroit." The Police Director stated he had received reports that "Negroes are buying guns from wholesale houses in our neighboring state of Arkansas." He also said that Negro youths "have been supplied for several weeks with specific instructions on how to make Molotov cocktails and firebombs."

KING'S ASSASSINATION

That evening, Martin Luther King was in his room on the second floor of the Lorraine Motel. He went outside, and leaned over the railing to chat with an associate, Rev. Jesse Jackson, standing just below him in a courtyard parking lot. Jackson introduced him to Ben Branch of Chicago, a musician who was to play that night at a rally in support of the striking sanitationmen. King asked Branch to play a Negro spiritual, "Precious Lord, Take My Hand," at the rally. Suddenly a shot burst out. King toppled to the concrete second-floor walkway. Blood gushed from the right jaw and neck area. His necktie had been ripped off by the blast. Later, Jackson recalled that King "had just bent over. If he had been standing up, he wouldn't have been hit in the face."

King was apparently still alive when he reached the St. Joseph's Hospital operating room. He was carried in on a stretcher, a bloody towel over his head. King received emergency surgery, but it was too late. He was pronounced dead at 7:05 p.m. Central Standard Time by staff doctors.

That night, Mayor Loeb reinstated a curfew which had been in effect, and declared: "After the tragedy which has happened in Memphis tonight, for the protection of all our citizens, we are putting the curfew back in effect. All movement is restricted except for health or emergency reasons." Governor Ellington called out the National Guard and pledged all necessary action by the state to prevent disorder. He stated, "I can fully appreciate the feelings and emotions which this crime has aroused, but for the benefit of everyone, all of our citizens must exercise restraint, caution and good judgment." Police said the murder of Martin Luther King had been followed by sporadic shooting, fires, bricks and bottles thrown at policemen, and looting that started in Negro districts and spread all over the city.

At this time, details about King's assassin were sketchy at best. Memphis Chief of Detectives W.P. Huston said a late model white Mustang was believed to have been the killer's get-away car. Police Director Holloman said the assassin had fired the fatal shot "50 to 100 yards away in a flophouse." A high-powered 30.06 caliber rifle was found about a block from the scene of the shooting. "We think it's the gun," Chief Huston said. All that was certain was that with the Memphis police patrolling the area, the killer made an incredibly perfect escape.

The days following the assassination were a grotesque nightmare, with eulogies approaching deification competing for newspaper coverage with reports of rioters running amok in over 100 cities. Sometimes in the same city, an integrated procession or service was being held while only blocks away store windows were being broken and stores looted. The mood of the ghetto would fluctuate from hour to hour, from day to day, from grief to fury to a bellicose cry for vengeance. A city might be tormented by rioters one day, quiet the next, then confronted by rioters the day after. Another city might be quiet in the first 24 hours after the assassination, then suddenly erupt into violence and looting. It was a frenzied grief coexisting precariously with a frenzied madness, with madness carrying the day. It was a funeral procession marching through a still smoking battlefield, a wake lit by the flames of a Molotov cocktail.

CHAPTER 4

King's Legacy

The Black Power Movement's Rejection of King's Nonviolent Strategy

Stokely Carmichael and Charles V. Hamilton

In their 1967 book *Black Power,* Charles V. Hamilton and the charismatic and militant civil rights activist Stokely Carmichael define what they mean by black power. While serving as the chairman of the Student Nonviolent Coordinating Committee (SNCC), Carmichael first introduced the slogan black power during a speech in Greenwood, Mississippi, on June 17, 1966. He defined it as a call for blacks to reject racist American values, to celebrate their heritage, and to establish their own goals. Many young black Americans interpreted Carmichael's black power as a plea for more aggressive protest.

Carmichael and Hamilton flatly reject King's approach to civil rights, a strategy they claim emphasizes an unworkable strategy of nonviolence and integration. Carmichael and Hamilton argue that King's approach caters to middle-class whites and does not fit the frustration and anger of urban blacks. In short, King's language of love and suffering will not suffice. The authors argue that gains made by King through civil rights legislation have been nullified by weak or nonexistent enforcement.

According to Carmichael and Hamilton, nonviolence is motivated by the fear of a white backlash and guided by white rules. Blacks must stop being patient, reject white lies about the American dream, and act on unified strength. Carmichael and Hamilton want whites to know that blacks will no longer remain passive. If the nation will not defend blacks, blacks must defend themselves. The authors conclude that whites do not deserve the luxury of black nonviolence.

Stokely Carmichael graduated from Howard University. He was the chairman of the Student Nonviolent Coordinating Committee, author, and organizer of black power liberation protests.

Charles V. Hamilton was the chairman of the Department of Political Science at Roosevelt University in Chicago. He has published numerous articles on civil rights and constitutional law.

A great deal of public attention and press space was devoted to the hysterical accusation of "black racism" when the call for Black Power was first sounded. A national committee of influential black churchmen affiliated with the National Council of Churches, despite their obvious respectability and responsibility, had to resort to a paid advertisement to articulate their position, while anyone yapping "black racism" made front-page news. In their statement, published in the *New York Times* of July 31, 1966, the churchmen said:

> We, an informal group of Negro churchmen in America, are deeply disturbed about the crisis brought upon our country by historic distortions of important human realities in the controversy about "black power." What we see shining through the variety of rhetoric is not anything new but the same old problem of power and race which has faced our beloved country since 1619.
>
> . . . The conscience of black men is corrupted because having no power to implement the demands of conscience, the concern for justice in the absence of justice becomes a chaotic self-surrender. Powerlessness breeds a race of beggars. We are faced with a situation where powerless conscience meets conscienceless power, threatening the very foundations of our Nation.
>
> We deplore the overt violence of riots, but we feel it is more important to focus on the real sources of these eruptions. These sources may be abetted inside the Ghetto, but their basic cause lies in the silent and covert violence which white middle class America inflicts upon the victims of the inner city.
>
> . . . In short, the failure of American leaders to use American power to create equal opportunity *in life* as well as *law*, this is the real problem and not the anguished cry for black power.
>
> . . . Without the capacity to participate with power, i.e., to have some organized political and economic strength to really in-

fluence people with whom one interacts, integration is not meaningful.

. . . America has asked its Negro citizens to fight for opportunity as *individuals,* whereas at certain points in our history what we have needed most has been opportunity for the *whole group,* not just for selected and approved Negroes.

. . . We must not apologize for the existence of this form of group power, for we have been oppressed as a group and not as individuals. We will not find our way out of that oppression until both we and America accept the need for Negro Americans, as well as for Jews, Italians, Poles, and white Anglo-Saxon Protestants, among others, to have and to wield group power.

It is a commentary on the fundamentally racist nature of this society that the concept of group strength for black people must be articulated—not to mention defended. No other group would submit to being led by others. Italians do not run the Anti-Defamation League of B'nai B'rith. Irish do not chair Christopher Columbus Societies. Yet when black people call for black-run and all-black organizations, they are immediately classed in a category with the Ku Klux Klan. This is interesting and ironic, but by no means surprising: the society does not expect black people to be able to take care of their business, and there are many who prefer it precisely that way.

In the end, we cannot and shall not offer any guarantees that Black Power, if achieved, would be non-racist. No one can predict human behavior. Social change always has unanticipated consequences. If black racism is what the larger society fears, we cannot help them. We can only state what we hope will be the result, given the fact that the present situation is unacceptable and that we have no real alternative but to work for Black Power. The final truth is that the white society is not entitled to reassurances, even if it were possible to offer them. . . .

REJECTION OF KING'S RHETORIC OF CHANGE

The advocates of Black Power reject the old slogans and meaningless rhetoric of previous years in the civil rights struggle. The language of yesterday is indeed irrelevant: progress, non-violence, integration, fear of "white backlash," coalition. Let us look at the rhetoric and see why these terms must be set aside or redefined.

One of the tragedies of the struggle against racism is that

up to this point there has been no national organization which could speak to the growing militancy of young black people in the urban ghettos and the black-belt South. There has been only a "civil rights" movement, whose tone of voice was adapted to an audience of middle-class whites. It served as a sort of buffer zone between that audience and angry young blacks. It claimed to speak for the needs of a community, but it did not speak in the tone of that community. None of its so-called leaders could go into a rioting community and be listened to. In a sense, the blame must be shared—along with the mass media—by those leaders for what happened in Watts, Harlem, Chicago, Cleveland and other places. Each time the black people in those cities saw Dr. Martin Luther King get slapped they became angry. When they saw little black girls bombed to death *in a church* and civil rights workers ambushed and murdered, they were angrier; and when nothing happened, they were steaming mad. We had nothing to offer that they could see, except to go out and be beaten again. We helped to build their frustration.

We had only the old language of love and suffering. And in most places—that is, from the liberals and middle class—we got back the old language of patience and progress. The civil rights leaders were saying to the country: "Look, you guys are supposed to be nice guys, and we are only going to do what we are supposed to do. Why do you beat us up? Why don't you give us what we ask? Why don't you straighten yourselves out?" For the masses of black people, this language resulted in virtually nothing. In fact, their objective day-to-day condition worsened. The unemployment rate among black people increased while that among whites declined. Housing conditions in the black communities deteriorated. Schools in the black ghettos continued to plod along on outmoded techniques, inadequate curricula, and with all too many tired and indifferent teachers. Meanwhile, the President picked up the refrain of "We Shall Overcome" while the Congress passed civil rights law after civil rights law, only to have them effectively nullified by deliberately weak enforcement. "Progress is being made," we were told.

REJECTION OF WHITE RULES

Such language, along with admonitions to remain nonviolent and fear the white backlash, convinced some that that course was the *only* course to follow. It misled some into believing that a black minority could bow its head and get whipped into a meaningful position of power. The very notion is absurd. The white society devised the language, adopted the rules and had the black community narcotized into believing that that language and those rules were, in fact, relevant. The black community was told time and again how *other* immigrants finally won *acceptance:* that is, by following the Protestant Ethic of Work and Achievement. They worked hard; therefore, they achieved. We were not told that it was by building Irish Power, Italian Power, Polish Power or Jewish Power that these groups got themselves together and operated from positions of strength. We were not told that "the American dream" wasn't designed for black people. That while today, to whites, the dream may *seem* to include black people, it cannot do so by the very nature of this nation's political and economic system, which imposes institutional racism on the black masses if not upon every individual black. A notable comment on that "dream" was made by Dr. Percy Julian, the black scientist and director of the Julian Research Institute in Chicago, a man for whom the dream seems to have come true. While not subscribing to "black power" as he understood it, Dr. Julian clearly understood the basis for it: "The false concept of basic Negro inferiority is one of the curses that still lingers. It is a problem created by the white man. Our children just no longer are going to accept the patience we were taught by our generation. We were taught a pretty little lie—excel and the whole world lies open before you. *I obeyed the injunction and found it to be wishful thinking.*" (Authors' italics)

REJECTION OF KING'S NONVIOLENCE

A key phrase in our buffer-zone days was non-violence. For years it has been thought that black people would not literally fight for their lives. Why this has been so is not entirely clear; neither the larger society nor black people are noted for passivity. The notion apparently stems from the years of marches and demonstrations and sit-ins where black people did not strike back and the violence always came from white mobs. There are many who still sincerely believe in that approach. From our viewpoint, rampaging white mobs and white night-riders must be made to understand that their days of free head-whipping are over. Black people should and must fight back. Nothing more quickly repels someone bent on destroying you than the unequivocal message: "O.K., fool, make your move, and run the same risk I run—of dying."

When the concept of Black Power is set forth, many people immediately conjure up notions of violence. The country's reaction to the Deacons for Defense and Justice, which originated in Louisiana, is instructive. Here is a group which realized that the "law" and law enforcement agencies would not protect people, so they had to do it themselves. If a nation fails to protect its citizens, then that nation cannot condemn those who take up the task themselves. The Deacons and all other blacks who resort to self-defense represent a simple answer to a simple question: what man would not defend his family and home from attack?

But this frightened some white people, because they knew that black people would now fight back. They knew that this was precisely what *they* would have long since done if *they* were subjected to the injustices and oppression heaped on blacks. Those of us who advocate Black Power are quite clear in our own minds that a "non-violent" approach to civil rights is an approach black people cannot afford and a luxury white people do not deserve. It is crystal clear to us—and it must become so with the white society—*that there can be no social order without social justice.* White people must be made to understand that they must stop messing with black people, or the blacks *will* fight back!

King's Response to the Black Power Movement

John J. Ansbro

During his Freedom March through Mississippi in June 1966, charismatic and militant civil rights activist Stokely Carmichael popularized the slogan "black power." John J. Ansbro argues that Martin Luther King Jr. supported the need for legitimate black power and all that it denotes: political strength, economic viability, and the freedom to rise above a submissive psychology. King, however, disliked the fact that the slogan "black power" connoted a sense of violence that could be used by racists and the media to isolate the black community and rationalize white hostility. Ansbro writes that King's definition of power meant political and economic strength, a force that is creative and works to implement justice and love. Ansbro reasons that King understood that in order for blacks to obtain power they must first break white society's insidious conditioning of unconditional submission, a legacy of slavery. Power, then, was the development of a new awareness of one's own values as a person.

Ansbro argues that King viewed Carmichael's black power as a pessimistic philosophy, one that conflicted with his own dedication to the power of justice and his belief that hope, not despair, provides the motivation for revolution. Ansbro concludes that King also felt that the shout for separatism inherent in black power was unrealistic since blacks needed to work within the system for large-scale political and economic reforms. King preached that there was no validity in riots and violence because violence imitated the worst in American white culture.

John J. Ansbro taught King's philosophy of nonviolence at Fordham University, Bronx, New York. He is an emeritus professor of philosophy at Manhattan College, Bronx, New York.

Excerpted from *Martin Luther King Jr.: The Making of a Mind*, by John J. Ansbro. Copyright ©1982 by Orbis Books, Maryknoll, NY 10545. Reprinted with permission.

"Black Power" was first used as a slogan in the civil rights movement by Stokely Carmichael during the Freedom March through Mississippi in June 1966. Outraged by the shooting of James Meredith, who had begun the march, Carmichael agreed to join with King and Floyd McKissick, national director of the Congress of Racial Equality (CORE), to continue the march. At a mass meeting in Greenwood, Carmichael delivered a speech to the marchers that denounced Mississippi "justice," and when he had sufficiently aroused the audience, he proclaimed, "What we need is black power." Willie Ricks of SNCC [Student Nonviolent Coordinating Committee] then mounted the platform and shouted to the crowd, "What do you want?" They responded, "Black Power." Again and again, Ricks repeated the question until the response "Black Power" reached fever pitch. The audience could not resist the appeal of the slogan. They had too long felt the pressure of white power. Moreover, they knew that the speakers who offered them the slogan were members of SNCC, the organization that had worked so courageously in their community during the turbulent summer of 1964. They knew Carmichael's history. In the struggle for their freedom he had been arrested twenty-seven times. When he had been director of the Freedom School in Greenwood in 1964, white terrorists firebombed the school and savagely beat nonviolent local black activists.

KING'S REACTION TO THE SLOGAN "BLACK POWER"

King thought that the term "Black Power," which had been used long before by Richard Wright and others, should not be adopted as a slogan for the march or the Movement. He witnessed how the slogan caused division in the ranks of the marchers as some speakers called for the chant of "Black Power" while others called for "Freedom Now." To resolve the problem, he met with Carmichael and McKissick to convince them to abandon the slogan. He advised them that the leader of a group has to be concerned about the problem of semantics. He explained that a term may have both a denotative meaning, that would be its explicit and recognized sense, and a connotative meaning, its suggestive sense. While granting that the *concept* of legitimate Black Power might be denotatively sound, he argued that the *slogan* "Black Power" conveyed the wrong connotations. He reminded them of how the press had already associated this slogan with violence and of how rash statements by a few of the marchers had tended to substantiate this interpretation by the press. Carmichael responded by declaring that the question of violence versus nonviolence was irrelevant. He indicated that the real issue was the need for blacks to consolidate their political and economic resources for the acquisition of power. He stated, "Power is the only thing respected in this world, and we must get it at any cost," and contended that almost every other ethnic group in America had acted on this conviction. King reminded Carmichael that the Jews, the Irish, and the Italians had not publicly chanted slogans referring to power, but rather had worked hard to achieve power through "group unity, determination, and creative endeavor." King maintained that blacks should do exactly the same, using every constructive means to obtain economic and political power and to build racial pride. While agreeing that a movement needs slogans, he argued that the slogan "Black Power" would only confuse allies, isolate the black community, and allow many whites who otherwise would be ashamed of their prejudice to rationalize their hostility to blacks. He felt that the slogan "Black Power" conveyed the impression that the Movement aimed at black domination. He proposed instead the slogan "Black Consciousness" or "Black Equality." Carmichael rejected these, claiming that "Black Power" was far more persuasive. When King saw that he could not convince them of the necessity of substituting a new slogan, he proposed that for the rest of the march they would not chant either "Black Power" or "Freedom Now." Carmichael and McKissick agreed to accept this compromise so that they would minimize the appearance of conflict within the Movement. However, Carmichael later chose to reject the spirit of this compromise when he engaged in abuse of white participants in the march.

BLACK POWER AS AN EMOTIONAL CONCEPT

King maintained that Black Power is essentially an emotional concept that can mean different things to different persons, and can vary in meaning even for the same person on different occasions. In his evaluation of the concept that attempted to go "beyond personal styles, verbal flourishes and the hysteria of the mass media," King explained that it was necessary to understand that "Black Power" was a cry of disappointment and that the causes of the disappointment were many. White power had left blacks empty-handed. Mississippi, where the slogan was born, symbolized the most blatant abuse of white power, with its unpunished lynchings, bombings of Negro churches, and murders of civil rights workers. King indicated that many of the young who proclaimed Black Power had been participants in the Nonviolent Movement and proponents of black-white cooperation. But as they labored and suffered courageously to expose the disease of racism, they came to feel that "a real solution is hopelessly distant because of the inconsistencies, resistance and faintheartedness of those in power." He attempted to understand how some of them in their anger could repudiate nonviolence even though he did not justify their position:

> If Stokely Carmichael now says that nonviolence is irrelevant, it is because he, as a dedicated veteran of many battles, has seen with his own eyes the most brutal white violence against Negroes and white civil rights workers, and he has seen it go unpunished.

King stated that members of SNCC, including Carmichael, had the impression that the life of a black in white America had no meaning. He recalled how this impression was reinforced during the Selma Movement when both Jimmy Lee Jackson, a Negro, and the Reverend James Reeb, a white Unitarian minister, had been killed by white racists, but President Johnson, in his "We Shall Overcome" speech, felt it appropriate to mention only Reeb.

King had no difficulty in adding to the list of disappointments that caused the frustrated to advocate Black Power. The refusal of the Federal Government to implement the civil rights laws helped lead the Black Power advocates to develop a contempt for the legislative process. As he indicated in 1967, although the 1965 Voting Rights Act required the appointment of hundreds of registrars and thousands of Federal marshals to protect the voters, fewer than sixty registrars were appointed, and not one Federal law officer with the power to arrest was sent into the South. As a result, the economic coercion, terrorism, and murder continued unchecked. He asserted that the disappointment of the Black Power advocates could only increase as they considered the educational, economic, and social conditions that oppressed blacks in Northern ghettos. These Black Power advocates could experience only further disappointment as they wit-

nessed a Government that was more concerned about winning the Vietnam War than about winning the war against
poverty and that praised blacks whenever they remained
nonviolent while it asked them to commit violence in Vietnam; a Christian Church that appeared to be more white
than Christian; white moderates who believed that they had
the right to set a timetable for the freedom of blacks; black
ministers more concerned about material rewards than
about the quality of their service to the black community; and
a black middle class that had forgotten its black brothers.

KING'S DEFINITION OF POWER

King explained that Black Power in its positive sense was a
call to black people to acquire the political and economic
strength to achieve their legitimate goals. He felt that the acquisition of legitimate power was crucial to the solutions of
the problems of the ghetto. "The problem of transforming the
ghetto is, therefore, a problem of power—a confrontation between the forces of power demanding change and the forces
of power dedicated to preserving the status quo." He was
careful to add that power should be creative and positive, and
should implement the demands of justice and love. Blacks
must not imitate those white Americans who had sought their
goals through power without love and conscience. He agreed
with the Black Power advocates on the necessity of develop-
ing political power in the black community. The many voter
registration campaigns conducted by SCLC [Southern Christian Leadership Conference] testified to his awareness of this
need. He agreed also with the Black Power advocates on the
necessity of blacks' pooling their resources to achieve economic security. While he called for a massive Federal program to help the poor, he contended that blacks could help
shape the policies of American businesses and thus improve
their own conditions by the ways in which they used the buying power in their collective annual income of $30 billion.

Given King's own dedication to the principle of the dignity
of the person, it was not difficult for him to find positive
value in Black Power as "a psychological call to manhood."
He recognized that the demand of the Black Power Movement that the black man should assert his manhood was a
reaction to the psychological indoctrination begun in slavery
and continued in segregation. He found a penetrating analysis of this indoctrination in *The Peculiar Institution* by the

historian Kenneth Stampp. To understand the indoctrination that the master used to develop a good slave, Stampp had consulted manuals on the training of slaves. He discovered certain recurring rules in these manuals. *First,* the master had to maintain strict discipline so as to achieve the unconditional submission of the slave to his absolute authority. *Second,* for the purpose of maintaining this control, the master was to inculcate in the slave "a consciousness of personal inferiority." Therefore he was to convince the slave that bondage was his natural status, that his African background had tainted him, and that his color was "a badge of degradation." *Third,* the master had to instill in the slave an awe of his enormous power. Though King did not indicate it, Stampp here referred to Frederick Douglass's contention that few slaves could free themselves altogether from the notion that their masters were "invested with a sort of sacredness." *Fourth,* the master had to attempt to persuade the slave to be concerned about his master's interests and to accept his standards of good conduct. *Fifth,* the master had to implant in the slave a sense of helplessness and to develop in him a habit of perfect dependence. King viewed the Black Power defiance of white authority as one that contained a legitimate concern of blacks to break away from the "unconditional submission" lingering from slavery, and to affirm one's own selfhood.

King saw the desire of the Black Power Movement to glory in blackness and in the African heritage as a further reaction to the system of slavery. Moreover, he acknowledged that although he felt that he could not justify how some Black Power advocates encouraged contempt for white authority and called for uncivil disobedience, he did understand how these responses could arise as alternatives to the system of slavery with its fear, awe, and obedience to the master. When proponents of Black Power went to the extreme of rejecting all forms of white help and the accepted "standards of good conduct," they were reacting against the slave pattern of total dependence on the master. Carmichael frequently attacked the systematic way in which whites continued their "colonization" of blacks in America by imposing their definitions on them. "They define what education is, they define what work is, they define how we move, what we do, and how we look—the oppressor defines even the standards of beauty for the victims of colonialism." Carmichael endorsed the contention of the French philosopher Albert Camus in *The Rebel* that it is only when a slave stops accepting definitions imposed on him by his master that he begins to move and create a life. While not endorsing the absolute independence and isolation in this reaction, King felt that it did have merit in that it emphasized the need for the black to develop a new awareness of his own value as a person:

> One must not overlook the positive value [in Black Power] in calling the Negro to a new sense of manhood, to a deep feeling of racial pride and to an audacious appreciation of his heritage. The Negro must be grasped by a new realization of his dignity and worth. He must stand up amid a system that still oppresses him and develop an unassailable and majestic sense of his own value. He must no longer be ashamed of being black.

KING'S OBJECTION TO BLACK SEPARATION

Even though King found positive values in the Black Power Movement, he believed that it had defects that were so serious that it could not become the basic strategy for the civil rights movement. At the foundation of the Black Power Movement he found a nihilistic philosophy that stood in sharp contrast to [Indian Nationalist Leader Mohandas] Gandhi's doctrine that hope and love must permeate an effective revolution. Some Black Power advocates rejected the possibility that blacks could find fulfillment within the American system. King tried to understand the depth of the frustration of blacks trapped in despair. He related that the only time he was booed by an audience was by young members of the Black Power Movement at a Chicago mass meeting, and that upon reflection he recognized that the youths were responding to the fact that promises of social justice had not been fulfilled. Nonetheless, he affirmed that, despite the lamentable rate of progress, blacks should not descend to a despair and a nihilism that seeks disruption for the sake of disruption. He stressed that hope is what keeps the fire of a revolution burning. God is in control of history, directs it toward righteousness, and demands our cooperation.

King contended that the implicit and often explicit belief of the Black Power Movement in separatism was totally unrealistic. He argued that if blacks chose to develop their political strength through separatism and by concentration on those few cities and counties where they constituted a majority, such a strategy would leave most blacks outside the mainstream of American political life. The Black Power Movement seemed to fail to realize that it was far more preferable for blacks to establish coalitions with white moderates to seek the election of fifteen or twenty representatives in Congress from Southern districts than for blacks on their own to secure the election of two or three black representatives from predominately black districts. King denounced any policy as morally unjustifiable and politically unsound that would elect candidates because they were black and reject all white candidates because they were white. He argued further that blacks could not achieve significant economic power through separatism. Though the proper use of black buying power could effect some improvements, only Federal programs involving billions of dollars could bring about the necessary basic reforms in jobs, housing, and education; blacks through their own efforts could not secure these programs. Only an alliance of liberal, labor, and civil rights forces could move the Government to create the necessary programs. Certain ethnic groups, such as the Jews, the Irish, and the Italians, did emphasize group unity, as the Black Power advocates maintained, but these groups also perceived the value of alliances with other groups such as political machines and trade unions. In recommending alliances, King stressed the need for vigilance against possible betrayal as well as the need to avoid an excess of skepticism that would constitute a denial of the contributions of some whites to the civil rights struggle and would cripple any alliance:

> While Negro initiative, courage and imagination precipitated the Birmingham and Selma confrontations and revealed the harrowing injustice of segregated life, the organized strength of Negroes alone would have been insufficient to move Congress and the administration without the weight of the aroused conscience of white America.

King denied that by entering alliances blacks were relying on white leadership or ideology. Rather, the black man was "taking his place as an equal partner in a common endeavor." King's Personalist belief in the interconnectedness of all humanity reinforced his conviction on the value of black-white alliances:

> There is no separate black path to power and fulfillment that does not intersect white paths, and there is no separate white path to power and fulfillment, short of social disaster, that does not share that power with black aspirations for freedom

and human dignity. We are bound together in a single garment of destiny.

In their desire for separatism many Negroes regarded themselves only as Africans. Others rejected their African heritage and defined goodness and beauty in terms of the standards of white society. King rejected the narrowness of each of these approaches and chose again to appeal to the Hegelian [German philosopher, Georg Friedrich Wilhelm Hegel] synthesis as "the best answer to many of life's dilemmas." "The American Negro is neither totally African nor totally Western. He is Afro-American, a true hybrid, a combination of two cultures." By this description he was attempting to respond to Carmichael's charge that "integration" meant that black people had to give up their identity and deny their heritage.

King felt that the Black Power Movement was deficient also because some of its members called for aggressive violence. In Atlanta and Chicago he had many dialogues with proponents of Black Power who argued for the validity of violence and riots. He not only denounced aggressive violence as morally wrong and practically absurd for the American Negro but he also opposed the unconscious and often conscious call for retaliatory violence in the Black Power Movement. He did not deny the right to defend one's home and person, but he rejected the role of retaliatory violence in a civil rights demonstration:

> It is dangerous to organize a movement around self-defense. The line of demarcation between defensive violence and aggressive violence is very thin. The minute a program of violence is enunciated, even for self-defense, the atmosphere is filled with talk of violence, and the words falling on unsophisticated ears may be interpreted as an invitation to aggression.

King uncovered a paradox in the Black Power Movement. While its members continued to insist on not imitating the "values" of white society, by advocating violence they were imitating the worst and the most brutal "value" of American life.

A Reevaluation of King's Policies

Rosemary R. Ruether

Rosemary R. Ruether writes that after King's death the tone of the civil rights movement became much more militant and frustrated. This change resulted partly from the perception that King's nonviolence is passive and slow moving. Ruether maintains that this is not true; in truth, nonviolence is direct action that actively coordinates the use of legal, economic, and moral pressure.

Ruether suggests that King's vision remains relevant for a variety of reasons. He appealed to a common American ideology based on Christianity and an American civic responsibility. More radical civil rights groups after King do not offer this broad appeal and consequently narrow their support. King also provided very specific economic and political solutions to America's race issue. He called for preferential hiring of blacks and loans for education, job training, housing, and business. In addition, King appealed to blacks to form voting blocs and vote against racist politicians.

Ruether claims that King broadened the context of his actions by acknowledging that the struggle of American blacks was morally connected to the struggle of all colonized peoples globally. In a similar fashion, King understood that the plight of the poor was an issue that went beyond civil rights. Near the end of his life King attacked the overall economic structure that generated large numbers of poor and, as a counteraction, attempted to coalesce the downtrodden of all races into a "rainbow coalition" to fight for common economic interests.

Rosemary R. Ruether is a Georgia Harkness Professor of Applied Theology at Garrett-Evangelical Theological Seminary in Evanston, Illinois. She also speaks internationally and writes articles for numerous periodicals.

Excerpted from Rosemary R. Ruether, "The Relevance of Martin Luther King for Today," in *Essays in Honor of Martin Luther King Jr.,* edited by John H. Cartwright. Copyright © Leiffer Bureau of Social and Religious Research 1977. Reprinted with permission.

In the period between 1963 and 1968 the mood of the Civil Rights Movement shifted from the inter-racial cooperation of the March on Washington to one of increasing frustration and militancy. The cry of Black Power emerged with Stokely Carmichael [militant activist and chairman of Student Non-violent Coordinating Committee, SNCC] and Rap Brown [activist who succeeded Carmichael as chairman of SNCC]. Ideologies of separatism replaced the earlier chants of "Black and White together." When Martin King was assassinated, his death touched off a modern 'passion week' of blood and fire. Yet, beneath the explosion of anger at his death, was the wide-spread suspicion that his methods and message had become 'obsolete'; that more militant leaders would carry the Movement farther than he had been able to take it. Today, almost a decade later [1977], it is possible to evaluate these assumptions with some objectivity. We can ask "was he really surpassed by Stokely or Malcolm X, or did these younger leaders fall below the high standards he had set? Did Martin King prove to be the 'naive' idealist, counting on too much good will from whites, and these others the 'hard-headed realists', or was it the other way around? They escalated the temper of the demands, but accomplished far less? Most of all, what aspects of this history emerge as the most promising lines into the future?"

NONVIOLENCE AS DIRECT ACTION

The impression that Martin King had been surpassed related, in large part to the issue of violence and non-violence. There is an assumption that non-violence is an expression of passivity, of vulnerability to the oppressor's evil. It is foolish to expect good will from white people. Black people have been vulnerable too long. They cannot make themselves victims any longer, nor assume that good will can be evoked from whites by such victimization. Black people must fight by whatever means necessary. This line of criticism rests on a misunderstanding of what is meant by non-violence as *direct action*. Non-violent direct action does call for a moral and spiritual rising superior to the oppressor, but it is not a capitulation to passivity or victimization. Direct action is a flexible component within a package of all the available tools of legal, economic and moral pressure that can be put on the rulers by the minority community. It works when the element of marches and confrontations are clearly delineated within this total strategy.

For example, a series of marches, together with a boycott, is designed to build up public pressure against discrimination in eating facilities. The white community is expected to crack at the point where repugnance against the extremes of police and officials in maintaining these unjust laws combines with the growing bite of the boycott upon the merchants. At the same time, national pressure is put on the local situation. Martin King understood that the white establishments were not all of one piece. The national government could be evoked against such local customs. Church and civic leaders could be mobilized nationally against their entrenched local representatives. Negotiations and litigation entered at the proper moment. Once the merchants could be split from police and elected officials by combined pressures, the merchants might be brought to the negotiating table to agree on steps to disband these customs. Meanwhile legal challenges could be made against such laws, as well as against ordinances evoked to block the demonstrations. All this involved strategy and timing as precise as any military campaign. . . .

KING'S BROAD-BASED APPEAL

King appealed to a broad common ideology shared by Americans; a combination of prophetic Christianity and the American civic creed. When the later black and peace movements shifted to ideological bases that most Americans did not share; such as black separatism or a Marxist support of the N.L.F. [South Vietnamese guerrilla fighters, National Liberation Front]; when they began to fly the flags of African nationalism or the Viet-Cong, they threw away this broad appeal. This does not mean there was not truth in the new ideologies. But, on tactical grounds, such ideologies narrowed the base of support greatly. The complex combination of negotiation, litigation, and coalition with liberal elites was discarded for mass rallies and street confrontations which had no such backup. So it is not surprising that the demonstrations of the later Movement appeared more and more impotent, easy to ignore or subject to police attack.

The later organizers of mass marches on Washington threw away most of the assets that had been coordinated with direct action in Martin King's strategy and relied on demonstrations in isolation. Demonstrations in themselves can be overused. They belong to the high pressure point of a campaign. But people cannot respond on high levels of intensity that take them out of their ordinary means of survival for long. Such tactics need to be used sparingly, and the day to day business of a struggle carried on by more conventional means. Part of the success of the Farm Workers' movement is that food boycotts on particular products allow large numbers of people to participate nation-wide without great shifts in their lives. Therefore I conclude that Martin King's methods are still useable today for a number of relevant issues. Nonviolent direct action may not be the method for transforming the macro-systems of American society. But it can be brought to bear in many cases where the conditions of a minority community differ markedly from the standards accepted as just and normal for the majority community. Needless to say, enclaves of poverty where Black, Brown and Red people live are rife with such issues. . . .

KING'S ECONOMIC AND POLITICAL STRATEGIES

In the last chapter of his book, *Why We Can't Wait*, King envisions a number of strategies for change that should be developed. These include many ideas that were later taken up under the rubric of Black Power. King suggests preferential hiring of Blacks to overcome the handicaps of a history of discrimination. He declares the need to develop Black economic power to make civil rights meaningful. What difference does it make if you can now drink a cup of coffee at an integrated lunch counter, if you don't have the money to pay for it? He suggests something like the GI Bill of Rights for disadvantaged persons to give them educational loans, job training, housing and business loans to compensate for the centuries and the earnings lost due to slavery and exploitative wages. America needs to pay these people back even more than it needed to pay back the servicemen who gave their time to their country during war. He calls for a variety of social service, such as Head Start [early childhood education], to break the cycle of poverty. He demands that the Federal government become the agent of enforcement of equal rights, rather than leaving it to the poor to litigate for their rights. Finally he suggests that Blacks organize politically and be prepared to engage in Black bloc voting in areas, such as Southern counties and inner cities, where Blacks form majorities. Blacks should not just vote individually within white choices and organizations, but organize the Black vote for Black interests and to turn racists out of government.

King was also a dedicated internationalist. He was always aware of the rise of American Blacks in relation to the worldwide struggle of colonized peoples in Africa and elsewhere against Western imperialism. Black pride in America could draw new strength from the new Black nations of Africa. Thus Martin King was not behind those who would see the American Movement in the context of Pan-Africanism.

But King went beyond the ideas advocated by Black Power at several points. First of all he remained always sensitive to the issue of war. All humanity had an urgent need to develop new values and ways of living together if it was to avert the nuclear holocaust that was being prepared by the cult of warfare. He hoped that the Black non-violent struggle might be a prelude to this larger need to end the world of war. At the conclusion of *Why We Can't Wait*, he wrote:

> More and more people have begun to conceive of this powerful ethic as a necessary way of life in a world where the wildly accelerated development of nuclear power has brought into being weapons that can annihilate all humanity. Political agreements are no longer secure enough to safeguard life against a peril of such devastating finality. . . .
>
> It is no longer merely the idealist or the doom-ridden who seeks for some controlling force capable of challenging the instrumentalities of destruction. Many are searching. Sooner or later all the peoples of the world, without regard to the political systems under which they live, will have to discover a way to live together in peace.
>
> Man was born into barbarism when killing his fellow man was a normal condition of existence. He became endowed with a conscience. And now he has reached the day when violence toward another human being must become as abhorrent as eating another's flesh.
>
> Non-violence, the answer to the Negro's need, may become the answer to the most desperate need of all humanity. (pp. 168–9)

THE COALITION OF THE POOR

Another important element in King's heritage that we need to re-examine today is his effort to create a coalition between the poor of all races: Black, Brown, Red and White. King understood the inter-structuring of racism and poverty. He also understood that poverty cannot be merely identified with racism. The American system is built on structural exploitation that has cast a large percentage of people at the bottom.

Today automation is making the poverty of the unskilled endemic. Without a significant change in the economic system, some 10–12 percent of the American population are doomed to permanent under- and un-employment. Racism ensures that people of color are disproportionately lumped at this bottom end of the scale, so that un-employment is likely to reach 30 percent in Black communities. But merely redistributing the structures of affluence more equally between the races would not end this systemic injustice. If Blacks were equally distributed among the classes, the injustice of poverty would remain.

King was concerned not to let the Black struggle be turned into a rivalry with other exploited communities—the school integration issue in South Boston being a classic case in point. In fact, this was exactly the original purpose of the Jim Crow laws. The Southern ruling class in the 1880's sought to prevent a populist coalition between Black and White poor by creating a special caste structure that set Blacks below even the poorest White. The white poor was thus given a stake in racism and was unable to unite with Blacks around their common economic interests. King was concerned that special compensation for Blacks reach out to the white disadvantaged community also, and not allow the system again to divide and conquer them. For this reason, when King proposed something like a GI Bill of Rights, he declared that this should be a Bill of Rights for the historically disadvantaged, including the white poor.

> To this day the white poor also suffer deprivation and the humiliation of poverty, if not of color. They are chained by the weight of discrimination, though its badge of degradation does not mark them. It corrupts their lives, frustrates their opportunities and withers their education. In one sense, it is more evil for them, because it has confused so many by prejudice that they have supported their own oppressors. (p. 152)

When the assassin's bullet struck him down, King was moving more directly down this path of creating alliances across racial lines in union struggles such as the garbage men's strike and the Poor People's March.

THE RESPONSE OF THE WHITE POWER STRUCTURE

As we survey the history of the nine years [1968–1977] that has elapsed since King's death, we can recognize the way in which the ruling classes have coopted not only Civil Rights into an 'integrationalism' that preserves white institutional power, but also has domesticated much that has gone under the rubric of Black Power. The White power structure appears to be more committed to the class structure of exploitative property relations, than to strict racial apartheid. That is to say, some redistribution of wealth and opportunity can be permitted between races within the middle class, but *not between classes*. Racial (and sexual) tokenism remains a policy of the federal government, but all that smacked of the 'War on Poverty' of the late 60's has been systematically dismantled under Richard Nixon and Gerald Ford. Redistribution of opportunities between white males, some black males and white females can be envisioned within the middle class because this consolidates and strengthens the middle class itself. But the basic economic profile of class exploitation is not touched by this.

The advocacy of Black Power, without an analysis of the class divisions that divide the whole society, dividing the Blacks internally as well; a Black Power that denies the possibility of coalition with whites and other races along class lines; all this allows Black Power to be coopted into a middle class framework. The white institution interprets this to mean that any Black, but preferably those fully qualified by middle class cultural and economic status, can be deployed as a token of the new 'racial justice'. The Black middle class is thus drawn into and scattered among White institutions to play this role of Black presence and therefore cut off from leadership of the Black community. (The same strategy can be observed among other ethnic groups, of course). Ironically enough, the Black Power refusal to recognize the significance of class divisions between Blacks, instead of building Black inter-class solidarity, allows the actual division to be ignored and mystified. The result today is the wide-ranging display of the Black presence in all major institutions and media. This is seen as the conquest of 'racism'. In this way the society turns away from the fact that the poor Black communities, far from being lifted by this process, are continually slipping into further marginality within the economic system.

This is not to suggest that middle class Black achievement is to be 'denegrated'. It is to be acclaimed in every way, for this is what gives the lie once and for all to the myth of racial inferiority. But we must also recognize the basic class structure of capitalism that prevents this middle class achievement from 'trickling down' to the poor community, and even sets it structurally against the poor. In addition to his challenge to the war-makers, the most radical and relevant aspect of King's heritage for us today is his decision toward the end of his life, to move beyond Civil Rights and to build a coalition among the poor. This would be the great alliance of the exploited that would unite the Black serfs of the South, the Black and Puerto Rican prisoners of the ghettos, the Chicanos and Blacks of the Migrant labor camps, the Appalachian whites shorn of their livelihood by strip mining, and the Indians who languish in the reservations. This was the 'rainbow coalition' of the poor that King envisioned building in 1968. Is it any accident that at that point Washington (and Wall Street?) decided that they could tolerate him no longer?

King's Relevance Today

Samuel DuBois Cook

Samuel DuBois Cook asks if King's positions are defensible and vindicated in a society seemingly moving away from them. After all, King called for nonviolence and died violently; he strove for racial justice, but black/white problems persist; and he fought against racism, but segregation remains. Nevertheless, Cook argues that King's legacy is as relevant today as it was when he was alive.

Cook suggests that King represents America at its best, an America that personifies equality, justice, and the celebration of community and individualism. King was an example of the transformative power of America, a nation that can transcend and correct its divided self. However, Cook acknowledges that King was, at times, too optimistic, particularly in his overestimation of the country's sense of justice and his underestimation of the depth of racial hatred in America.

Cook believes that one of King's greatest attributes was his belief in the higher possibilities of the human spirit. King's fight to celebrate and nurture the human spirit made a creative difference in history by touching the hearts and aspirations of all people, both the oppressed and the oppressors. He worked to emancipate all people, for he saw an interdependence and oneness of humankind. Cook argues that King's character provided an example for all people, exemplifying impeccable standards of humility, sensitivity, morality, and, most importantly, love. Cook writes that King's greatest legacy was his ability to draw upon the redemptive power of love, transforming it from an abstraction to an authentic foundation for everyday life.

Samuel DuBois Cook was a classmate of Martin Luther King Jr. at Morehouse College. He was a professor of political science at Duke University, Durham, North Carolina, and is currently working with the Ford Foundation.

Excerpted from Samuel DuBois Cook, "Is Martin Luther King Jr. Irrelevant?" in *New South*, Spring 1971. Reprinted by permission of the author.

He did not have much time. But is the legacy of Martin Luther King, Jr. both timely and timeless? He preached and practiced love and nonviolence, but his own life, in its noon-day brightness and zest, was snuffed out by hate and violence. Does this mean that love and nonviolence are not the way to the betterment of human life? With prophetic eloquence and passion, he proclaimed a vision of the beloved community, but polarization and other forms of human estrangement, like angry ghosts and vengeful gods, increasingly stalk and haunt this troubled land.

THE RELEVANCE OF KING'S IDEAS TODAY

Nonviolence was a key to his philosophy, but the cult of violence is steadily winning converts, and there has been an upsurge in acts of terrorism and barbarism. Does this mean that nonviolence has lost its creative role, staying power, moral weight, and practical validity? He taught and lived by the principle that means and ends are intimately wedded in the whole context of life and hence are inseparable, but it is increasingly fashionable to deny that organic unity and to insist, instead, on the philosophy of "any means necessary" or the philosophy that ends, somehow, flow from or grow out of means, that means, through some mysterious process, generate or create ends. Does this indicate that the former position is no longer capable of rational defense, moral justification, and pragmatic vindication?

He was an apostle and uncompromising champion of racial justice, but, because of the depth and persistence of white racism, the country's mood on the black man's quest for equality of citizenship and humanity has gone from hope to despair, from optimism to pessimism. Does it follow that the situation is hopeless, that the light of creative possibility has gone out, that black men are trapped between the twin perils of the Scylla of self-defeating acts of desperation and the Charybdis of romantic schemes of escapism? Or perhaps slow and painful spiritual, psychological, and intellectual death through the continuity of oppression?

In ringing tones, he was an exponent of integration, but segments of the black community see separatism as the wave of the future, and the vast majority of whites have demonstrated no inclination to escape from the prison of a preconceived, narrowly restricted, alienated, and controlled life and culture of blacks. Does this mean that integration, conceived in terms of equality of shared power and purpose, is either unworthy of pursuit or impossible of attainment?

He was the chief engineer, symbolic figure, and unifying focus in the formation and execution of the powerful and remarkable coalition of the Civil Rights Movement, but is not that coalition a thing of the distant past, a faded memory, and has not the Movement itself been duly awarded an official death certificate? He was the major architect and patron saint of the Black Revolution, but, oh come now, do not the land, great causes, and the future belong to the living, not the dead?

KING'S DEDICATION TO HIS CAUSE

In a speech delivered on April 8, 1968, Coretta Scott King reflected on the meaning of her husband's death and his commitment to a higher goal.

He often said, unearned suffering is redemptive, and if you give your life to a cause in which you believe, and which is right and just—and it is—and if your life comes to an end as a result of this, then your life could not have been lived in a more redemptive way. And I think that this is what my husband has done.

But then I ask the question: How many men must die before we can really have a free and true and peaceful society? How long will it take? If we can catch the spirit, and the true meaning of this experience, I believe that this nation can be transformed into a society of love, of justice, peace, and brotherhood where all men can really be brothers.

Coretta Scott King, *My Life with Martin Luther King, Jr.* New York: Holt, Rinehart and Winston, 1969.

In his tragic absence, Martin Luther King, Jr., exerts a powerful and agonizing presence. He is, somehow, as troubling in death as he was in life. Have history and destiny caught up with and overrun Dr. King and his legacy? Some say that he and his ideas, once meaningful, useful, necessary, indeed a godsend, have become irrelevant, but is it more valid to assert that they are today more relevant than ever?

On January 15, 1971, he would have been, incredibly, only 42 years old, not exactly a point in the autobiographical journey when men worry about the joy and pain of retirement and the perils and uncertain certainties of the aging process.

In order are reflections on the meaning and relevance of his life, character, philosophy, and legacy. . . .

KING'S LEGACY DEFINES AMERICA

Martin Luther King, Jr. and his legacy are about what America, at its best and in its ultimate dimensions, is about: freedom, justice, equality, the value and dignity of the human person, and community which, in turn, are essential to the experience and enjoyment of the larger, deeper, and higher possibilities, meanings, and values of the human mind and spirit.

He and his legacy are about the America which ought to be and which, through human intelligence, will, organization, leadership, imagination, priority, and commitment, can be. They are about America's transcendence over its divided, estranged, and contradictory self, born of the radical gulf and tension between promise and fulfillment, ideal and reality, commitment and performance. They are deeply rooted in the fertile soil of the American liberal, democratic, humanistic, and idealistic tradition. What does America mean? What does it mean to be an American? What are American ideals, goals, and principles? What are the promises of the land?

KING'S OPTIMISM

In view of the record of tragedy and ambivalence, it is significant, and perhaps somewhat strange, that Martin Luther King, Jr., until the darkness of death engulfed him, maintained robust faith in the creative and redemptive possibilities of the land. Despite his epic struggles, disappointments, frustrations, bitter defeats, and perhaps occasional dashes of disillusionment, he, in terms of general outlook and basic pattern of belief and conduct, kept the faith. And he was able to impart that faith to others. Doubts, from time to time, there could have been, but of faith there was always much more. Time, experience, and reflection moderated and sobered his exuberant faith, but pervasive optimism remained. He doggedly believed that the country would, at last, kick the terrible habit of racism and do justice by black people. This strong and stubborn faith in America, the character of her people, the viability and self-corrective quality of her institutions and processes, and the creative power of her ideals is an integral and chief part of the King legacy. He believed. His soaring optimism was, by the way, characteristically American.

That kind of faith is not easy for a black man. It is indeed hard to come by. The evidence for such a faith is mixed and ambiguous. It provides partial justification and partial refutation. Symbolic and indicative of the duality and ambivalence of the realities of experience, the black man must believe and doubt and combine hopefulness and skepticism. It is not easy to be a black American.

Dr. King's optimism raises an intriguing question: the functional relationship of belief and power, will and reality. Was his faith one of the secrets of his phenomenal power? Did it help the country better see itself and its higher possibilities, enlarge its imagination and heighten its sensitivities? Did it enable the country to develop a little more self-belief, self-integrity, and self-appreciation? Belief and mood can make a difference in the outcome of social movements and other human encounters; they affect, at times, the structure, distribution, and process of power—the allocation of benefits and rewards.

In general, Dr. King was, I think, excessively optimistic. He overestimated the country's active sense of justice, moral and rational resources, will for a new order in race relations, and sense of guilt and shame over the dehumanized role of black people. He underestimated—as we all once did—the radical depths, persistence, intensity, and self-contained character of racism. Ironically, progress disclosed the naked depths, complexities, and subtleties of racism and hence was a master teacher of us all. Thus Dr. King's optimism was indeed understandable, though events and experience proved it not entirely justifiable.

But the court of truth is still out and thus has not rendered a final verdict. Although in a heated and cruel race with destiny, the future, which is in large part open and filled with alternative choices and possibilities, will make the final judgment. In the ultimate analysis, the brute realities of time and experience will determine the validity of Dr. King's optimism about the country. The answer, in truth, is largely in the hands of white America—White Power. Judged from the current mood, leadership, direction, priorities, and commitment, the prospects, at this critical juncture, are bleak. Qualified pessimism is not only justifiable but an essential, rational, and healthy imperative. Sober reflection insists on the conditional mood.

KING'S FAITH IN THE HUMAN SPIRIT

Martin Luther King, Jr., was a passionate and actively committed moralist and prophet who, as [French philosopher] Jacques Maritain said of the Angelic Doctor, was always about his Father's business. That business was enrichment and enlargement of the quality of the human condition. In grappling with the massive and complex problems of human conflict, aspiration, and community, his life discloses something profound, enduring, and ennobling about the *higher possibilities* of the human spirit. I cannot reflect upon his life, character, and work without a deep sense of awe and wonder.

His life made a *creative difference* in history, touching the longings of the human heart and aspirations of the human spirit. He inspired. He moved men, events, institutions, and forces. He led. He combined protest and affirmation, rebellion and solidarity, realism and idealism, power and morality, criticism and construction, vision and technique, love and militance. What a man!

Not the least of his contributions was his service as catalyst of, and model for, non-black social movements involving groups who, too, cry bitterly for justice, social reform, and a new day of meaning, value, and self-realization. We refer to Mexican-Americans, American Indians, Puerto Ricans, poor whites, students and other young people, the women's liberation movement, and the peace movement.

KING'S CHARACTER

The character of the man was as remarkable, significant, and fascinating as his ideas and leadership. He was an exceptionally good, civilized, and sensitive human being. His character, integrity, spiritual strength, and moral courage were of genuinely rare quality. He was an embarrassment to us ordinary mortals. I admired his humility; he was singularly devoid of arrogance and self-worship. He was haunted by a sense of his own frailties and limitations. His self-standards were high. He was more concerned with his private reality than his public image.

I was moved by his selfless public service, self-sacrificial commitments, sense of personal responsibility, willingness to accept the consequences of his choices and conduct, feeling of moral urgency, moral outrage at social injustice, identification with the poor, weak, powerless, and disinherited regardless of race, culture, or nationality, inordinate compassion for human suffering and pity for human folly, and rock-like determination not to add to the miseries, tragedies, and woes of the world.

I admired Dr. King's staggering moral self-mastery and purity of motives in avoiding bitterness, hatred, ill-will, and poison and meanness of spirit and hence the ability to overcome the "natural" and "understandable" desire for revenge and retaliation against racial oppression, and his boundless love of, and good will toward, all men—including various kinds and degrees of enemies. He sought not to "do in" his enemies but to convert them into friends. "Love your enemies" is the most difficult, mind-jarring, ego-transcending, and revolutionary ethical imperative ever uttered. In earnest, Dr. King sought desperately to do just that. No one knows how well or poorly he succeeded, but everyone knows that it takes a lot of moral character and guts to try and to judge one's self by that standard. The motive and goal are embarrassing and painful enough. The effort is worthy of the divine. I do not believe that Dr. King hated or harbored ill-will toward any man or group. This is moral character of the highest order.

Dr. King had a rare capacity to forgive, even those who sought, in every conceivable way, to destroy him, his family, the ideals he cherished, the causes he espoused, and the Movement he led. His leadership, involving the power, ideological, and personality clashes of the contemporary scene, was saturated with these magnificent personal qualities. The man was both too wise and too foolish to forget that the Movement he led was ultimately moral, and that the moral element is the capstone of public leadership.

In view of human nature and the psychology of power and prestige—specifically, the corruptibility of power and prestige—I was always struck by M.L.'s (in college, we called him M.L.) remarkable humility. To my amazement, his monumental achievements to the contrary notwithstanding, he avoided, at least from my angle of vision (which was not always distant), the tragic corruptions of power. He displayed, until the flame of his life was extinguished, the same gentleness, sense of humor, friendliness, warmth, personal charm, down-to-earthness, and just plain sweetness of personality that marked our years in college. Inevitably, I thought, with the cocksureness of Thrasymachus [a philosopher in Plato's *The Republic*], the psychology of power and fame would get to and intoxicate him. I couldn't have been more wrong. At the height of his power and fame in 1964, I said to my wife, Sylvia, that "M.L. has more humility than the average college professor—including this one—and other professional persons I know." He did not succumb to the sin of *hubris*. He took seriously [Medieval Church father and theologian] St. Augustine's assertion that humility is the first virtue, the second, and the third.

In all his mighty struggles of power and ideology, Dr. King demonstrated character, integrity, and moral courage. He did not compromise his principles. Unity, continuity, and integrity marked his character, thought, and action. There was no moral hypocrisy or guile in him. He believed what he taught and put it into the brutal engagements of the stubborn and cruel realities of power and confrontation with which he wrestled. *He sought to moralize power struggles, phenomena, and relations.* His philosophical, social, and ethical tenets were an integral part of the structure of his being. "The ideals cherished in the souls of men," said [English mathematician and philosopher] Alfred North Whitehead, "enter into the character of their actions."

Some men are literally slaves of principles and ideals, which define and structure their lives, meaning, freedom, needs, and whole being. Dr. King was such a man. I could have been wrong, but I always got the feeling that he was so deeply and totally committed to love and nonviolence that if, through some strictly mysterious, private, and personal process, he could have brought about the beloved community and the Kingdom of God in history by means of a little hate and violence he would have, after prayer and meditation, refused the opportunity. He had too much integrity and character for that. "*Oh yes,*" I think he would have said, "but what about my soul?" On the question of fidelity to principles, the man was indeed an "extremist." Not a few—and they all were not his enemies—called him a fool.

THE IMPORTANCE OF LOVE

Love was the key to the character, thought, and labors of Martin Luther King, Jr. It is the supreme law of human life. It is creative and redemptive. By love he meant nothing about the romanticization of life. He meant neither *eros* (sensual, romantic, sentimental) nor *philia* (mutuality, reciprocity, fraternity). He had in mind, rather, active human understanding, good will, redemptive concern for others, sympathetic imagination and identification with human needs beyond self-interest. This love, he held, is the proper motivation, norm, end, and means.

What is striking about Dr. King was his interpretation, application, and extension of the ancient ideal of love—how he sought to use it and to let it use him. He sought desperately to bring love to bear on social conflict and the struggles, processes, and structures of power in history. The attempt to unite love and power not in the quiet and solitary adventures of philosophic discourse, ethical contemplation, and theological speculation but in the hurly-burly, the pushing and shoveling, the claims and counter-claims, and tensions and ambiguities of the marketplace of daily encounter and power relations—that is the heroic legacy of Martin Luther King, Jr.

Love, in Dr. King's view, is supremely relevant to methods and processes of social change and stability. It is more than a way of avoiding social conflict; it is also a way for the management and resolution of social conflict. A chief office of love is the direction and control of power. A major office of power is to be the servant of love—and never love's master. The way of love in social movements expresses strength, not weakness, courage, not cowardice, militance, not subservience. Love is crucial because the end of action is sovereign. The ultimate end is, after all, reconciliation, redemption, and creation of the beloved community. Efforts at social change are meaningful and justifiable only in terms of a better world.

Hate is a mighty poor basis for a social philosophy and methodology of social change and progress. It is ultimately self-defeating. It can destroy but cannot build. After destruction, what? What new system will replace the old? What follows the revolution? Hate can tear apart, but it cannot heal. Hate is a self-feeding cancer in the body politic. "Along the way of life, someone must have sense enough and morality enough to cut off the chain of hate." Hate militates against community.

> He who works against community is working against the whole of creation. Therefore, if I respond to hate with a reciprocal hate I do nothing but intensify the cleavage in broken community. I can only close the gap in broken community by meeting hate with love. If I meet hate with hate, I become depersonalized, creation is so designed that my personality can only be fulfilled in the context of community.

The human person is at once too large and too small, too creative and too destructive, and too full of both virtue and defect to make hate the basis of life and the foundation of choice and conduct. This applies, even more so, to groups and collective relationships.

Inherent in Dr. King's philosophy of love is a profound sense of human community. With the increased polarization, fragmentation, conflict, tension, intolerance, fanaticism, hate, and ill-will in the land, Dr. King's ideas remind us of the common basis of life and the solidarity of the human enterprise. Crises tend to obscure the deep bonds of the common life. Community is precious. And the sense of community is the antidote to destructive conflicts, irrational divisions, and various forms of fratricide.

Martin Luther King, Jr. sought to find himself by losing himself in the needs, aspirations, miseries, and agonies of his fellows—both the oppressors and the oppressed, both whites and blacks, both rich and poor. For, according to him, freedom and justice are indivisible, and hence oppression enslaves the oppressor as well as the oppressed. Emancipation of the oppressed is a necessary condition of the liberation of the oppressor. Human solidarity, mutuality, moral autonomy, and self-realization are impossible under conditions of oppression and other forms of social injustice. "Injustice anywhere," he said, "is a threat to justice everywhere. We are caught up in an inescapable network of mutuality, tied in a single garment of destiny. Whatever affects one directly, affects all indirectly." I like that.

The interdependence and oneness of mankind Dr. King saw operating on a number of levels. Poverty, hunger, starvation, and malnutrition in this rich land with a GNP (Gross National Product) of a trillion dollars are a moral scandal, social disgrace, and political shame. Dr. King viewed the existence of poverty not only in terms of the material misery and degradation of millions of men, women, and children but also in the larger perspective of militating against, and subversion of, community, the kinship and solidarity of human life. "In a real sense, all life is interrelated. The agony of the poor impoverishes the rich; the betterment of the poor enriches the rich. We are inevitably our brother's keeper because we are our brother's brother."

The Impact of King's "I Have a Dream" Speech

Nicolaus Mills

Nicolaus Mills assesses the power and impact of King's most famous speech, "I Have a Dream," delivered at the 1963 civil rights protest March on Washington. Mills suggests that the purpose of the speech was to pressure Congress into passing President John F. Kennedy's civil rights legislation. In order to avoid antagonizing Congress, King designed a speech that was inspirational and visionary but would not incite his listeners to violent or disruptive behavior.

According to Mills, King's speech was self-conscious until King began to speak extemporaneously. King offered his dream, a dream that pushed beyond civil rights to present a civil religion, a nation's destiny, and God's will. In short, Mills writes that it was one of America's finest tributes to hope.

Mills believes that King's speech was crucial to the civil rights movement because it worked to unite black leaders, it forced the public and media to reflect on the need for protest, and it inspired biracial coalitions. The speech also had a tremendous impact on President Kennedy. Prior to the March on Washington, Kennedy was afraid of the negative impact the protest might have on his presidency and he worked to discourage the crusade's organizers. But the march's success and King's popularity redeemed Kennedy, shedding a positive light on his image and the president's civil rights strategy. Mills claims that Kennedy shared in the optimism and Americanism that King eloquently portrayed in his landmark speech.

Nicolaus Mills is a professor of American Studies at Sarah Lawrence College in Bronxville, New York. His books include *The New Journalism, Culture in an Age of Money,* and *The Crowd in American Literature.*

Excerpted from *Like a Holy Crusade: Mississippi 1964: The Turning of the Civil Rights Movement in America,* by Nicolaus Mills. Copyright ©1992 by Nicolaus Mills. Reprinted by permission of Ivan R. Dee, Publisher.

It is difficult to recall a political demonstration so associated with one man as the 1963 March on Washington. By the time he finished his "I have a dream" speech, the day was Martin Luther King's. The most prophetic speech given that hot August afternoon was not, however, King's. It was that of John Lewis, the new SNCC [Student Nonviolent Coordinating Committee] chairman. In his tone, in his deliberate distancing of himself from the civil rights establishment, Lewis forecast the event that in 1964 would transform the civil rights movement in the Deep South—the Mississippi Summer Project.

But it is with King, not Lewis, that the drama of the March on Washington begins. From the start King wanted his speech to be brief, "sort of a Gettysburg Address." He would, he knew, be following a long list of speakers. A fiery sermon would not do, not for this audience. The aim of the march was to pressure Congress into passing President Kennedy's civil rights bill. Demonstration, not civil disobedience, the march sponsors agreed, would be the order of the day. It was crucial to make sure the crowd that came to Washington stayed calm and did nothing to offend the congressmen on whom final passage of civil rights legislation depended. In an earlier meeting with the leaders of the march, the president had gone out of his way to warn against "the wrong kind of demonstration at the wrong time."

KING'S SPEAKING STYLE

Once King took the microphone and looked at the two hundred thousand people gathered around the reflecting pool of the Lincoln Memorial, however, he knew that neither he nor any of the march sponsors had imagined a gathering on this scale. Downtown Washington was deserted, but everywhere King looked there were people. They were even perched in the trees bordering the reflecting pool. The marchers had begun assembling at the Washington Monument in the early dawn. By 10:30 there were fifty thousand of them, by noon more than one hundred thousand. Opening the program, A. Philip Randolph, the seventy-four-year-old director of the march, announced, "We are gathered here in the largest demonstration in the history of this nation." King, too, was awed. As he waited for the applause that greeted him to die down, his movements were stiff, almost jerky. He started out reading his prepared speech; only after he had gotten through most of it did he begin to speak extemporaneously.

It was a decision that made all the difference in the world. Until his "I have a dream" peroration, there was little in King's speech that moved his audience. He had tried too hard to write an updated Gettysburg Address. As he began reading from his prepared text, what emerged was not moral passion but historical self-consciousness. It was a speech so dominated by carefully crafted metaphors that it left little room for spontaneity. In Lincolnesque fashion King began, "Five score years ago, a great American, in whose symbolic shadow we stand today, signed the Emancipation Proclamation." Next came an even more elaborate historical reference—to the promissory note signed by the Founding Fathers when they wrote the Declaration of Independence and the Constitution. "It is obvious today that America has defaulted on this promissory note, insofar as citizens of color are concerned," King declared. "Instead of honoring this sacred obligation, America has given the Negro people a bad check, a check which has come back marked 'insufficient funds.'"

"But we refuse to believe that the bank of justice is bankrupt," King continued. "*Now* is the time to make real the promises of Democracy. *Now* is the time to rise from the dark and desolate valley of segregation to the sunlit path of racial justice." Then, after a litany of all that was wrong with black life in America, King moved on to another appeal for action. "We cannot be satisfied so long as the Negro in Mississippi cannot vote and the Negro in New York believes he has nothing for which to vote," he insisted. "No, we are not satisfied, and we will not be satisfied until justice rolls down like waters and righteousness like a mighty stream."

KING'S CALL FOR A CIVIL RELIGION

Once King began to speak of his dream, however, what he had to say became an altogether different story. "I'd used it many times before, that thing about 'I have a dream,'" King later acknowledged. But in the context of the March on Washington, there was nothing used about King's peroration. It transformed his words so that his speech no longer had a clear-cut beginning, middle, and end. It became instead a dialogue between him and the crowd. King offered a dream. The crowd answered back with applause. King responded with a new dream. It was no longer just civil rights that King was talking about now, it was civil religion—the nation's destiny as the accomplishment of God's will. God's purposes, American history, and the fate of the nation's black population became inseparable as King described his dream. His "I have a dream" refrain was the Bible made political, the Southern revivalist tradition linked to the idea of equality.

King cited the Declaration of Independence, then pictured the sons of former slaves and the sons of former slave owners sitting down together at the table of brotherhood. He quoted Isaiah, "Every valley shall be exalted and every hill and mountain shall be made low," and imagined freedom ringing from "every hill and molehill of Mississippi." He called for the day when "all of God's children will be able to sing with new meaning, 'My country 'tis of thee, sweet land of liberty.'" And he ended by envisioning a future in which the entire nation would "join hands and sing in the words of the old Negro spiritual, 'Free at last. Free at last. Thank God, Almighty, we are free at last.'"

King's vision took the country from its beginnings to the present, and as he repeated his "I have a dream" peroration (four times in the first paragraph that he used it, eight times in all), the momentousness of what he was saying began to build. Each dream stood on its own yet melted into the others. And as the process repeated itself, the hope King was expressing became more tenable. During the Revolution and later during the Civil War, the country had been tested, King made clear, as to whether it believed all men are created equal. Now it was being tested again, and it was not too much to think it could triumph again, that the heritage of Washington and Lincoln was alive in 1963.

In the next day's *New York Times,* columnist James Reston summed up King's speech by comparing his words with those of Roger Williams, Sam Adams, Henry Thoreau, William Lloyd Garrison, and Eugene Debs. "Each time the dream was a promise out of our ancient articles of faith: phrases from the Constitution, lines from the great anthem of the nation, guarantees from the Bill of Rights, all ending with the vision that they might one day all come true," Reston wrote. It was the kind of front-page analysis political speeches rarely receive in this country, but King had created a context in which Reston's praise did not seem extravagant. By the time King finished, there was no base he had failed to touch. Built on repetition, his speech grew stronger as it was replayed on television in homes across the country. One did

not have to be in the crowd at the Lincoln Memorial to iden-
tify with the hope it expressed.

IMPACT OF THE MARCH ON WASHINGTON

King's success at the March on Washington was especially
crucial for the civil rights movement. Plans for the march
had been in the works since 1962, when A. Philip Randolph,
the founder and president of the Brotherhood of Sleeping
Car Porters, proposed a "mass descent" on Washington that
would draw public attention to the economic plight of blacks
in America and the need for more civil rights legislation. But
by early 1963 it seemed unlikely that such a march would
happen. Randolph could not get other civil rights leaders to
agree that the time was right. Only in June, when Martin
Luther King concluded that the civil rights demonstrations
he had been leading in Birmingham against Public Safety
Commissioner Bull Connor and the city's merchants needed
the support of national protests, did prospects for holding
the march revive. Even then, the civil rights leadership was
divided over how the march should be conducted and who
should pay for it. The expense problem was removed when
Stephen Currier, president of the liberal Taconic Foundation, proposed the establishment of the Council for United
Civil Rights Leadership (CUCRL), which would serve as a
clearing house for allocating the larger contributions that
Currier himself promised to solicit on behalf of the march.
But not until June 24 was the date for the march set, and
even then infighting continued. The NAACP's [National Association for the Advancement of Colored People] Roy
Wilkins [NAACP executive secretary] objected to the appointment of [protest organizer] Bayard Rustin as director of
the march because Rustin had spent time in prison for refusing to serve in the army and had an arrest record for ho-
mosexuality. (Rustin was instead given the title of deputy director.) The leadership of SNCC was unhappy with the
decision of the march sponsors to forbid civil disobedience.

King's speech did not erase such internal differences, but
it did deflect public attention from what divided the march's
black leaders, who, in addition to Randolph and King, included Roy Wilkins of the NAACP, John Lewis of SNCC,
James Farmer of CORE [Congress of Racial Equality], and
Whitney M. Young, Jr., of the National Urban League. King's
vision of a civil rights movement rooted in a belief in Amer-

ican justice forced the public and the media to think about the reasons for the march. After King finished speaking, it was easy for Bayard Rustin to step to the podium and get the crowd to roar its approval of the goals of the march. The nation was put in the same position. In the face of King's dream, it seemed petty to dwell on the divisions among the march's six black sponsors.

King's speech also furthered the kind of biracial coalition which the established civil rights movement believed was needed in order to get action from Congress. In addition to the black sponsors of the march, there were four key whites: Walter Reuther, president of the United Automobile Workers; Matthew Ahmann, director of the National Catholic Conference for Interracial Justice; Rabbi Joachim Prinz, president of the American Jewish Congress; and the Reverend Eugene Carson Blake from the National Council of Churches. King's speech not only said they were welcome; it said that in a country where racial justice was both a religious and a secular concern, the kinds of organizations these men represented had an obligation to participate in the civil rights movement.

THE RELATIONSHIP BETWEEN KING AND PRESIDENT KENNEDY

Finally, King's triumph at the March on Washington was crucial for the Kennedy administration. The relationship between King and Kennedy had become extremely complicated by 1963. During the 1960 presidential campaign Kennedy publicly intervened to have King released from a Georgia jail. In 1963, when King was jailed in Alabama, Kennedy acted again, this time calling his wife Coretta King to assure her that the FBI had ascertained that her husband was safe. The calls earned Kennedy the gratitude of the King family as well as a great many black votes. But the calls did not make King look the other way when the Kennedy administration sought to keep "order" in the South rather than support black protest. In early June, King made headlines when he described the president's record on civil rights as "inadequate" and charged him with not living up to his campaign promises.

Only reluctantly did the president commit himself to supporting the March on Washington. It was not until June 22, after plans for an August march were announced, that the president asked its leaders to the White House. At that meeting he did everything in his power, short of asking them to call off the march, to discourage them from going ahead with it. "It seemed to me a great mistake to announce a March on Washington before the [civil rights] bill was even in committee," the president told the march leaders. "Now we are in a new phase, the legislative phase, and results are essential. . . . We have, first, to oppose demonstrations which will lead to violence, and, second, give Congress a fair chance to work its will." Three weeks passed before the president gave his formal blessing to the march. In doing so, he pointed out to the press that he viewed it as "not a march on the capital" but a "peaceful assembly calling for a redress of grievances."

Kennedy was gambling. By blessing the march in advance, he wanted to make sure that its target would be the Southern senators who opposed his civil rights bill and not his own record on civil rights. The national reaction to King's "I have a dream" speech redeemed that strategy. The optimism of King's speech, its equation of civil rights and Americanism, was tailor-made to the political image the Kennedy administration wished to project. The order maintained by the marchers added to that image. Neither the two thousand National Guardsmen called to duty in Washington nor the troops standing by in Maryland and Virginia needed to be brought to the march. Indeed, there was scarcely a need for the twenty-nine hundred Washington police whose leaves were canceled on the day of the march. A five-hundred-man cleanup squad organized by Bayard Rustin picked up the trash the huge crowd had left behind. At the end of the day the president no longer had to worry that he had made a mistake in supporting the march. He could share in the march's triumph by inviting its leaders to the White House and announcing, "This nation can properly be proud of the demonstration that has occurred here today. The leaders of the organizations sponsoring the march and all who have participated in it deserve our appreciation for the detailed preparations that made it possible and for the orderly manner in which it has been conducted."

Discussion Questions

Chapter One

1. Aldon D. Morris identifies three social institutions that worked to develop black leaders like Martin Luther King Jr. Name the three and explain how each worked to strengthen the black community.

2. Coretta Scott King explained that Martin's visit to India to study the teachings of Gandhi was an awakening for him. Discuss how Martin was impacted by the trip.

3. Although Martin Luther King Jr. had a wide understanding of western theology, James H. Cone argues that the preacher was admired primarily for his embodiment of the black church tradition. Clarify how King drew upon the tradition of the black church.

Chapter Two

1. Hanes Walton Jr. argues that King's code of ethics is partially built on a Greek form of love called *agape*. Discuss how *agape* connects to King's commitment to nonviolence.

2. Ira G. Zepp Jr. writes that King promoted a vision of society called the beloved community. Define the beloved community by identifying its primary characteristics.

3. Adam Fairclough suggests that King had philosophical ties to the ideas of democratic socialism. Explain how this view brought King to the belief that racism is a product of economic stratification.

Chapter Three

1. At the start of the Montgomery bus boycott, Stephan and Abigail Thernstrom write, King was just twenty-six years old and a newcomer to Montgomery. Outline the events at Montgomery that moved King into the position of a prominent national civil rights leader.

2. Before the March on Washington, President John F. Kennedy was opposed to it. According to James Colaiaco,

what were Kennedy's reasons for opposing the protest? Were they justified?

3. Why does Stephen B. Oates argue that King made one of the most momentous decisions in black history when he allowed children to participate in the Birmingham demonstrations?

4. Compare and contrast King's participation in Albany and his campaign in Birmingham. In your answer explain why John A. Salmond considers Albany a failure and why Stephen B. Oates considers Birmingham a strategic success.

CHAPTER FOUR

1. Stokely Carmichael and Martin Luther King Jr. have two different definitions of black power. Compare Carmichael's definition with King's as it is presented in the John J. Ansbro article.

2. Using both the Samuel DuBois Cook and Rosemary R. Ruether articles, list the key components of King's legacy. Discuss King's relevance today.

3. Nicolaus Mills believes that King's "I Have a Dream" speech was crucial to the civil rights movement. Explain Mills's assertion and then assess the impact the speech has on you as you read it.

Appendix

Excerpts from Original Documents Pertaining to Martin Luther King Jr.

Document 1: Letter from a Birmingham Jail on Just and Unjust Laws

In an open letter to his fellow clergymen written from a Birming-ham, Alabama, jail cell on April 16, 1963, King explains the differ-ence between just and unjust laws. He writes that to break an unjust law, one must do it openly and lovingly and, subsequently, be will-ing to accept the penalty for breaking it.

One may well ask, "How can you advocate breaking some laws and obeying others?" The answer is found in the fact that there are two types of laws: there are *just* and there are *unjust* laws. I would agree with [early Christian church father and philosopher] Saint Augus-tine that "An unjust law is no law at all."

Now what is the difference between the two? How does one de-termine when a law is just or unjust? A just law is a man-made code that squares with the moral law or the law of God. An unjust law is a code that is out of harmony with the moral law. To put it in the terms of Saint Thomas Aquinas, an unjust law is a human law that is not rooted in eternal and natural law. Any law that uplifts human personality is just. Any law that degrades human personal-ity is unjust. All segregation statutes are unjust because segrega-tion distorts the soul and damages the personality. It gives the seg-regator a false sense of superiority, and the segregated a false sense of inferiority. To use the words of Martin Buber, the great Jewish philosopher, segregation substitutes an "I-it" relationship for the "I-thou" relationship, and ends up relegating persons to the status of things. So segregation is not only politically, economically and sociologically unsound, but it is morally wrong and sinful. Paul Tillich [American theologian and philosopher] has said that sin is separation. Isn't segregation an existential expression of man's tragic separation, an expression of his awful estrangement, his ter-rible sinfulness? So I can urge men to disobey segregation ordi-nances because they are morally wrong.

Let us turn to a more concrete example of just and unjust laws.

An unjust law is a code that a majority inflicts on a minority that is not binding on itself. This is a difference made legal. On the other hand a just law is a code that a majority compels a minority to follow that it is willing to follow itself. This is sameness made legal.

Let me give another explanation. An unjust law is a code inflicted upon a minority which that minority had no part in enacting or creating because they did not have the unhampered right to vote. Who can say that the legislature of Alabama which set up the segregation laws was democratically elected? Throughout the state of Alabama all types of conniving methods are used to prevent Negroes from becoming registered voters and there are some counties without a single Negro registered to vote despite the fact the Negro constitutes a majority of the population. Can any law set up in such a state be considered democratically structured?

These are just a few examples of unjust and just laws. There are some instances when a law is just on its face and unjust in its application. For instance, I was arrested Friday on a charge of parading without a permit. Now there is nothing wrong with an ordinance which requires a permit for a parade, but when the ordinance is used to preserve segregation and to deny citizens the First Amendment privilege of peaceful assembly and peaceful protest, then it becomes unjust.

I hope you can see the distinction I am trying to point out. In no sense do I advocate evading or defying the law as the rabid segregationist would do. This would lead to anarchy. One who breaks an unjust law must do it *openly, lovingly* (not hatefully as the white mothers did in New Orleans when they were seen on television screaming, "nigger, nigger, nigger"), and with a willingness to accept the penalty. I submit that an individual who breaks a law that conscience tells him is unjust, and willingly accepts the penalty by staying in jail to arouse the conscience of the community over its injustice, is in reality expressing the very highest respect for law.

Martin Luther King Jr., *Why We Can't Wait.* New York: Harper & Row, 1963. In *I Have a Dream: Writings and Speeches that Changed the World.* Ed. James Melvin Washington. San Francisco: HarperCollins, 1992.

DOCUMENT 2: PRESIDENTIAL ADDRESS TO THE SOUTHERN CHRISTIAN LEADERSHIP CONFERENCE ON NONVIOLENCE

King asserts that only nonviolence will offer substantive changes for American blacks. Violence, he contends, may stop a hater but it will not eradicate hate.

It is perfectly clear that a violent revolution on the part of American blacks would find no sympathy and support from the white population and very little from the majority of the Negroes themselves. This is no time for romantic illusions and empty philosophical debates about freedom. This is a time for action. What is needed is a strategy for change, a tactical program that will bring the Negro into the mainstream of American life as quickly as possible. So far, this has only been offered by the nonviolent movement. Without recognizing this we will end up with solutions that don't solve, answers that don't answer and explanations that don't explain.

And so I say to you today that I still stand by nonviolence. And I am still convinced that it is the most potent weapon available to the Negro in his struggle for justice in this country. And the other thing is that I am concerned about a better world. I'm concerned about justice. I'm concerned about brotherhood. I'm concerned about truth. And when one is concerned about these, he can never advocate violence. For through violence you may murder a murderer but you can't murder murder. Through violence you may murder a liar but you can't establish truth. Through violence you may murder a hater, but you can't murder hate. Darkness cannot put out darkness. Only light can do that.

Martin Luther King Jr., *Where Do We Go from Here: Chaos or Community?* New York: Harper & Row, 1967. In *I Have a Dream: Writings and Speeches that Changed the World.* Ed. James Melvin Washington. San Francisco: HarperCollins, 1992.

DOCUMENT 3: ACCEPTANCE SPEECH AFTER RECEIVING THE NOBEL PEACE PRIZE

On December 10, 1964, Martin Luther King Jr. received the Nobel Peace Prize in Oslo, Norway. In his acceptance address he insisted that nonviolence is not servile passivity; instead, it is a powerful moral force.

After contemplation, I conclude that this award [Nobel Peace Prize] which I receive on behalf of that movement [the civil rights movement] is profound recognition that nonviolence is the answer to the crucial political and moral question of our time—the need for man to overcome oppression and violence without resorting to violence and oppression.

Civilization and violence are antithetical concepts. Negroes of the United States, following the people of India, have demonstrated that nonviolence is not servile passivity, but a powerful moral force which makes for social transformation. Sooner or later, all people of the world will have to discover a way to live together in peace, and thereby transform this pending cosmic elegy into a creative psalm of brotherhood.

If this is to be achieved, man must evolve for all human conflict a method which rejects revenge, aggression and retaliation. The foundation of such a method is love.

Reprinted by arrangement with The Heirs to the Estate of Martin Luther King Jr., c/o Writers House, Inc., as agents for the proprietor, from King's Nobel Prize acceptance speech, Oslo, Norway, December 10, 1964. Copyright ©1964 by Martin Luther King Jr.; copyright renewed 1992 by The Estate of Martin Luther King Jr.

DOCUMENT 4: SPEECH AT A MEETING OF CLERGY AND LAITY CONCERNING THE VIETNAM WAR

A persistent theme in King's protest against the war in Vietnam was his claim that the war was just another symptom of the growing moral dysfunction in American life and policy.

As we counsel young men concerning military service we must clarify for them our nation's role in Vietnam and challenge them with the alternative of conscientious objection. I am pleased to say that this is the path now being chosen by more than seventy students at my own alma mater, Morehouse College, and I recommend it to all who find the American course in Vietnam a dishonorable and unjust one. Moreover I would encourage all ministers of draft age to give up their ministerial exemptions and seek status as conscientious objectors. These are the times for real choices and not false ones. We are at the moment when our lives must be placed on the line if our nation is to survive its own folly. Every man of humane convictions must decide on the protest that best suits his convictions, but we must all protest.

There is something seductively tempting about stopping there and sending us all off on what in some circles has become a popular crusade against the war in Vietnam. I say we must enter the struggle, but I wish to go on now to say something even more disturbing. The war in Vietnam is but a symptom of a far deeper malady within the American spirit, and if we ignore this sobering reality we will find ourselves organizing clergy- and laymen-concerned committees for the next generation. They will be concerned about Guatemala and Peru. They will be concerned about Thailand and Cambodia. They will be concerned about Mozambique and South Africa. We will be marching for these and a dozen other names and attending rallies without end unless there is a significant and profound change in American life and policy. Such thoughts take us beyond Vietnam, but not beyond our calling as sons of the living God.

Martin Luther King Jr., "A Time to Break the Silence," *Freedomways* 7, Spring 1967: 103–17. In *I Have a Dream: Writings and Speeches that Changed the World.* Ed. James Melvin Washington. San Francisco: HarperCollins, 1992.

DOCUMENT 5: SERMON AIRED BY THE CANADIAN BROADCASTING CORPORATION PROTESTING THE WAR IN VIETNAM

In addition to moral issues, King's opposition to the war in Vietnam is based on the fact that it is diverting funds and energy from important poverty programs at home. The extraordinarily high proportions of poor blacks who are fighting and dying in Vietnam also dismay King.

Since I am a preacher by calling, I suppose it is not surprising that I had several reasons for bringing Vietnam into the field of my moral vision. There is at the outset a very obvious and almost facile connection between the war in Vietnam and the struggle I and others have been waging in America. A few years ago there was a shining moment in that struggle. It seemed as if there was a real promise of hope for the poor, both black and white, though the poverty program. There were experiments, hopes, new beginnings. Then came the buildup in Vietnam, and I watched the program broken and eviscerated as if it were some idle political plaything of a society gone mad on war, and I knew that American would never invest the necessary funds or energies in rehabilitation of its poor so long as adventures like Vietnam continued to draw men and skills and money like some demoniacal destructive suction tube. And so I was increasingly compelled to see the war not only as a moral outrage but also as an enemy of the poor, and to attack it as such.

Perhaps a more tragic recognition of reality took place when it became clear to me that the war was doing far more than devastating the hopes of the poor at home. It was sending their sons and their brothers and their husbands to fight and die and in extraordinarily higher proportions relative to the rest of the population. We were taking the black young men who had been crippled by our society and sending them eight thousand miles away to guarantee liberties in Southeast Asia which they had not found in southwest Georgia and east Harlem. And so we have been repeatedly faced with the cruel irony of watching Negro and white boys on TV screens as they kill and die together for a nation that has been unable to seat them together in the same schools. We watch them in brutal solidarity burning the huts of a poor village, but we realize that they would never live on the same block in Detroit. I could not be silent in the face of such cruel manipulation of the poor.

Martin Luther King Jr., *The Trumpet of Conscience.* New York: Harper & Row, 1967. In *A Testament of Hope: The Essential Writings of Martin Luther King, Jr.* Ed. James Melvin Washington. San Francisco: Harper & Row, 1986.

DOCUMENT 6: ARTICLE ON BLACK POWER

In a 1967 New York Times Magazine *article King writes that power is not a white man's birthright; rather, power is a social force that must be harnessed and organized by a growing black population.*

We must turn more of our energies and focus our creativity on the useful things that translate into power. We in this generation must do the work and in doing it stimulate our children to learn and acquire higher levels of skill and technique.

It must become a crusade so vital that civil rights organizers do not repeatedly have to make personal calls to summon support. There must be a climate of social pressure in the Negro community that scorns the Negro who will not pick up his citizenship rights and add his strength enthusiastically and voluntarily to the accumulation of power for himself and his people. The past years have blown fresh winds through ghetto stagnation, but we are on the threshold of a significant change that demands a hundredfold acceleration. By 1970 ten of our larger cities will have Negro majorities if present trends continue. We can shrug off this opportunity or use it for a new vitality to deepen and enrich our family and community life.

We must utilize the community action groups and training centers now proliferating in some slum areas to create not merely an electorate, but a conscious, alert and informed people who know their direction and whose collective wisdom and vitality commands respect. The slave heritage can be cast into the dim past by our consciousness of our strengths and a resolute determination to use them in our daily experiences.

Power is not the white man's birthright; it will not be legislated for us and delivered in neat government packages. It is a social force any group can utilize by accumulating its elements in a planned, deliberate campaign to organize it under its own control.

DOCUMENT 7: SERMON ON THE NEED TO ADDRESS POVERTY IN AMERICA

In his last Sunday morning sermon delivered on March 31, 1968, at the National Cathedral in Washington, D.C., King reminds the nation that it has a moral responsibility to help the poor. He asserts that his scheduled poor people's march in Washington, D.C., is designed to call attention to the great gulf between governmental promises and fulfillment.

In a few weeks some of us are coming to Washington to see if the will is still alive or if it is alive in this nation. We are coming to Washington in a poor people's campaign. Yes, we are going to bring the tired, the poor, the huddled masses. We are going to bring those who have known long years of hurt and neglect. We are going to bring those who have come to feel that life is a long and desolate corridor with no exit signs. We are going to bring children and adults and old people; people who have never seen a doctor or a dentist in their lives.

We are not coming to engage in any histrionic gesture. We are not coming to tear up Washington. We are coming to demand that the government address itself to the problem of poverty. We read one day—We hold these truths to be self-evident, that all men are created equal, that they are endowed by their creator with certain inalienable rights. That among these are life, liberty and the pursuit of happiness. But if a man doesn't have a job or an income, he has neither life nor liberty nor the possibility for the pursuit of happiness. He merely exists.

We are coming to ask America to be true to the huge promissory note that it signed years ago. And we are coming to engage in dramatic nonviolent action, to call attention to the gulf between promise and fulfillment; to make the invisible visible.

Why do we do it this way? We do it this way because it is our experience that the nation doesn't move around questions of genuine equality for the poor and for black people until it is confronted massively, dramatically in terms of direct action.

Great documents are here to tell us something should be done. We met here some years ago in the White House conference on civil rights, and we came out with the same recommendations that we will be demanding in our campaign here, but nothing has been done. The president's commission on technology, automation and economic progress recommended these things some time ago. Nothing has been done. Even the urban coalition of mayors of most of the cities of our country and the leading businessmen have said these things should be done. Nothing has been done. The Kerner commission [Governmental Report on Civil Disorders] came out with its report just a few days ago and then made specific recommendations. Nothing has been done.

And I submit that nothing will be done until people of good will put their bodies and their souls into motion. And it will be the kind of soul force brought into being as a result of this confrontation that I believe will make the difference. Yes, it will be a poor people's campaign. This is the question facing America. Ultimately a great nation is a compassionate nation. America has not met its obligations and its responsibilities to the poor.

One day we will have to stand before the God of history and we will talk in terms of things we've done. Yes, we will be able to say we built gargantuan bridges to span the seas, we built gigantic buildings to kiss the skies. Yes, we made our submarines to penetrate oceanic depths. We brought into being many other things with our scientific and technological power.

It seems that I can hear the God of history saying, "That was not enough! But I was hungry and ye fed me not. I was naked and ye clothed me not. I was devoid of a decent sanitary house to live in, and ye provided no shelter for me. And consequently, you cannot enter the kingdom of greatness. If ye do it unto the least of these, my brethren, ye do it unto me." That's the question facing America today.

Martin Luther King Jr., *Congressional Record* 114 (9 April 1968): 9395–97. In *A Testament of Hope: The Essential Writings of Martin Luther King, Jr.* Ed. James Melvin Washington. San Francisco: Harper & Row, 1986.

DOCUMENT 8: PROPOSAL TO SOLVE POVERTY

In his book, Where Do We Go from Here: Chaos or Community? *King warns America that it must strive for a more equitable distribution of goods by helping the poor to become consumers. King's solution is the enactment of a guaranteed income.*

I am now convinced that the simplest approach will prove to be the most effective—the solution to poverty is to abolish it directly by a now widely discussed measure: the guaranteed income.

Earlier in this century this proposal would have been greeted with ridicule and denunciation as destructive of initiative and responsibility. At that time economic status was considered the measure of the individual's abilities and talents. In the simplistic thinking of that day the absence of worldly goods indicated a want of industrious habits and moral fiber.

We have come a long way in our understanding of human motivation and of the blind operation of our economic system. Now we realize that dislocations in the market operation of our economy and the prevalence of discrimination thrust people into idleness and bind them in constant or frequent unemployment against their will. The poor are less often dismissed from our conscience today by being branded as inferior and incompetent. We also know that no matter how dynamically the economy develops and expands it does not eliminate all poverty.

We have come to the point where we must make the nonproducer a consumer or we will find ourselves drowning in a sea of consumer goods. We have so energetically mastered production that we now must give attention to distribution. Though there have been increases in purchasing power, they have lagged behind increases in production. Those at the lowest economic level, the poor white and Negro, the aged and chronically ill, are traditionally unorganized and therefore have little ability to force the necessary growth in their income. They stagnate or become even poorer in relation to the larger society.

The problem indicates that our emphasis must be twofold. We must create full employment or we must create incomes. People must be made consumers by one method or the other. Once they are placed in this position, we need to be concerned that the potential of the individual is not wasted. New forms of work that enhance the social good will have to be devised for those for whom traditional jobs are not available.

Martin Luther King Jr., *Where Do We Go from Here: Chaos or Community?* New York: Harper & Row, 1967. In *A Testament of Hope: The Essential Writings of Martin Luther King, Jr.* Ed. James Melvin Washington. San Francisco: Harper & Row, 1986.

DOCUMENT 9: ESSAY ON THE TENACIOUSNESS OF RACISM

In an essay published posthumously, King acknowledges that many whites adhere to the ideals of the Declaration of Independence and want to see blacks have equal opportunities. He also writes that many whites have displayed great heroism in the civil rights struggle. Nevertheless, King asserts that the poison of racism is so ingrained in the American character that it is hard to win white allies.

It is time that we stopped our blithe lip service to the guarantees of life, liberty and pursuit of happiness. These fine sentiments are embodied in the Declaration of Independence, but that document was always a declaration of intent rather than of reality. There were slaves when it was written; there were still slaves when it was adopted; and to this day, black Americans have not life, liberty nor the privilege of pursing happiness, and millions of poor white Americans are in economic bondage that is scarcely less oppressive. Americans who genuinely treasure our national ideals, who know they are still elusive dreams for all too many, should welcome the stirring of Negro demands. They are shattering the complacency that allowed a multitude of social evils to accumulate. Negro agitation is requiring America to reexamine its comforting myths and may yet catalyze the drastic reforms that will save us from social catastrophe.

In indicting white America for its ingrained and tenacious racism, I am using the term "white" to describe the majority, not *all* who are white. We have found that there are many white people who clearly perceive the justice of the Negro struggle for human dignity. Many of them joined our struggle and displayed heroism no less inspiring than that of black people. More than a few died by our side; their memories are cherished and are undimmed by time.

Yet the largest portion of white America is still poisoned by racism, which is as native to our soil as pine trees, sagebrush and buffalo grass. Equally native to us is the concept that gross exploitation of the Negro is acceptable, if not commendable. Many whites who concede that Negroes should have equal access to public facilities and the untrammeled right to vote cannot understand that we do not intend to remain in the basement of the economic structure; they cannot understand why a porter or a housemaid would dare dream of a day when his work will be more useful, more remunerative and a pathway to rising opportunity. This incomprehension is a heavy burden in our efforts to win white allies for the long struggle.

Martin Luther King Jr., "Testament of Hope," *Playboy* 16 (January 1969): 175 ff. In *A Testament of Hope: The Essential Writings of Martin Luther King, Jr.* Ed. James Melvin Washington. San Francisco: Harper & Row, 1986.

DOCUMENT 10: SERMON AT EBENEZER BAPTIST CHURCH ON THE CAUSES OF RACISM

In a 1968 sermon to his congregation, King preached that prejudice has prevented poor whites from seeing that the forces that oppress blacks are also oppressing them.

I always try to do a little converting when I'm in jail. And when we were in jail in Birmingham the other day, the white wardens all enjoyed coming around to the cell to talk about the race problem. And they were showing us where we were so wrong demonstrating. And they were showing us where segregation was so right. And they were showing us where intermarriage was so wrong. So I would get to preaching, and we would get to talking—calmly, because they wanted to talk about it. And then we got down one day to the point—that was the second or third day—to talk about where they lived, and how much they were earning. And when those brothers told me what they were earning, I said, now "You know what? You ought to be marching with us. You're just as poor as Negroes." And I said, "You are put in the position of supporting your oppressor. Because through prejudice and blindness, you fail to see that the same forces that oppress Negroes in American society oppresses poor white people. And all you are living on is the satisfaction of your skin being white, and the drum major instinct of thinking that you are somebody big because you are white. And you're so poor you can't send you children to school. You ought to be out here marching with every one of us every time we have a march."

Now that's a fact. That the poor white has been put into this position—where through blindness and prejudice, he is forced to support his oppressors, and the only thing he has going for him is the false feeling that he is superior because his skin is white. And can't hardly eat and make his ends meet week in and week out.

Martin Luther King Jr., "The Drum Major Instinct," Flip Schulke, ed. *Martin Luther King, Jr.: A Documentary . . . Montgomery to Memphis* (New York and London: Norton, 1976), 220–22. In *A Testament of Hope: The Essential Writings of Martin Luther King, Jr.* Ed. James Melvin Washington. San Francisco: Harper & Row, 1986.

DOCUMENT 11: RACISM AS AN INTERNATIONAL PROBLEM

Racism and the economic exploitation that feeds it are not unique to America; they are, according to King, an international problem. In South Africa and many other countries around the world, white men are exploiting people of color to build empires.

Among the moral imperatives of our time, we are challenged to work all over the world with unshakable determination to wipe out the last vestiges of racism. As early as 1906 [American educator] W.E.B. DuBois prophesied that "the problem of the twentieth century will be the problem of the color line." Now as we stand two-thirds into this exciting period of history we know full well that racism is still that hound of hell which dogs the tracks of our civilization.

Racism is no mere American phenomenon. Its vicious grasp knows no geographical boundaries. In fact, racism and its perennial ally—economic exploitation—provide the key to understanding most of the international complications of this generation.

The classic example of organized and institutionalized racism is the Union of South Africa. Its national policy and practice are the incarnation of the doctrine of white supremacy in the midst of a population which is overwhelmingly black. But the tragedy of South Africa is not simply in its own policy; it is the fact that the racist government of south Africa is virtually made possible by the economic policies of the United States and Great Britain, two countries which profess to be the moral bastions of our Western world.

In country after country we see white men building empires on the sweat and suffering of colored people. Portugal continues its practices of slave labor and subjugation in Angola; the Ian Smith government in Rhodesia continues to enjoy the support of British-based industry and private capital, despite the stated opposition of British government policy. Even in the case of the little country of South West Africa we find the powerful nations of the world incapable of taking a moral position against South Africa, though the smaller country is under the trusteeship of the United Nations. Its policies are controlled by South Africa and its manpower is lured into the mines under slave-labor conditions.

Martin Luther King Jr., *Where Do We Go From Here: Chaos or Community?* New York: Harper & Row, 1967. In *A Testament of Hope: The Essential Writings of Martin Luther King, Jr.* Ed. James Melvin Washington. San Francisco: Harper & Row, 1986.

DOCUMENT 12: ADDRESS TO THE NATION ON JUSTICE AND FREEDOM

As the keynote speaker at the March on Washington, D.C., August 28, 1963, King delivered his most famous speech, "I Have a Dream." Standing before the Lincoln Memorial, King outlined his vision of an America transformed into a nation free of racism, segregation, and injustice.

I am happy to join with you today in what will go down in history as the greatest demonstration for freedom in the history of our nation.

Fivescore years ago, a great American, in whose symbolic shadow we stand today, signed the Emancipation Proclamation. This momentous decree came as a great beacon light of hope to millions of Negro slaves who had been seared in the flames of withering injustice. It came as a joyous daybreak to end the long night of their captivity.

But one hundred years later, the Negro still is not free; one hundred years later, the life of the Negro is still sadly crippled by the manacles of segregation and the chains of discrimination; one hundred years later, the Negro lives on a lonely island of poverty in the midst of a vast ocean of material prosperity; one hundred years later, the Negro is still languished in the corners of American society and finds himself in exile in his own land.

So we've come here today to dramatize a shameful condition. In a sense we've come to our nation's capital to cash a check. When the architects of our republic wrote the magnificent words of the Constitution and the Declaration of Independence, they were signing a promissory note to which every American was to fall heir. This note was the promise that all men, yes, black men as well as white men, would be guaranteed the unalienable rights of life, liberty, and the pursuit of happiness.

It is obvious today that American has defaulted on this promissory note in so far as her citizens of color are concerned. Instead of honoring this sacred obligation, America has given the Negro people a bad check; a check which has come back marked "insufficient funds." We refuse to believe that there are insufficient funds in the great vaults of opportunity of this nation. And so we've come to cash this check, a check that will give us upon demand the riches of freedom and the security of justice.

We have also come to this hallowed spot to remind America of the fierce urgency of now. This is no time to engage in the luxury of cooling off or to take the tranquilizing drug of gradualism. Now is the time to make real the promises of democracy; now is the time to rise from the dark and desolate valley of segregation to the sunlit path of racial justice; now is the time to lift our nation from the quicksands of racial injustice to the solid rock of brotherhood; now is the time to make justice a reality for all God's children. It would be fatal for the nation to overlook the urgency of the moment. This sweltering summer of the Negro's legitimate discontent will not pass until there is an invigorating autumn of freedom and equality.

Nineteen sixty-three is not an end, but a beginning. And those who hope that the Negro needed to blow off steam and will now be content, will have a rude awakening if the nation returns to business as usual.

There will be neither rest nor tranquility in America until the Negro is granted his citizenship rights. The whirlwinds of revolt will continue to shake the foundations of our nation until the bright day of justice emerges.

But there is something that I must say to my people who stand on the warm threshold which leads into the palace of justice. In the process of gaining our rightful place we must not be guilty of wrongful deeds.

Let us not seek to satisfy our thirst for freedom by drinking from the cup of bitterness and hatred. We must forever conduct our struggle on the high plane of dignity and discipline. We must not allow our creative protest to degenerate into physical violence. Again and again we must rise to the majestic heights of meeting physical force with soul force.

The marvelous new militancy which has engulfed the Negro community must not lead us to a distrust of all white people, for many of our white brothers, as evidenced by their presence here today, have come to realize that their destiny is tied up with our destiny and they have come to realize that their freedom is inextricably bound to our freedom. This offense we share mounted to storm the battlements of injustice must be carried forth by a biracial army. We cannot walk alone.

And as we walk, we must make the pledge that we shall always march ahead. We cannot turn back. There are those who are asking the devotees of civil rights, "When will you be satisfied?" We can never be satisfied as long as the Negro is the victim of the unspeakable horrors of police brutality.

We can never be satisfied as long as our bodies, heavy with fatigue of travel, cannot gain lodging in the motels of the highways and the hotels of the cities. We cannot be satisfied as long as the Negro's basic mobility is from a smaller ghetto to a larger one.

We can never be satisfied as long as our children are stripped of their selfhood and robbed of their dignity by signs stating "for whites only." We cannot be satisfied as long as a Negro in Mississippi cannot vote and a Negro in New York believes he has nothing for which to vote. No, we are not satisfied, and we will not be satisfied until justice rolls down like waters and righteousness like a mighty stream.

I am not unmindful that some of you have come here out of excessive trials and tribulation. Some of you have come fresh from narrow jail cells. Some of you have come from areas where your quest for freedom left you battered by the storms of persecution and staggered by the winds of police brutality. You have been the veterans of creative suffering. Continue to work with the faith that unearned suffering is redemptive.

Go back to Mississippi; go back to Alabama; go back to South Carolina; go back to Georgia; go back to Louisiana; go back to the slums and ghettos of the northern cities, knowing that somehow this situation can, and will be changed. Let us not wallow in the valley of despair.

So I say to you, my friends, that even though we must face the difficulties of today and tomorrow, I still have a dream. It is a dream deeply rooted in the American dream that one day this nation will rise up and live out the true meaning of its creed—we hold these truths to be self-evident, that all men are created equal.

I have a dream that one day on the red hills of Georgia, sons of former slaves and sons of former slave-owners will be able to sit down together at the table of brotherhood.

I have a dream that one day, even the state of Mississippi, a state sweltering with the heat of injustice, sweltering with the heat of oppression, will be transformed into an oasis of freedom and justice.

I have a dream my four little children will one day live in a nation where they will not be judged by the color of their skin but by the content of their character. I have a dream today!

I have a dream that one day, down in Alabama, with its vicious racists, with its governor having his lips dripping with the words of interposition and nullification, that one day, right there in Alabama, little black boys and black girls will be able to join hands with little white boys and white girls as sisters and brothers. I have a dream today!

I have a dream that one day every valley shall be exalted, every hill and mountain shall be made low, the rough places shall be made plain, and the crooked places shall be made straight and the glory of the Lord will be revealed and all flesh shall see it together.

This is our hope. This is the faith that I go back to the South with.

With this faith we will be able to hear out of the mountain of despair a stone of hope. With this faith we will be able to transform the jangling discords of our nation into a beautiful symphony of brotherhood.

With this faith we will be able to work together, to pray together, to struggle together, to go to jail together, to stand up for freedom together, knowing that we will be free one day. This will be the day when all of God's children will be able to sing with new meaning—"my country 'tis of thee; sweet land of liberty; of thee I sing; land where my fathers died, land of the pilgrim's pride; from every mountain side, let freedom ring"—and if America is to be a great nation, this must become true.

So let freedom ring from the prodigious hilltops of New Hampshire.

Let freedom ring from the mighty mountains of New York.

Let freedom ring from the heightening Alleghenies of Pennsylvania.

Let freedom ring from the snow-capped Rockies of Colorado.

Let freedom ring from the curvaceous slopes of California.

But not only that.

Let freedom ring from Stone Mountain of Georgia.

Let freedom ring from Lookout Mountain of Tennessee.

Let freedom ring from every hill and molehill of Mississippi, from every mountainside, let freedom ring.

And when we allow freedom to ring, when we let it ring from every village and hamlet, from every state and city, we will be able to speed up that day when all of God's children—black men and white men, Jews and Gentiles, Catholics and Protestants—will be able to join hands and to sing in the words of the old Negro spiritual, "Free at last, free at last; thank God Almighty, we are free at last."

CHRONOLOGY

1929

Martin Luther King Jr. is born in Atlanta, Georgia.

1947

Jackie Robinson breaks the "color line" in major league baseball; the Truman Doctrine and the Marshall Plan are announced; the cold war intensifies.

1948

King graduates from Morehouse College in Atlanta.

1949

NATO is founded.

1950

Senator Joseph McCarthy increases fears of Communist infiltration in American life; Korean War begins.

1951

King graduates from Crozer Theological Seminary, Chester, Pennsylvania.

1952

Dwight D. Eisenhower is elected president.

1953

King marries Coretta Scott.

1954

Brown v. Board of Education Supreme Court decision; King becomes pastor at Dexter Avenue Church in Montgomery, Alabama.

1955

Bus boycott begins in Montgomery, Alabama; Martin Luther King gains national recognition as president of the Montgomery Improvement Association.

1956

King's house is bombed; King delivers his first major national address during the prayer pilgrimage in Washington, D.C.; Civil Rights Act signed by Congress concerning voting rights; sit-ins begin in Greensboro, North Carolina.

1957

King is elected as the president of the Southern Christian Leadership Conference (SCLC); nine black students are admitted to an all-white school in Little Rock, Arkansas; Russia launches the satellite *Sputnik.*

1958

King is stabbed at a book signing in Harlem, New York.

1959

King travels to India to study the teachings of Mahatma Gandhi.

1960

John F. Kennedy is elected president; King deliberates with President Kennedy; King is arrested in Atlanta.

1961

Freedom riders are attacked in Alabama; King is arrested during a demonstration in Albany, Georgia; Bay of Pigs invasion in Cuba.

1962

King is again arrested in Albany, Georgia, during a prayer vigil; James Meredith attempts to attend the University of Mississippi; Cuban missile crisis; John Glenn orbits the earth.

1963

King is arrested in Birmingham, Alabama, and while in jail he writes his famous "Letter from Birmingham Jail"; Medgar Evers, NAACP state chairman, is murdered in Jackson, Mississippi; thousands attend the March on Washington, where King delivers his "I Have a Dream" speech; President Kennedy is assassinated.

1964

King receives the Nobel Peace Prize; Lyndon B. Johnson is elected president; the Tonkin Gulf Resolution is passed and American involvement in Vietnam escalates.

1965

Malcolm X is murdered in New York; marchers are attacked

during a demonstration in Selma, Alabama; President Johnson signs the Voting Rights Act; riots break out in Watts, a district of Los Angeles, California.

1966

King delivers a national statement against the Vietnam War; Stokely Carmichael introduces the slogan "black power"; King is attacked in Chicago.

1967

Riots explode in Jackson, Mississippi; Newark, New Jersey; and Detroit, Michigan; King is convicted of contempt-of-court charges for his 1963 Birmingham demonstration; King leads an anti–Vietnam War march in Chicago, Illinois; war between Israel and Egypt.

1968

Riots break out during King's demonstration in Memphis, Tennessee; King is murdered by a sniper, James Earl Ray; the Tet offensive in Vietnam further divides public opinion concerning the Vietnam War; Richard M. Nixon is elected president.

1983

Congress declares the third Monday in January a holiday in honor of Martin Luther King Jr.

FOR FURTHER RESEARCH

BOOKS BY MARTIN LUTHER KING JR.

Martin Luther King Jr., *Stride Toward Freedom: The Montgomery Story.* New York: Harper & Row, 1958.

———, *The Measure of a Man.* Philadelphia: Christian Education Press, 1959.

———, *Strength to Love.* New York: Harper & Row, 1963.

———, *Why We Can't Wait.* New York: Harper & Row, 1963.

———, *Where Do We Go from Here: Chaos or Community?* New York: Harper & Row, 1967.

———, *The Trumpet of Conscience.* New York: Harper & Row, 1967.

BIOGRAPHICAL WORKS

Lerone Bennett Jr., *What Manner of Man: A Biography of Martin Luther King, Jr.,* 3rd. ed. Chicago: Johnson Publishing, 1968.

James Bishop, *The Days of Martin Luther King, Jr.* New York: G.P. Putnam's Sons, 1971.

Robert Bleiweiss, ed., *Marching to Freedom: The Life of Martin Luther King, Jr.* New York: New American Library, 1969.

Coretta Scott King, *My Life with Martin Luther King, Jr.* New York: Holt, Rinehart & Winston, 1969.

David Lewis, *King: A Critical Biography.* Baltimore: Penguin Books, 1963.

C. Eric Lincoln, ed., *Martin Luther King, Jr.: A Profile.* New York: Hill & Wang, 1970.

Lionel Lokos, *House Divided: The Life and Legacy of Martin Luther King.* New Rochelle, NY: Arlington House, 1968.

William Robert Miller, *Martin Luther King, Jr.: His Life, Martyrdom and Meaning for the World.* New York: Weybright and Talley, 1968.

Lawrence D. Reddick, *Crusader Without Violence: A Biography of Martin Luther King, Jr.* New York: Harper & Row, 1959.

Flip Schulke and Penelope McPhee, *King Remembered.* New York: W.W. Norton, 1968.

Alan F. Westin and Barry Mahoney, *The Trial of Martin Luther King.* New York: Thomas Y. Crowell, 1974.

John William, *The King God Didn't Save: Reflections on the Life & Death of Martin Luther King.* New York: Coward, McCann & Geoghegan, 1970.

William R. Witherspoon, *Martin Luther King, Jr.—To The Mountaintop.* Garden City, NY: Doubleday, 1985.

HISTORICAL WORKS

Herbert Aptheker, *A Documentary History of the Negro People in the United States.* New York: Citadel Press, 1951.

Floyd B. Barbour, ed., *The Black Power Revolt.* Boston: Porter Sargent, 1968.

Numan V. Bartley, *The Rise of Massive Resistance: Race and Politics in the South During the 1950s.* Baton Rouge: Louisiana State University Press, 1969.

Inge P. Bell, *CORE and the Strategy of Nonviolence.* New York: Random House, 1968.

Edward Clayton, *The Southern Christian Leadership Conference.* Atlanta: SCLC, 1964.

Eyes on the Prize: America's Civil Rights Years. Public Television Series, production of Blackside, Inc., Boston, 1986.

James C. Harvey, *Civil Rights During the Kennedy Administration.* Jackson: University & College Press of Mississippi, 1973.

John Herbers, *The Black Dilemma.* New York: John Day, 1973.

Alton Hornsby Jr., *Milestones in 20th-Century African-American History.* Detroit: Visible Ink Press, 1993.

Lewis M. Killian, *The Impossible Revolution?: Black Power and the American Dream.* New York: Random House, 1968.

Charles D. Lowery and John F. Marszalek, eds., *Encyclopedia of African-American Civil Rights: From Emancipation to the Present.* New York: Greenwood Press, 1992.

William L. O'Neill, *Coming Apart: An Informal History of America in the 1960s.* Chicago: Quadrangle Books, 1964.

Edward Peeks, *The Long Struggle for Black Power.* New York: Charles Scribner's Sons, 1971.

Nathan Wright Jr., *Black Power and Urban Unrest.* New York: Hawthorn Books, 1967.

INDEX